D1572111

TO MARYLAND FROM OVERSEAS

*A Complete Digest of the Jacobite Loyalists Sold into
White Slavery in Maryland, and the British and
Continental Background of Approximately
1400 Maryland Settlers from 1634 to the
Early Federal Period with Source
Documentation*

By

Harry Wright Newman

Baltimore
GENEALOGICAL PUBLISHING CO., INC.
1985

Originally published: Annapolis, 1982
Copyright © 1982 by Harry Wright Newman
Copyright © transferred (1984) to Genealogical Publishing Co., Inc.
Baltimore, Maryland. All Rights Reserved.
Reprinted: Genealogical Publishing Co., Inc.
Baltimore, 1985
Library of Congress Catalogue Card Number 84-82536
International Standard Book Number 0-8063-1109-6
Made in the United States of America

PREFACE

The British and Continental background of Maryland colonists has maintained my interest for nearly sixty years. During the many hours spent among Maryland records as well as source records in Britain and on the Continent whenever a reference was cited as to European origin of a Maryland colonist, notation was carefully made.

The results will offset the all-too-often statement that Maryland settlers were of a low social and economic status and that Maryland like the other Colonies was a haven for criminals turned out of English jails. It gives subjective satisfaction to debunk our heritage, especially those only a few generations on our shores or those from the peasantry and ghettos of Europe.

Statements furthermore are made that the early Maryland settlers were not aware of their ancestry or had come to America to forget it. While it is conclusively accepted that all colonials were not of ennobled blood or scions of the squirarchy and county gentry, many were of high social standing in Britain and the Continent and continued to emulate that culture in Maryland.

Many brought their credentials with them or letters of introduction from folks at home to friends or kinsmen who had emigrated to Maryland. Such documents have mostly been lost through the vicissitudes of time, but a few survive to this day.

Recall Lord Baltimore stated that nearly "Twenty Gentlemen of Fashion" had sailed on the Ark and the Dove in 1633. Many so-called convicts sold in Maryland after the internal wars in Britain between 1715-1775 were principally political and religious prisoners who had been condemned to banishment whose blood was in many cases as proud as any in Britain.

Some convicts, it cannot be denied, were common criminals, but it should not be overlooked that, according to Blackstone, 160 offences in Britain were punishable by death. We are therefore prepared with reason to accept that many of the offenders shipped to Maryland were in most cases victims of stringent laws compatible with the times or subject to torts and misdemeanors rather than serious crimes.

Harry Wright Newman

Annapolis, Maryland.

ATTENTION

For the most part this compilation does not contain the naturalization records of the great number of German and Swiss-born settlers who came into Maryland through the generous offers of Lord Baltimore and who became British subjects under the Naturalization Act of 1740 (13 George 11). The complete record of these adjurations is on file at the Hall of Records, Annapolis, Md.

In a few instances natives of the Continent with distinctive English names such as Bishop, Boone, Hammond and others bearing the names of early prominent Maryland families were included. This proves that some foreign born cannot be attached to the early colonial families of similar names.

Attention is called to the Stansbury section where discussion is made of Maryland emigrants from the Continent with Anglo-Saxon names and the possibility of British background.

TABLE OF CONTENTS

Conditions of Prisoners Captured at Preston 1

List of Prisoners Sold in 1716 3

Prisoners Captured at Culloden 6

List of Prisoners Sold in 1747 8

Felons Shipped to Maryland in 1749 9

Some Maryland Emigrants and Their Background 11

Index (prisoners or rebels only) 187

AUCTION OF JACOBITE PRISONERS

Many Jacobites, Scottish loyalists, who fought unsuccessfully to place the Stuarts on the throne of Britain in 1715 and 1746 were captured by the English, shackled, shipped and sold at Maryland docks to the highest bidder into servitude or white bondage for seven years. Many were of ancient and honourable lineage. Some returned to Scotland at the end of their period of slavery, while others remained and became loyal tenants of the Lord Proprietary.*

SCOTTISH PRISONERS SOLD IN MARYLAND BY THE ENGLISH

After the defeat of the Jacobites or Scottish Loyalists at the decisive battle of Preston, Lancashire, on 13 November 1715, to place James Stuart, the Old Pretender, on the British throne after the death of Queen Anne in 1714, hundreds of Scottish captives were thrown into unsanitary prisons and ultimately tried at Carlisle by an English jury. A number, however, rather than be tried for treason opted to be shipped to the American plantations "Beyond the Seas" and sold into bondage.

In anticipation a session of the Council held at Annapolis 11 January 1715/6, passed the following proclamation which was duly signed by Governor Hart relative to the arrival of the ship *Friendship*. "Whereas His most Sacred Majesty out of the abundant Clemency has caused eighty Rebbells (most of them Scotsmen) lately taken at Preston in Lancashire in the ship *Friendship* of Belfast, Michael Mankin, Commander...that the said Rebbells to number aforesaid be sold to the Asignes of the Merchants who should purchase them for the full term of Seven Years and not for any lesser time".

The proclamation furthermore stated that the rebels "shall give security for their abiding in this province and be of good behaviour for the Term of Seven Years".

A second proclamation was issued by Governor Hart at Annapolis "the eleventh day of January in the 2d year of his Lordship Dominion (Benedict Leonard Calvert, 4th Baron Baltimore, and 3d Lord Proprietary) & c. Annon

---

*Provincial Court Records, Liber TP no. 4, (1709-19), folios 395-97; 405-7, contain the names of those who were taken at the battle of Preston in 1715 and shipped to Maryland.

1

Domini 1716". "Whereas There has been transported into this province by his Majesty Royal Command, fifty-five persons, most of them Scots, men taken in the late Rebellion at Preston and Imported in the Ship the *Good Speed* of Liverpool,,,,, concerning whom his Majesty has graciously . . . to me by letter from the Right Honourable James Stanhope, Esq. one of the principal Secretaries of State, dated Whitehall the fourth day of May last, that it was his Royal pleasure that the Rebbells so taken & Imported as aforesaid should either enter into Indentures to serve such persons would purchase them for the term of Seven Years or otherwise that on the Sale of such who should refuse so to do I should grant to the respective purchasers or Masters under my hand and Seale a proper Certificate that it was the Majesty's pleasure the said Rebbells so transported into this province should be sold by the factor of Messrs. Richard Guildard & Company to serve the term aforesaid. . . ."

John Ramsey writing of his experience 10 December 1716, to _____ Wallkington of Barrowfield, Glasgow, stated "You can't imagine the bad treatment we had from the Master (that is, Master of the ship), while he had us in his power, having all been kept in chains except one and myself who had bought our freedom".

Instrument or Document by which the Jacobite Prisoners were sold to Their Maryland Masters in 1716

John Hart, Esq Capt Generall and Govn Chief in and over the Province of Maryland & C.

To all to these presents Shall Come Greeting. Know Yee that whereas Henry Murray haveing been Concerned and taken in the late Rebellion against His Majty in Lancashire in Great Britain and Submitted to his royall pleasure.

Where upon his Majty by the right honble James Stanhope Esq., one of the principall Secretaries of State Signified to me his Royall will and pleasure that the said Henry Murray now Transported into this Province in the Ship Friendship of Belfast whereof Michael Mankin is Commander at the Charge and Expense of Messr William Greenway and Company is to serve abide and Continue in this province as a Servant for and dureing the full space and Term of Seaven Years and not for any Lessor Term or Space or Time And now whereas William Holland, Esq. of Anne Arundel County has purchased the said Henry Murray of Mr. Thomas Lewis of factor and Agent for the Messrs Greenway and Compy for a Valuable consideration. It is His Majestys pleasure and ordered to me as afsd that the said Henry Murray Shall Serve William Holland, Esq. who has so purchased him as afsd and Dureing the term and Space of Time as afsd Given at the City of Annapolis under my hand and Seale this 25th day of Augt ye 3d year of the reign of Our sov Lord George by the Grace of God & of Great Britain, France and Ireland Annoq Dom 1716.

2

A List of Rebells Transported in the Shipp the Friendship of Belfast, Michael Mankin, Commander, the 20th of August 1716.

Rebells' Name	By whom purchased
John Pitter, James Nithery, Dugall Macqueen	William Holland, Esq.
Alexa Smith	Samuel Chew, Jr.
Abraham Lowe	Thomas Larkin
Henry Wilson, Alexander Gordon	John Gresham
John Hay	William Homes
William Smith, Alex'der Spalding	William Nicholson
Leonard Robinson	Thomas Doccra
John Blandell	Benjamin Wharfield
John Sinckar	Joseph Hill
William Grant	Thomas Davis
Thomas Spark	Philip Dowell
James Webster	Steph. Warman
Wm Cummins, Allin Machen Jno Robertson	Thos Macnemara
Farq. Macgilvary	Samuel Young, Esq.
David Mills	Evan Jones
Patrick Cooper	Albert Greening
Jeremiah Dunbar	Hugh Kenneday
John Degedy, William McBean, Thomas Lowry	Phile. Lloyd, Esq.
John Glaney	Hugh Spedden
Wm Macgilvary	Robert Ungle, Esq.
Alexander Nave	Thomas Breadhurst
James Hindry	John Oldham
William Mobbery	Henry Tripp
James Small, James White	Samuel Peele
John Macbayn	John Ford
Rot Henderson	Edward Penn
Thomas Potts, George Thompson John Ramsey, Alexander Reind, Thomas Forbus	Wm Bladen, Esq.
William Davidson	Mordecai Moor
James Mitchell, James Lowe	Benjamin Tasker
James Denholne	John Clark
James Allen	Eliz Brown

Rebells' Name	By whom purchased
James White	Benjamin Dunbar
Thomas Donelson	John Cheney
James Hill	Humphrey Godman
David Steward, Henry Iansdale	Jacob Henderson
Arch. Macdonall, alias Kennedy	W. FitzRedmond
Charles Donalson, William Mare, Hecton MacQueen	Aaron Rawlings
John Maclean	Edward Parish
John MacIntire, William Onan, Alex Macqueen, Alex. Macdugall	Daniel Sherwood
David Macqueen, John Macdonald	Robert Grundy
John Poss	Edgar Webb
Robert Stobbs	John Valiant
Finley Cameron	Wm Elbert
John Mertison	Peter Anderson
Alex, Swinger	Phil Sherwood
Wm Macgilvary	Thomas Mackall
Patrick Hunter	James Calston
Henry Farchaser	Darley Dullany
Alex. Mortimer	Henry Ennalls
Jas Robertson	Joseph Hopkins
Thomas Butler, Andrew Davidson	Francis Bullock
Thos Smith	Joseph Bullock
Thos MacNabb	Wm Thomas
James Shaw, Donald Robertson	Thomas Robbins
Andrew Daw	Roger Woolforde
John Couchan	Philip Kersey
Henry Murry	William Holland, Esq.

In all 80 Rebells

A List of the Rebell Prisoners Transported into this Province in the Ship Good Speed on the 18th Day of October Anno Domini 1716 with the Names of the Persons who Purchased Them

Rebels	Purchasers
Will McPherson, Thomas Shaw, Milis Boggs	Mr. Nichl Martin
Richd Whittingham, Tho Berry, James Learn	Mr. Randall Garland
John McGregor, Danl Stewart	Mr. Richd Eglon
Duncan Ferguson, John McKewan	Capt. John Fendall
William Ferguson, James Dixon	Mr. John Brice
Rowland Robertson, Ninian Brown	Mr. Thomas Jameson
David Graham, William Johnson, James Maltone, George Nicolson John Chambers	Mr. Charles Diggs
Danll Kennedy, Patt McKoy, Angus McDormott	Mr. John Courts
James McIntosh, Hugh McDugall	Mr. Robert Hanson
James Sinclair, Alex Orack, Humphrey Sword	Mr. Henry Warton
John Stewart	Mr. John Middleton
James Crampson	Mr. Fran Calvo
John McCollinn, Willm Shaw	Mr. John Hawkins
Patt Smith, Ja: Somervill	Dr. Gustavus Brown
George Hodgson	Mr. John Nelty
Malcolm McColon	Mr. John Wilder
James McIntosh	Mr. Hene Holld Hawkins
John Cameron	Mr. Willm Penn
David Lander	Mr. Francis Goodrick
Fran McBean	Mr. Charles Boon
Wm Simpson	Mr. John Rogers
Ja: Bow	Mr. John Phillpotts
John Kenny	Mr. Marmaduke Simm
Lauglin McIntosh	Mr. Hen Miles
Alex McIntosh	Mr. Danll Steward
Hugh Macintire	Mr. John Vincent
Finlow Macintire	Mr. John Penn
Richd Birch	Mr. Benj Tasker
James Shaw	Mr. John Donnellson

5

Rebels	Purchasers
Danll Grant	Mr. Will: McConhie
Hugh White	Mr. Danll Bryan
Ja: Rutherford	Mr. Arthur Smith
Tho: Hame	Mrs. Judith Bruce
James Renton	Kannar McKenny
Alex McGiffon	Runaway

In all 54 Prisoners ye above prisoners where Imported by His Majesties Command in ye Ship Good Speed Arthur Smith Commander where disposed of according to my Instructions from Mr. Richard Gilbert and Compt Mercht p Liverpoole.

Richard Done

Ja. Somerivill
Humphrey Sword } Agreed by and Ordered p my owners not to be sold.

Governor Hart writing to King George I on the 28th April 1717, stated that "some of the Rebell Prisoners have run away from their Service, but on Complaint of their Masters I have given strict orders for the Apprehending of them whenever they shall be found in this Province".

ARRIVALS OF 1747

At the surrender of the Scottish Loyalists under Charles Edward, the Young Pretender, at the disastrous battle of Culloden Moor, Inverness, on April 16, 1746, to William Augustus, Duke of Cumberland, son of George II, ended any future attempt of the Jacobites to place the Stuarts on the throne. Cumberland slaughtered the Highlanders with unrelenting cruelty and gained for himself the name of "Butcher". The captives were dispatched by Cumberland to various destinations such as Preston, Garstang, Wigon, Manchester and Liverpool to suffer the indignities of the gallows. About 600 submitted to the King's Mercy and "were offered indentures to sign for seven years service in the Plantations".

Richard Gilbert of Liverpool, Lancashire, Esq., contracted with His Majesty's Treasurer to undertake the transportation of the prisoners at £5 per head. Upon their arrival they were to be sold on the auction block (as was done with black arrivals from Africa) to the highest bidder in white bondage or slavery for seven years of serviture and none less.

On May 5, 1747, Captain William Pemberton commanding the *Johnson* sailed from Liverpool with one contingent for Maryland. They were brought from prisons at Carlisle and Chester, but eight from Chester were drowned accidentally while being taken in small boats to the ship. The *Johnson* arrived at Oxford on July 17, 1747.

Sailing also from Liverpool in the *Gilbert* commanded by Captain Richard Holme, a short time later, another contingent of so called Rebells was destined for "Port North" on the Potomac. The ship arrived on August 5, 1747, in the lower Potomac.

Four ships in all landed at "Wecomeca" in St. Mary's, where a number of rebels were advertised for sale to planters under the direction of Robert Horner, a Maryland Gentleman and Planter. In all seven ships of Jacobite prisoners anchored in Maryland waters, the first having been the "Potomac" on February 10, 1747.

One Jacobite wrote of his experience, ". . . as to everything else we all fared alike, our meal being a salt bough of beef for five and a biscuit to every one once a day, and an allowance of stinking water as red as blood, having been kept in claret cask. Our beds were every answerable to our Diet".

Alexander Stewart, one of the prisoners, has left an interesting narrative of the event and stated that he was the first to be put in irons, and the last to have them taken off: "the carpenter go and take off all our irons. . . . James Strachen and me the last that got them off".

Upon the ship's arrival on July 19, 1747, after the irons had been removed, Horner spoke "a quiet word to us" and ordered all the prisoners below deck. "Horner came down and made a vertie fine speech concerning the goodness of the countrie". The auction occurred on shipboard on July 22, 1747. He stated that the purchasers were "gentlemen" except "two common buckskins then that are born in the countrie".

Alexander Stewart was bought by Benedict Calvert, Esq., for £9/6/– Sterling, and was immediately granted his freedom by his benefactor. While in Maryland he found old friends, especially John Mushet and his brother Dr. Mushet, formerly of Stirlingshire. Also Dr. Stewart and his brother William both living in Annapolis. In 1748 he sailed on the *Peggis of Dumfries* for Dumfries, Scotland, a free subject of King George.*

---

*For the entire narrative, see Maryland Historical Magazine.

Scottish Rebels Transported to Maryland in 1747
Transported in the "Johnson" of Liverpool

James Allen
John Arbuthnot
William Beverly
John Bowe
Robert Boy
John Brandy
Alexander Buchanan
John Burnett
Donald Cameron
Duncan Cameron
John Cameron
John Cameron
John Cameron
Alexander Campbell
Saunders Campbell
Alexander Carnagee
William Chambers
James Chaperton
William Connell
William Cowan
Robert Craigin
Jane Cumming
Charles Davidge
Robert Davis
John Duff
John Dunkin
James Erwin
Dunkan Ferguson
Dunkan Ferguson
Patrick Ferguson
John Foster
Peter Gardiner
Allen Grant
Angus Grant

John Grant
John Gray
Robert Hamilton
John Hector
James Herring
George Irwin
James King
Arch McAnnis
Hugh McClean
Alexander McCloud
Angus McCloud
Peter McCloughton
William McCown
Peter McCoy
Gilbert McCullum
Angus McDaniel
Daniel McDaniel
John McDoniel
Mary McDaniel
James McDuff
Roderick McFerrist
Daniel McGelis
John McGregor
Duncan McGregor
John McGregor
John McGregor
Patrick McIntergath
Archie McIntire
Danold McIntire
Dunkan McIntosh
Ann McKinsey
Kate McKown
John McNab
John McQuerrish

Roderick McGaerrist
Flora McQuin
Alexander Marr
John Mean
William Melvil
James Mill
Patrick Morgan
William Murdoch
Patrick Murray
John Nesmith
John Newton
Adam Norvil
Alice Pinmurray
Nalle Robertson
Thomas Ross
Pater Ruddock
David Russell
Margaret Shaw
Mary Shaw
Alexander Smith
Michael Steel
James Stretton
William Stuart
John Suter
Adam Sutherland
John Taylor
Saunders Taylor
Andrew Tillery
John Warner
Saunders Walker
George Watson
John Watt
Ninian Wise
William Yeats

Transported in the Gilbert of Liverpool 1747

John Allen
Alexander Annon
William Atkin
George Bailey
William Beard
James Black
John Bower
James Brand
John Brodey
Andrew Brown
John Buccanon
Dougle Cameron
Malcum Cameron
John Campbell
John Carrey
James Chop
James Cristy
James Critton
David Dick
James Donaldson
John Dow
Robert Duff
John Duncan
Peter Duncan
Alexander Fleming
Alexander Gaddish
Nicholas Gardner

John Gibson
John Golder
William Grant
John Gray
John Halton
Richard Johnson
James Keath
Joseph Kemno
William Knoles
John Lammon
Thomas Land
William Lawson
John Lucky
Alexander Mac Donald
Anguish MacDonald
Angus MacDonald
Donald MacDonald
John MacDonald
John MacDonald
Ronald MacDonald
Alexander MacInny
Alexander MacIntosh
Donald MacKiney
John MacLain
Malcolm MacLain
John MacPherson

Duncan Magrigr
Mark Magriger
Kenard Macluff
Farquar Miller
George Mitchell
John Ogilvie
John Paddy
John Patent
Ralph Price
Daniel Roninson
John Russell
David Scott
William Shade
John Shippard
Andrew Smith
Andrew Smith
James Smith
William Smith
Alexander Steward
Alexander Steward
James Stroon
William Thompson
George Wallace
Robert White
David Wood
Francis Yates

Convicted Persons and Felons imported in the Ship St. George Capt. James Dobbins Commanding arrived 22 March 1748

NOTE: In evaluating British crimes in the eighteenth century, it should not be overlooked that 160 offences were punishable by death. Felons and political prisoners were not only transported to Maryland but to all the Thirteen Colonies.

John Bennett
William Bilby
Mary Bagwell

Charles Franklin
James Fitzsimmonds
John Fling

Sarah Lowther
Joseph Longdin
Elizabeth Murray

Elizabeth Ball	Annie Flower	James Magham
Elizabeth Bennett	Jasper Godby	Lackland McGuire
John Brace	Ann Gregory	Margaret Matthews
Ann Angus	Ann Gover	Elizabeth Mitchell
Mary Baker	Thomas Hargrove	William Newman
Mary Barber	William Haughton	Anne Page als Willis
Sarah Bottle	John Henry	Mary Pebworth als Smith
William Clark	Charles Health	Hugh Roberts
Samuel Courtney	James Hodges als Pison	Robert Randwell
Bridget Craith	Thomas Holden	John Read als Surep
Thomas Cooke	William Jones	Charles Roberts
Mary Carnes	Benjamin Jukes	William Studder
Ann Boswell	Cornelius Jacob	William Seall
Ann Connack	Judith Judge	John Studder
Susannah Crawford	John Kent	Ann Strong
Sarah Crisp als Ridge	Mary Kendall	Susan Thompson
Sophia Cudday	Hannah Killigrew	Peter Tuker
Davis Deleney	John Lamb	Edward Vaughan
John Davis	Nathaniel Lawrence	Ann Wright
Jane Ellis	Edmond Low	John Welch
Joseph Wethersher	William Williams	Ann Wheeler
John Williams	John Wright	Elizabeth White

From London and Middlesex — Thomas Lemon, John Mason, Edward Aloule, William Mullings, John Sheriers, Mary Clarke

From Sarum — William Sawyer, John Collins, John Harvie, Samuel Jones, Thomas Jones, Richard Lawrence, George Massey, Edward Rose, William Whiteby, Frances Montgomery, Jane Thaker

From Essex — William Bennett, Nathaniel Cooke, John Fairall.

From Sussex — Richard Waters, John Cameron, Samuel Gazey, James Mitchell, William Paddison, Mary Wall.

From Surrey — William Harrison, Jane Clarke, Nathaniel Robins, James Sawyer.

From Winton — Ann White, Robert Clover als Temple, John Jones.

From Warwick — William Webb.

From Bucks — John Taylor.

From Yarmouth — Mary Shaw.

From Kent — Samuel Prior.

From Deal — Mary Hiags.

REF: Prov. Crt Deeds, Liber EI no. 8, folio 404-406, Hall of Records, Annapolis.

BACKGROUND OF MARYLAND EMIGRANTS OR SETTLERS

ABINGTON

John Abington of London, Merchant, and Calvert Co., Md., was the son and heir of Anthony Abington of Dowdeswell, Gloucestershire, He held manorial rights on Abington Manor and likewise possessed Dowdeswell Plantation, both in Calvert Co. He married in 1628 Muriel, daughter of Sir Richard Berkeley of Stoke-Gifford, Gloucestershire. He resided for a time in St. Mary's Co., but returned to England, where he died in 1693, without issue, styling himself of the Parish of St. Faith the Virgin. He appointed his nephew, John Abington of William, the executor of his estate. He was also the brother to Katharine, the Dowager Countess of Carnwarth. John Abington of this family settled in Prince George's Co., died 1739, leaving issue and an affluential estate.

REF: Waters' Gleanings, vol. 1, p. 600; Md. Hist. Soc. Mag., vol. 25, p. 253; Heraldic Marylandiana, by Newman.

ACHILLIS

Peter Achillis in 1675 when he petitioned for naturalization stated that he was "borne att Amsterdam in Holland under the said Dominion" of the States General.

REF: Md. Archives, vol. 2, p. 460.

ADAMS

Mark Adams left Ireland about 1772 and served in the 4th Md. Regt., Revolutionary War, later of Gloucester Co., N.J.

REF: Rev. Pension Claim W 2896, National Archives, Wash.

Thomas Adams of Kent Co., Md., Gent. deposed in May 1640 that he was aged 29 and had been born in Bodenham Parish, Herefordshire, and had arrived on Kent Isle in 1636 or 1637.

REF: Md. Archives, vol. 5, p. 229.

Valentine Adams, a German Protestant, received the sacrament of the Reformed Church at Frederick Town and under the Act of George II (13th) at court in Apr. 1763, took the Oath of Abjuration.

REF: Crt Judgements, Liber DD no. 3, folio 136.

William Adams of Co. Somerset, on January 5, 1684, was bound to James Fawcett for 4 years in Maryland.

REF: Ghirelli, folio 1.

11

ADDISON

The Rev. Henry Addison (died Maryland 1789) who studied at Oxford, England, grandson of Colonel John Addison, the Emigrant, recorded in his note-book that he was descended from the Rev. Launcelot Addison I of the Established Church and that the Rev. Launcelot Addison II, Dean of Litchfield, was his great-uncle as well as the Rev. Anthony Addison, chaplain to the Great Duke of Marlborough, who was also rector of St. Helen's Church, Abington, Berks. Joseph Addison, nephew of John the Emigrant, married Charlotte, the Dowager Countess of Warwick. The seat of the elder Addison was Mauldismeaburn, Parish of Crosby Ravensworth, Co. Westmoreland.

REF: National Dictionary of Biographies; "One Hundred Years Ago", by Elizabeth Hessilius Murray, pub. 1895; Md. Hist. Mag., vol. 14, p. 389.

ADENBROOKE

Edward Adenbrooke of London, Merchant, received a proprietary grant of land August 26, 1663.

REF: Patents, Liber 6, folio 42.

ALCOCK

Thomas Alcock, late of Maryland, (1709) was of Walthamstow, Essex, England.

REF: Prov. Crt Deeds. Liber TP no. 4 (1709-1719), folio 35.

ALEXANDER

Robert Alexander, Annapolis, Merchant, 13 May 1732, devised land to Mr. William Alexander of Antigo, Merchant, legacy to cousin Mr. Hugh McBryde of Beechland and also bequeathed legacy to Mr. Hugh Rogers, Merchant, in Glasgow".

REF: Wills, Liber 20, folio 576.

William Alexander, Cecil Co., 29 July 1738, ". . . late of that part of the Kingdom of Great Brittain called Scotland but now of Cecil County", Merchant, named his "Sister Margaret Cleland of the parish and Town of Whithern, Shire of Galloway and Kingdom of Scotland", also cousin Mary Donaldson in the parish of Kirkcoubright in the Stewartry of Galloway, referred also to a "Deed of Gift from my said wife [Araminta] unto her son Ephraim Augustine Herman".

REF: Wills, Liber 24, folio 75.

ALISON

Patrick Alison, Princess Anne, Somerset Co., Jan. 14, 1748, devised estate in Donegal "to the children of my brothers James, William and John Alison and also the children of my sister Jean Smith in Ireland".

REF: Wills, Liber 26, folio 121.

ALLANSON

Thomas Allanson, Gent., of Charles Co., who was granted by Lord Baltimore Court Baron on a manorial estate is possibly the fifth son of John Allanson of Norwood, Middlesex, Gent., who is listed in the 1633-34 Visitation of London, a family originally of Yorks. John Allanson, the Younger and son and heir of the armorial registrant, was of the Middle Temple, Gent. Thomas Allanson of Maryland named his manor "Christian Temple".

REF: Visitation of London 1633, pub. 1880 by the Harleian Soc., London.

ALLEN

Thomas Allen, Prince George's Co., Nov. 3, 1775, "I give and bequeath to my daughter Mary Allen now living in Devonshire in England £40 Sterling...to my sister Elizabeth Allen also living in England £3".

REF: Wills, Liber 41, folio 168.

ALLENBY

Philip Allenby, Anne Arundel Co., Glasier, Oct. 12, 1664, "...unto my Wife Jane Allenby and my Daughter Joyce Allenby in Cockermouth in the County of Cumberland in England one moyety of my estate".

REF: Wills, Liber 1, folio 263.

ALLEYNE

Francis Edmund Alleyne, one-time rector of All Hallow's Parish, Anne Arundel Co., was the son of Colonel Alexander Alleyne, Seventh Dragoon Guards, British Army.

REF: Bible of Richard Lockerman Harwood, imprint dated May 20, 1854.

ALVEY

Joseph Alvey was transported to St. Mary's County as an indenture in 1657 and his brother emigrated in 1670. The court records of Bedfordshire contain misdemeanors by the Alvey family for not conforming to the Established Church of England. Ancient orthography was Alway as it appeared in early Bedfordshire Visitations. Joseph Alvey named his plantation "Knotting", a parish on the northern borders of Bedfordshire and another plantation "Rome". The family was thus associated with the Roman Catholic community.

REF: Patents, Liber Q, folio 18; Liber 12, folio 550; Original manuscripts, British Museum.

ALWARD

In 1682 a bill was introduced and passed for the naturalization of John Alward of Charles Co.

REF: Md. Archives, vol. 7, pp. 287, 330.

AMBROSE

Abraham Ambrose and Abraham his son of Kent Co. were naturalized in 1694, by an act of the General Assembly.

REF: Md. Archives, vol. 19, pp. 85, 103.

AMES

Sarah Ames daughter of Thomas Ames of Leather Lane, St. Andrews Holbourne, London, was bound by her father to William Worthington of Maryland.

REF: Ghirello p. 1.

AMIES

Anthony Amies, son of Lazarus, scrivener, on August 13, 1684, was bound to Thomas Tench of Maryland for 4 years.

REF: Ghirelli, folio 2.

ANDERSON

John Anderson by will of Jan. 16, 1803, named his father Alexander Anderson and brother George Anderson of the Kingdom of Ireland.

REF: Balto. Co. Wills, Liber 7, folio 141.

Mounts Anderson in 1674 upon naturalization stated that he was a native of Sweadland [Swedish settlements on the Delaware].

REF: Md. Archives, vol. 2, p. 400.

The progenitor of the Anderson family of Anne Arundel and Prince George's Counties who is identified with the plantation "Providence" and who does not appear in Maryland records until about 1731 is placed as William Anderson of the Orkney Islands, Scotland, who on August 20, 1718, at the age of 18 years, contracted with John Williams of Lambeth, Surrey, Tobacconist, as agent for a 5-year indenture for emigration to Maryland. He signed the contract.

REF: List of Emigrants from England to America 1718-1758, transcribed from microfilms of the original records at Guildhall, London, by Kaminkow, pub. 1966.

ANDREWS

John Andrews of Anne Arundel Co., by will dated March 6, 1738/9, devised his wife Alice whom he appointed executrix and his unnamed sister in England the residuary heirs. To his sister Eleanor Horton and Sarah Caulton who may or may not be domiciles of Maryland he bequeathed 40 shillings each. The English heirs by Feb. 22, 1748/9, had made Daniel Dulany of Annapolis their attorney.

REF: A.A. Co. Deeds, Liber RD no. 3, folio 95; Wills, Liber 22, folio 518.

William Andrews of Frederick Co., was naturalized a British subject in April 1763, after subscribing to the Oath of Abjuration and submitting certification that he had received the sacrament of the Church of England at St. Anne's, Annapolis.

REF: Prv. Crt Judgements, Liber DD no. 3, folio 128-9.

ANLETON

An act for the naturalization of Peter Anleton [Anesone, Auelson] and his unnamed children passed the Lower House of Maryland in 1683.

REF: Md. Archives, vol. 7, pp. 487, 488.

ANNISON

Edward Annison of Hackney, Middlesex, on July 18, 1684, bound himself to Richard Fyfe of Maryland for 4 years.

REF: Ghirello, folio 3.

APOLLO

Lewis B. Apollo, a native and refugee from Santo Domingo, escaped to Maryland from the 1793 insurrection, died Oct. 16, 1821, in Frederick Co.

REF: History of Western Maryland, by Scharf, vol. 1, p. 472.

ARCHER

Peter Archer of Calvert Co., by his will dated June 22, 1683, named his mother, Mary Archer, of Waymouth [Weymouth, Dorset], England.

REF: Wills, Liber 4, folio 19.

ARENSON

Cornelius Arenson in 1674 upon his petition for naturalization stated that he was born "under the Dominion of the States General of the united Provinces", now The Netherlands.

REF: Md. Archives, vol. 2, p. 400.

ARNAUD

John Peter Arnaud, born Marseille, France, about 1753, enlisted 1781 in Baltimore Co. Militia for the Revolution, later settled in Savannah, Ga.

REF: Rev. Pension Claim S 31523, National Archives, Wash.

ARNOLD

Alicia Arnold, daughter of Michael Arnold Jr. and Anne Knipe his wife of Westminster, London, married John Ross and settled in Annapolis. The said Michael Arnold was born circa 1675, died November 3, 1735, and was buried in St. Margaret's Westminster. His wife, Anne, the daughter of the Rev. Thomas Knipe, was born 1676/7, married February 16, 1696/7, to the said Michael Arnold, and was buried September 30, 1703, in St. Margaret's Westminster. The said Rev. Mr. Knipe was Prebendary of Westminster and Headmaster of Westminster School and was buried in Westminster Abbey.

REF: Register of The Abbey and St. Margaret's; Md. Hist. Soc. Mag., vol. 9, p. 118; Heraldic Marylandiana, by Newman.

ARTHUR

Michael Arthur, a German Protestant of Baltimore Co., on 10 April 1765, received communion at St. Paul's Church, according to the Act of Parliament and subscribed to the Oath of Abjuration.

REF: Prv. Crt Judgement, Liber DD no. 7, folio 280.

ASBURY

On 7 June 1813, Francis Asbury declared himself "a native of Great Britain at Great Bar Handsworth Parish, Stafford Shire, County Superendendent and Bishop of the Methodist Episcopal Church in America".

REF: Balto. Co. Wills, Liber 10, folio 172.

ASBY

Rudolph Asby, of Frederick Co., a German Protestant, received the sacrament of the Congregation at Camgocheque, on 12 Sept. 1762, and at court on 30th Sept., subscribed to the Oath of Anjuration.

REF: Prov. Crt Judgements, Liber DD no. 2, folio 355.

ASH

Henry Ash took the sacrament in St. Anne's Parish, Annapolis, and in September 1765, subscribed to the Oath of Abjuration and became a British subject.

REF: Prov. Crt Judgements, Liber DD no. 9, folios 2-16.

ASHTON-DENT

The 1634 Visitation of London lists Walter Aston [Ashton], 4th son of Walter Aston of Longdon, Staffordshire, Gent., "in the West Indies". He died April 6, 1656, in Virginia, according to his tomb in Charles City Co.

Members of the Ashton family settled later in Maryland and intermarried with the Dents of Southern Maryland.

REF: Harleian Soc. Pub., vol. 15, p. 29; History of Staffordshire, by Wm. Salt Archaeological Soc., vol. 3, p. 37.

ASKEW

Thomas Askew, Baltimore Co., Mariner, Nov. 2, 1754, ". . .to my Beloved Father William Askew now living at Whitehaven in the County of Cumberland in the Kingdom of Great Britain during natural life of father and after the decease of my said Father William Askew I give and bequeath the Same unto my Dear Cousin John Hardy at present my second mate".

REF: Wills, Liber 29, folio 271.

ATKINS

John Atkins, aged 12, son of Robert Atkins, Perewigmaker of London, deceased, was bound on Aug. 31, 1685, to Henry Robinson for 10 years in Maryland; witnessed by Elizabeth Robinson his mother.

REF: Ghierlli, folio 3.

AUSTIN

Elizabeth Austin, aged 23, spinster, on Oct. 4, 1685, was bound to Anthony Cornwell of Maryland for 4 years, also her brother, John, aged 22, for 4 years.

REF: Ghirelli, folio 3, 4.

AYLEWAY

Hercules Ayleway on June 24, 1731, declared himself of Annapolis, but late of the Isle of St. Christopher, then returned to St. Kitts and sold his negroes to Robert Carrington, also late of St. Kitts.

REF: Prov Crt Deeds, Liber PL no. 8, folio 1.

BACON

Thomas Bacon, born Isle of Man circa 1700, ordained a priest of the Anglican Church "in order to go into the Plantations", was brother to Anthony Bacon of Maryland who returned to England in 1740; was rector of St. Pater's Church, Talbot Co. and also All Saints, Frederick Co.; married Elizabeth Bosman; died May 24, 1768, Frederick Co. leaving three daughters as coheiresses.

REF: Thomas Bacon, by William E. Diebert, Spring 1978 edition, p. 79, Md. Historical Soc., Magazine.

Thomas Bacon of Maryland became one of the heirs of his brother, Anthony Bacon, late of Cyfarthfa, Glamorganshire, Wales, as of June 14, 1785.

REF: Anne Arundel Co. Wills, Liber JG no. 1, folio 203.

BAKER

Joseph Baker of Calvert Co., Apr. 3, 1699, "As for my worldly Estate I bequeath unto my Brother William Baker living in Gilford in the County of Surry in England".

REF: Wills, Liber 13, folio 329.

Mary Baker, daughter of Gyles Baker of Yarmouth, England, tailor, was bound Aug. 10, 1685, to Henry Hawkins of Maryland, for 4 years.

REF: Ghirelli, p. 17.

Roger Baker of Wapping, Middlesex, Eng., by will dated Aug. 15, 1676, recorded in Maryland 1688 willed all property in Maryland and Virginia to his brother-in-law Abraham Hughes of Oakingham, Berks, whom he appointed executor, and to his two daughters, Honor and Mary. If the daughters died without issue or before marriage, then to the four unnamed daughters of his sister Mary Cleve and to the children of his brother, John Baker.

REF: Wills, Liber 6, folio 41.

BAKER-ENGHAM

Ancestry of Mary Baker, first wife of Robert Brooke, of Calvert Co., Esq., appears in the 1619 Visitation of Kent.

REF: Harleian Soc. Pub., vol. 42, p. 50.

BALE

Anthony Bale of Baltimore Co., Gent. was brother and heir-at-law of Thomas Bale of Withicomb Rawleigh Parish, Devonshire. By the will of the said Anthony Bale, dated Apr. 10, 1720, he bequeathed "unto my Dear Sister now in England Mary Wootten and to her heirs £10...unto my Amacible Mother if alive £10". His sister, Mary Wootton, in 1729 was of Exmouth, Devonshire, widow.

Anthony Bale "of the Parish of Withicomb Rawleigh", Devonshire, Gent., purchased lot in London Town, August 6, 1717, from Nicholas Gassaway.

REF: Harleian Soc. Pub., vol. 2, p. 141; Anne Arundel Co. Deeds, Liber IB no 2, folio 405; Wills, Liber 16, folio 16; Balto. Co. Deeds, Liber IS no. 1, folio 428.

NOTE: Bale later became corrupted as Beale and was used as a Christian name in many Anne Arundel and Baltimore Cos. families.

BALTZELL

Charled Baltzell, born c1736 in one of the German States, although no naturalization on record in Maryland, settled in Frederick Co., and died near Woodborough, aged 77, on December 31, 1813. In his youth he served in the Seven Years' War and served as Captain of General DeArendt's Continental Regiment. He was one of the Original Members of the Society of the Cincinnati.

REF: Obituary, see also Scharf's History of Western Maryland, vol. 1, p. 471.

BANEUF

John Payan Baneuf, a 1793 refugee from Santa Domingo settled in Frederick Co. and became a large land and slave owner. He died in 1819.

REF: History of Western Maryland, vol. 1, p. 471, by Scharf.

BANNISTER

John Bannister of Somerset Co., by will of November 1, 1725, declared himself to be late of the City of Liverpool.

REF: Wills, Liber 18, folio 456.

BARBERY
Thomas Barbery a "Subject to the Kingdome of Portugal" on October 12, 1666, was granted letters of denization.

REF: Md. Archives, vol. 3, p. 557.

BARCLAY
The Rev. John Barclay, rector of St. Peter's Parish, Talbot Co., was the son of David and Christian Barcley of Kincardinshire, Scotland.

REF: St. Peter's Parish Register, Talbot Co.

BARECROFT
John Barecroft, St. Mary's Co., 4 July 1693, "I give and bequeath my well beloved and Dear Brother Mr. Stephen Barecroft, Merchant, in London what money Soever is belonging to me in England of my proper Estate but I doe hereby declare that if my said Dear Brother shall...the Legacy which is Given me...by my father or by my mother or by both of them than I do hereby declare that my will is that I give £50 of this legacy unto the Parish of St. Ellinor in Worchester County in England".

REF: Wills, Liber 6, folio 43a.

BARGMAN
Michael Bargman, born October 29, 1738, in Europe, died December 17, 1878; and his wife Eva Brockonier, born November 30, 1752, at Hanau, Province of Hess-Nassau, Germany, died May 18, 1827.

REF: Gravestone, Roman Catholic Cemetery, Hagerstown.

BARKER
Thomas Barker of Liverpool received land rights in 1680.

REF: Patents, Liber WC no. 2, folio 201.

BARNES
Thomas Barnes, son of Thomas, of Chichester, butcher, deceased, was bound to Richard Moss of Maryland for four years; Aug. 6, 1684.

REF: Ghirello, p. 6.

BARRET
Joseph Barret, subject of the King of France, on June 10, 1791, declared himself a Christian and took the Oath of Naturalization. County domicile not cited.

REF: Council Proceedings, Md. Archives, vol. 72, p. 203.

HARTELL
John Hartell, born Oct. 22, 1833, Goditz, Kingdom of Bavaria, died May 11, 1873, Allegany Co.

REF: Headstone, Methodist Cemetery, Allegany.

BARTLEY
Thomas Bartley, born Downmere Yards, near Charing Cross, London, Apr. 9, 1759, settled in Baltimore at the age of 13, and served in the Maryland Line during the Revolution, later domiciled in the Edgefield District of S.C.

REF: Revolutionary Pension Claims S18708, National Archives.

BARTON

William Barton, Mattawoman, Charles Co., 13 Nov. 1708, "If my said son William Barton should die without heirs lawfully begotten then it is my will that it should fall to the Bartons of Warwickshire in England from heir to heir".

REF: Wills, Liber 12, pt. 2, folio 60a.

BARTRAND

Paul Bartrand and his brother, natives of France, settled first in England but later came to the Colonies. John settled in Gloucester Co., Va., while Paul settled in Calvert Co., Md., west of the Patuxent (now in Pr. Geo. Co.), where he died leaving a widow and son Paul. The latter returned to England and died at Bath 1753.

REF: Va. His. Mag., vol. 23, p. 430.

BASLIN

On Dec. 7, 1660, Pater Baslin, a native of the Kingdom of France, demanded land for his transportation into Maryland, having performed his service in Virginia.

REF: Patents, Liber 6, folio 89.

BASS

Charles Bass, Cecil Co., Sept. 6, 1701, "I give and bequeath unto my brother and sister Robert and Sarah Bass living in Leicester, England, all my personal estate", providing that they emigrated to Maryland within two years.

REF: Wills, Liber 11, folio 168.

BATE

James Batie, M.D., Frederick Co., Nov. 4, 1779, "I give and bequeath unto my dear Sister Philippa Lesslie for use of her son Andrew Lesslie the one hundred pounds Sterling left me by the will of the late Rev. Mr. James Young of Catrick [Catterick] in County of York and Kingdom of Great Britain . . . at the age of 21 years".

REF: Fred. Co. Wills, Liber GM no. 1, folio 163.

BATEMAN

Nov. 18, 1674, Mary Bateman of London, spinster and daughter and heiress of John Bateman late of London, Haberdasher, otherwise John Bateman late of the Province of Maryland and Mary Bateman his wife and afterwards widow of the said John Bateman and Henry Scarborough of North Walsham, County York, Gent., assigned to Richard Pery of the Patuxent River, Maryland, Merchant, "Resurrection Manor" with all improvements for £100. The Bateman family was registrant at the 1634 Visitation of London.

REF: Provincial Court Deeds, Liber PL no. 6, folio 238; Harleian Soc. Pub., vol. 40, p. 55.

BATEMAN-PERY

Aug. 8, 1664, Captain Thomas Harwood swore that he witnessed the signature of Margaret Pery of Westminster, Middlesex, widow, mother of

Mary Bateman, the relict of John Bateman "late Cittizen and Haberdasher of London", deceased, but who died in St. Mary's Co., 1663.

REF: Md. Archives, vol. 7, folio 53; Visitation of London 1664, Harleian Soc., vol. 65, p. 14.

BATHE

Peter Bathe, Apr. 12, 1661, "My will is that my Brother Christopher Bathe shall take unto his care and custody all the Estate that belonged to my ffather in Ireland . . . and the rest of what is left to be Sent to one Mr. Edward Arthur, Merchant, Livein at the Signe of the Ship Just before the entrance to the Old Exchange that he may give the same to my Brother Christopher Bathe for the use of my Son Richard Bathe".

REF: Wills, Liber 1, folio 124.

BAULDRY

Jean Bauldry and Elizabeth his wife on Aug. 4, 1685, were bound to Marmaduke Larkin of Maryland for 4 years.

REF: Ghirelli, folio 7.

BAUX

Jean Baux, a subject of France, on June 1, 1793, declared himself a Christian and subscribed to the Oath of Naturalization. County domicile not cited.

REF: Council Proceedings, Md. Archives, vol. 72, p. 338.

BAYARD

At the 1684 Assembly an act was introduced to naturalize Peter Bayard.

REF: Md. Archives, vol. 13, p. 126.

BAYLIE

William Baylie, Charles Co., 7 August 1702, confirmed his will made in England and named "Brother John Bayley" heir to his estate in England and Virginia.

REF: Wills, Liber 11, folio 209.

BAYLY

Ananias Baylie, cordwainder, was bound to Marmaduke Larkin on July 23, 1685, for 4 years; witnessed by Caleb Dutch of Southwark. Elizabeth Bayly (sic) wife of Ananias on Aug. 4, 1685, became bound to Marmaduke Larkin for 4 years.

REF: L. Ghirelli, folio 7.

BAYNE

Ellinor Bayne, widow, Charles Co., 5 Nov. 1700, "I give to my Sister in England one mourning ring".

REF: Wills, Liber 11, folio 298.

"John Bayne Son of Daniel and Mary Bayne, was born at Popescastle near Cockemouth in the County of Cumberland in England the 23 day of March A.D. 1726". "20 Aug. 1749. On this day was married Mr. John Bayne late of Popescastle near Cockermouth in the Cty of Cumberland in England and Miss Mary Noble of Piscataway".

REF: Transcript of register of St. John's Piscataway Parish, Pr. Geo., Co., Md. Hist. Soc., folios 288-289.

BEALL

Members of the Beall family, that is, Ninian, Thomas, Alexander, James and Robert, were natives of St. Andrew's Parish, Fifeshire, Scotland, where their births or baptisms are registered in the parish archives. The naming of their Maryland plantations also attested to their Scottish heritage. The Scottish spelling was "Bell" and was so used in early Maryland records. Why "a" was inserted is unknown, but after the first generation Beall was consistently used by all members of the family.

The Scottish research was conducted by the late Alexander Graham Bell who invented the telephone and phonograph, although he was not a scion of the Fifeshire.

REF: Research by Alexander Graham Beall at the Library of Congress; Parish Register of St. Andrew's, Fifeshire, Registration House, Edinburgh.

BEANE, BAYNES

Ralph Beane, no county cited, 12 November 1654, named George Cerye Smith of Southwark, Eng., and Joseph Ward at the Sign of the White Hart, Eng., executor and "overseer of estate of daughter Sarah until of age...and my will is that if my beloved brother Walter Beane goeth for England this present year and arrived safe home then my desire is that he should dispose of the Tobacco and beaver for the use of my daughter...wife Elizabeth Bean the whole estate she hath present in her possession in England".

REF: Wills, Liber 1, folio 61.

BEARD

Robert Beard, born in Scotland, substituted for Abraham Claude, in accordance with the "Act to procure Troops for the American Army", passed March Session 1778.

REF: Militia List, Md. Hist. Soc., Balto.

BEAUCHAMP

Edmond Beauchamp who wrote his will of January 5, 1716/7, Somerset Co., was listed in the 1633 Visitation of London as the third son of John Beauchamp of London, Merchant.

REF: Harleian Soc. Pub., vol. 15, p. 59; Heraldic Marylandiana, by Newman.

BEDLO

Isaack Bedlo "late of England and of Dutch Parents" on January 22, 1662/3, was declared a "ffree dennizen".

REF: Md. Archives, vol. 3, p. 466.

BELL

Peter Bell, a native of Germany, and member of the Lutheran Church of Frederick Co., subscribed to the Oath of Abjuration on Sept. 13, 1765, and became a subject of the King of England.

REF: Prov. Crt Judgement, Liber DD no. 9, folio 20.

BELLVILL

Louis Bellvill, subject of France, declared himself a Christian and on Nov. 6, 1793, subscribed to the Oath of Naturalization; county domicile not cited.

REF: Council Proceedings, Md. Archives, vol. 72, p. 357.

BEMAN

John Beman, Anne Arundel Co., 2 October 1690, "...give unto my Daughter Ellinor Beman all the rest of my Estate, but if she should died without heirs...I give my said Plantacon whereon I now Live unto my Cusin Edward Godsby in England...Now for as much as I the said John Beman being Right and Lawfull heir to a Certain Estate of Land in England in Somerset Shire I do give and bequeath to my said Daughter Ellinor Beman....Cusin Edward Godsby and Mr. Thomas Gibbes to be Guardian to my said Daughter".

REF: Wills, Liber 2, folio 208.

BENDER

George Bender, a German Protestant, took the sacrament of the Church of England in St. Anne's Church, and on Sept. 16, 1765, took the Oath of Abjuration and became a British subject.

REF: Prov. Crt Judgements, Liber DD no. 9, folio 18.

BENER

Elizabeth Bener, wife of John Pritchell, whom she married Mar. 2, 1701, was a native of Stepney Parish, Middlesex.

REF: Transcript of St. John's Piscataway Parish, Pr. Geo. Co., Md. Hist. Soc., Balto.

Peter Bender of Frederick Co. after certification that he had received the sacrament of the Calvinistc Church of Geneve on Aug. 29, 1762, took the Oath of Abjuration under the Act of George II on Sept. 15th, and thus was declared a naturalized subject.

REF: Prov. Crt Judgements, Liber DD no. 2, folios 347-9.

BENNETT

The Bennett family of Virginia and then Maryland appears in the 1633 Visitation of London as an armorial family, showing that Richard Bennett, the progenitor, as "of London now living 1634".

REF: Harleian Soc. Pub., vol. 40, p. 64.

BENNIE

Alexander Bennie Emigrated to Maryland from the Barbadoes 1674.

REF: Patents, Liber 18, folio 1.

BENSON

Thomas Benson, Somerset Co., Tailor, November 21, 1736, "to my brother John Benson and his heirs living near Whitehaven in Cumberland £140 Maryland cash to be put into Coll. Leving Gale hands till he can conveniently turn it into bills of Exchange and send it to him".

REF: Wills, Liber 21, folio 738.

BERRIDGE

William Berridge, son of William and Elizabeth Berridge of Gainsborough, Co. Lincoln, England, born April 15, 1744, married December 30, 1773, Grace Macmahan, daughter of John and Elizabeth Macmahan, born Sept. 29, 1751.

REF: St. Peter's Parish Register, Talbot Co.

BERRY

Samuel Berry of Kent Co., Carpenter, "borne under the Dominion of the king of Sweden", was naturalized in 1713.

REF: Md. Archives, vol. 38, p. 181.

William Berry, a native of England, substituted for Joseph Eastman in accordance with the "Act to procure Troops for the American Army", passed March Session 1778.

REF: Militia List, Md. Hist. Soc.

BERTE

An act of the 1686 Assembly made Paul Berte and Mary his wife naturalized subjects of England.

REF: Md. Archives, vol. 13, p. 144.

BESSON

Stephen Besson of Dorchester Co., in 1671 declared himself a native of the Kingdom of France upon application for naturalization.

REF: Md. Archives, vol. 2, p. 270.

BIGGS

Sarah Webb of Bristol, England, widow, on Jan. 13, 1711, declared herself the only sister and heir of Seth Biggs, late of Anne Arundel Co.

REF: Prov. Crt Deeds, Liber TP no. 4, folio 84.

BILLINGSLEY

January 1679, Capt. John Coalbreath deposed that in 1658 or 59 he carried letters from John Billingsley, then living in Cuchahuck in Nansemond Co., Va., to his mother, Agatha Billingsly, of Rotterdam, Holland. John Trester deposed that John Billingsly was the son of Agatha Billingsley of Rotterham, Holland.

George Billingsley "of Choskatuck in ye County of Upper Norfolk in Virginia", though he maintained a landed estate in Maryland and his will probated in Maryland, 13 Feb. 1681/2 "It's my Will and desire to dispose of ye Money left to me by my Grand mother Mrs. Agatha Billingsley as a legacie in ye hands of Mr. John Griffith's Drugster in Rotterdam her Executrix".

REF: Wills, Liber 4, folio 118; Testamentary Proceedings, Liber 11, folio 283, Hall of Records, Annapolis.

BIRCH

Thomas Birch, born in Ireland 1746, settled in Montgomery Co., where he served in the militia during the Revolution, later lived in Fayette Co., Penn.

REF: Revolutionary Pension Claim W3380, National Archives.

BIRD

John Bird, Charles Co., May 26, 1704. about to sail for England, "I give and bequeath one half of my real and personal estate in Maryland and England unto my Loving sister Elizabeth Flye in London".

REF: Wills, Liber 3, folio 638.

BIRKHEAD

Behamina Birkhead of Anne Arundel Co., was heir in the will of his father, Christopher Birkhead of Bristol, Mariner, dated Nov. 11, 1675, and probated Oct. 25, 1676, at the Prerogative Court of Canterbury, receiving 500 acres of "Birkhead" in Anne Arundel Co. at the death of Joane Birkhead, the testator's widow, and one-sixth of his father's ships, also "Little Bristol" on the north side of the Great Choptank, Talbot Co.

Abraham Birkhead, Quaker, who died testate Anne Arundel Co. 1685, was brother to Nehemiah Birkhead of Bristol, Mariner, and was made a contingent executor of his brother's estate, probated 1676.

REF: Public Record Office, Bence 127.

BIRNEY

Mary, daughter of William Birney and Jane his wife, late of the Parish of Clownis in Ireland, buried 9 June 1719.

REF: Original Register of St. Anne's Parish, Anne Arundel Co., p. 44.

BIRNIE

Hugh Birnie, born c1746, near Templepatrick, Co. Antrim, Ireland, son of Clothworthy and Margaret (Dove) Birnie, settled in Baltimore prior to the Revolution; nephew of Dr. Upton Scott of Annapolis.

REF: Md. Hist. Mag., vol. 72, p. 413.

BISHOP

Jacob Bishop, a native German, took the sacrament of the Lutheran Church of Frederick Co., and in Sept. 1765, became a subject of Great Britain.

REF: Prov. Crt Judgements, Liber DD no. 9, folio 14.

John Bishop on Apr. 14, 1762, received the sacrament of the Church of England at St. Anne's, Annapolis, and on Sept. 10, 1762, at court he subscribed to the Oath of Abjuration under the Act of George II (13th year) in order to become a naturalized subject.

REF: Prov. Crt Judgements, Liber DD no. 2, folios 89, 91.

BISSETT

James Bissett, Baltimore Co. Jan. 10, 1760, devised the residue of his estate to his father Thomas Bissett of Glen Clover [Scotland].

REF: Wills, Liber 33, folio 431.

April 16, 1764. "Thomas Bissett of Glen Albert of the Parish of Little Dunkeld and Shire of Perth in that part of Great Britain called Scotland Father to James Bissett of Baltimore Co. and Province of Maryland, Attorney, deceased . . . appointed Alexander Stenhouse Surgeon and Apothecary in the Province and County, aforesaid, and at present in Scotland to be my true and lawful Attorney".

REF: Wills, Liber 32, folio 220; Wills, Liber 33, folio 431.

BJEAN

Paul Bjean of Baltimore, died Feb. 23, 1822, aged 93, "one of those persecuted Acadians who were depossed of their property by Great Britain when Nova Scotia was taken from the French in 1756".

REF: National Intellenger, Mar. 8, 1822.

BLACK

Alexander Black, London Town, Anne Arundel Co., Dec. 17, 1740, bequeathed substantial legacies to the following kinsmen: mother unnamed; sister Mary Black of Edinburgh; sister Christian Williams and her daughter Hannah Williams; sister Jeany Campbell of London; brother William Black of London; niece Mary Tate of Edinburgh daughter of sister Margaret; cousin James Dick.

REF: Wills, Liber 30, folio 295.

BLACKISTONE (BLACKSTON)

The Blackistones of St. Mary's Co. and the Eastern Shore were of Newton Hall, Co. Durham. George Blackiston [Blakiston], Esq., later of St. Mary's Co., was the son of the Rev. Marmaduke Blakiston who was son of Judge John Blakiston, one of the Judges to sign the death warrant of Charles I.

REF: Surtees' Durham, vol. 3, pp. 402-3.

Thomas Blackston presumably one-time of Calvert Co. died testate in Great Britain on May 25, 1741, sized of property in Maryland and Great Britain. He appointed Samuel Spurrier of the County of Surrey, England, his executor, and Gabriel Parker of Calvert Co. his Maryland executor. Samuel Spurrier of Surrey granted power of attorney to Alexander Lawson of Baltimore Co. to act in his behalf.

REF: Testamentary Proceedings, Liber 31, folio 339.

BLADEN

Thomas Bladen of the Parish of St. James within the Liberty of Westminster, County Middlesex, on July 8, 1724, deeded to Thomas Colmore of London, Merchant, for £370/6/3 "Fort Kent Manor" on Kent Isle with Court Baron and Court Leet and all profits of the said court.

On February 1, 1724/5, Thomas Bladen of London, Gent., son and heir of William Bladen, late of the Province of Maryland, deceased, conveyed to William Staveley and James Bennett of London, Gent., for £600 "Fort Kent Manor" of 2000 improved acres on the Isle of Kent, Queen Anne's County.

REF: Provincial Court Deeds, Liber PL no. 6, folio 67, 107.

Colonel William Bladen (1673-1718), Secretary and Attorney General of Maryland, was son of Nathaniel Bladen of Hemsworth, Yorks, Esq., and Isabelle, daughter of Sir William Fairfax of Steeton, Yorks, Knt.

At London Apr. 19, 1742, Thomas Bladen "of the Parish of St. James in the Liberty of Westminster & County of Middlesex, Esq." was appointed Lieutenant General & Chief Governor" of the Provinces of Maryland & Avalon.

REF: History of Antiquities of Co. of Rutland, by Thomas Blore, pub. Eng. 1811, p. 180; Notes & Queries 3d series, vol. 7, p. 326; Visitation of Yorks; Prov. Crt Deeds, Liber EI no. 3, folio 330, Hall of Records, Annapolis.

BLADEN-JANSSEN

Barbara Janssen, wife of Thomas Bladen, 7th Governor of Maryland, was daughter of Sir Theodore Janssen, Bart, of Wimbledon, and sister to Mary Jannssen, wife of Charles, 5th Baron of Baltimore.

BLAKE

Charles Blake, Queen Anne's Co., 24 Aug. 1723, "And whereas my father has promised me and given me an Estate in England by his last will and has also given me leave to dispose of it by will. . .if it should please God I die before him", the testator made provisions for the distribution to his heirs.

REF: Wills, Liber 20, folio 597.

BLAND

Thomas Bland, attorney, who became the second husband of Margaret Larkin, second wife of Colonel Edward Dorsey (died 1705), was of the Inner Temple of London.

REF: Bond's Maryland Court of Appeals, vol. 1, p. xxxiii.

BLANKENSTEINE

Bill for the naturalization of William Blankensteine of St. Mary's County was presented to the General Assembly on Nov. 1, 1682.

REF: Archives of Maryland, vol. 7, pp. 345, 405, 444.

BLANGEY, BLANGY

In 1681, an Act was introduced in the Assembly to naturalize Lewis Blange (sic) and was passed accordingly under the name of Lewis Blangey. He died testate in Kent Co. 1684, and made his brother, Jacob Blangy, of London, contingent heir to his Maryland plantations.

REF: Md. Archives, vol. 7, pp. 151, 157, 187, 216; Wills, Liber 4, folio 101.

BLOCKLEY

On May 30, 1766, "Thomas Blockley heretofore of Hampstead. . .in the County of Middles South Britain but now of Frederick County, Schoolmaster, to John Johnstown of London, Mariner. . .three Messingers or Tenements. . .lying in Hempstead in the occupation of James Mackclellan, Alexander Cloye and John Sutton to which said Premises the said Thomas Blockley and Thomas Blockley my late father now deceased were admitted Tenements at Special Court Baron holden in and for the said manor to Thomas Blockley [Sr.] during life and at his decease to me the said Thomas Blockley". Mary Blockley, wife, waived her dower rights.

REF: Fred. Co. Deeds, Liber J, folio 815.

BOARMAN

William Boarman, Lord of Boarman's Manor, Charles Co., is listed in the 1634 Visitation of Hampshire, as the second son of William Bourman of Brooke and his wife Barbara Worsley.

REF: Visitation of Hampshire, Harleian Soc., Pub., vol. 64, pp. 162, 193.

BODIEN

In October 1727 petition was filed in the Assembly for the naturalization of "Francis Rudolph Bodien of Kent County Chirurgeon. . . . Born under the Emperour of Germany and his children Anne, Elizabeth, Henry, Augustus, Sophie, Sidonia and Hannah already born".

REF: Md. Archives, vol. 36, pp. 14, 66.

BODKIN

James Bodkin of Charles Co., by will of August 23, 1683, devised his mill to his brother, Dominick Bodkin of the Isle of Antigua, but if he be dead then to brother, Augustus Bodkin, then to cousin, Andrew Bodkin son and heir of Uncle Dominick Bodkin, then to sisters Ann, Jane and Eleanor Bodkin. Named father Patrick Bodkin, mother Monica, brother Edward Bodkin and cousin James Bodkin. All apparently domiciled outside of Maryland.

REF: Wills, Liber 4, folio 184.

BOHLAYER

John Bohlayer, born Dec. 29, 1793, in Germany, emigrated to America Dec. 6, 18—, died District of Columbia, May 26, 1850.

REF: Congressional Cemetery, Washington, D.C.

BOISMOSIN

Francois Christopher Ambrose Deichemin Boismosin, Baltimore Town, 1 August 1816, by will stated "born in Lavel in the Province of Maine in France the 31 of January 1749, lawful son of James Reni Christopher Deichmen Boismosin and Frances Susanna Guidi Dubourgneuf", bequeathed 9 lots in Washington City which were bequeathed him by Arnold Gouges as real estate belonging to the widow of Raymond Gouges residing in Saint Croix Dumont near to Bordeaux in France".

REF: Balto. Co. Wills, Liber 10, folio 466.

BOISNEUF

Jean Payen Boisneuf on Dec. 23, 1792, stated that he was formerly of the French portion of Santo Domingo, but "now of Frederick Co." and that three servants had been sent to him from his former domicile. He died 1815.

REF: Hartridge; Fred. Co. Deeds, Liber WR no. 11, folio 755.

BOISSON

Jeanne Marie Francoise Adelaide Boisson, refugee from Santo Domingo about 1793, married Dr. Pierre Chatard, also from Santo Domingo.

REF: Hartridge.

BOND

Barnet Bond "late of Maryland in America but now of St. Anne's Lime House, Co. Middlesex, Mariner", by will of January 25, 1741/2, devised his "freehold estates at Gunpowder River at the head of Bush River and at Nodd fforest in the place called Land of Nodd" to his wife, Alice, and his two daughters, and made his wife, Alice, the trustee of his estate, but in the event that his widow, Alice, married his "cousin Mr. William Bond of Maryland", then he was to act as the trustee. In event that his widow and daughters died without issue, then the testator's brothers, Peter and William Bond, were to inherit.

REF: Public Record Office, London, List 100.

BONE

Handeal Bone of Frederick, Nov. 1, 1761, "about to depart for a voyage to Germany".

REF: Wills, Liber 32, folio 187.

BOON

Nicholas Boon took the sacrament of the Church of England in St. Anne's Church, Annapolis, and subscribed to the Oath of Abjuration on Sept. 11, 1765, as a subject of Great Britain.

REF: Prov. Crt Judgements, Liber DD no. 9, folios 2-16.

BOOTH

John Booth, subject of Great Britain, on Sept. 5, 1785, declared himself a Christian, and subscribed to the Oath of Naturalization.

REF: Council Proceedings, Md. Archives, vol. 71, p. 135.

BOOTH-PYE

Madam Mary Pye, nee Booth, consort of Charles Pye of Cornwallis Neck, was the daughter of Charle Booth of Breinton, Herfordshire, and sister and ultimate sole-heiress of James Booth of Lincoln's Inn, Middlesex, England, who died testate 1771, leaving over £3000 to the heirs of his sister.

REF: Provincial Court Deeds, Liber JG no. 7, folio 19; Pr. Geo. Co. Deeds, Liber IRM no. 9, folio 205; Heraldic Marylandiana, by Newman.

BORDLEY

Thomas Bordley of Annapolis, Esq., 29 June 1726, "I Thomas Bordley of the Citty of Annapolis in the Province of Maryland, Esq., the Youngest Child of the Rev. Stephen Bordley Clerk late prebendary of St. Paul's and Rector of St. Mary's Newington London. . . . I release my Dear Sister Mary & Elizabeth Bordley in Newcastle upon Tyne all Claines or Demands whatsoever".

REF: Wills, Liber 19, folio 99.

BOSTON

Samuel Boston, Baltimore Co., 6 Jan. 1676/7, "I give unto my Sonne in Law George Goldsmith one gold Ring with a Seale on it" and referred to kinsmen in the Parist of Pinchback, Lincolnshire.

REF: Wills, Liber 5, folio 175.

BOUCHER

The Rev. Jonathan Boucher, rector of St. Anne's Parish 1770 Tory was born Mar. 1, 1731, at Bancogo, a small hamlet in the Parish of Bronfield, Co. Cumberland, Eng.

REF: Md. Hist. Mag., vol. 7, p. 1.

BOUQUET

Colonel Henry Bouquet, an Officer of His Majesty's Royal American Regiment, "a foreigner of the Protestant or Reformed Religion" was naturalized in 1762.

REF: Md. Archives, vol. 48, p. 206.

BOURNE

Thomas Bourne, Calvert Co., Aug. 4, 1703, "And as to willing all my messuages and houses in White Beare Court in London which are Mortgaged to Jacob Crawford deceased I give. . .to my wife", and to my wife the Personal estate in England.

REF: Wills, Liber 3, folio 251.

BOUYER

Balthazard Bouyer, subject of France, declared himself a Christian and subscribed on Sept. 17, 1793, to the Oath of Naturalization; county domicile not cited.

REF: Council Proceedings, Md. Archives, vol. 72, p. 350.

BOWER

Christian Bower took the sacrament of the Church of England in St. Anne's Church in Sept. 1765, and became a British subject.

REF: Prov. Crt Judgements, Liber DD no. 9, folio 15.

Stephen Bower became a naturalized subject on Sept. 10, 1762, after subscribing to the Oath of Abjuration under the Act of George II (13th year) and certifying that he had taken the sacrament on Apr. 14, 1762 at St. Anne's Church, Annapolis.

REF: Prov. Crt Judgements, Liber DD no. 2, folios 89-90.

BOWES

George Bowes, Talbot Co., Quaker, July 4, 1719, ". . .unto my youngest Sister named Agnes Bowes being altered by marriage I know not what her Surname is. . .she was married near Grarigg in Westmoreland".

REF: Wills, Liber 16, folio 369.

BOWLES

John Bowles of St. Mary's Co., Gent., who declared himself to be the son of Valentine Bowles of Deal, Co. Kent, England, Gent., bequeathed March 27, 1750, ". . .to my beloved Brother George Bowles, Gent., of the Parish of All Faith in St. Mary's County all Such money Rents and Arrears of Rents from the Estate in the Parish of Iskham in the co. of kent. . .in default to Mrs. Elizabeth Smith of Deal, Co. Kent, wife of Cornelius Smith, Merchant, daughter of my brother, Anthony Bowles, deceased".

REF: Wills, Liber 28, folio 347.

James Bowles, of the Patuxent, Merchant, only son of Tobias Bowles, sugar and tobacco merchant of London and Deal, England, died in Maryland circa 1727. He canceled all debts of his Uncle George [Bowles] and his poor relations in England and elsewhere. He was nominated, but not confirmed, for governor after the death of his Uncle John Seynour (1649-1709).

REF: Liber 19, folio 50.

At the distribution of the personal estate of Silas Bowles of St. Mary's Co., in 1775, a legacy was earmarked for "John Watson and his three Sisters in Scotland".

REF: Balances, vol. 7, p. 44.

On Feb. 19, 1705/6, Tobias Bowles of Deal, Co. Kent, England, Merchant, granted power of attorney to James Bowles of Patuxon River, Md., Merchant. No relationship was stated.

REF: Crt Deeds, Liber TP no. 4, folio 74.

BOWMAN

Samuel Bowman, Talbot Co., Aug. 27, 1768, "I give & bequeath to my affectionate sister Jane Bowman now or late of County Cumberland in Great Britain £15 Sterling".

REF: Wills, Liber 36, folio 530.

BOYES

In 1681 a bill for the naturalization of Cornelius Boyes of Baltimore Co. was introduced and passed.

REF: Md. Archives, vol. 7, pp. 149, 216.

BRADFORD

John Bradford, Prince George's by will dated 26 March 1726, "I give and bequeath unto my beloved son John Bradford one cottage house with a Small orchard...lying in open fields near the Village of Thinkinson in the County of Leicester in the Kingdom of Great Britain all which was bequeathed unto me by the will of my Uncle John Smith of the town of One Leap in the County of Leicester...unto my son John Bradford all that parcel of land being pasture lying in the town of Stoak Golding in the aforesaid County of Leicester now in the possession of my honoured father John Bradford of Stoak Golding". He furthermore named his kinsmen, John Carroll and Thomas Gantt executors of his estate.

By the will of Charles Carroll, the Emigrant, of 1 December 1718, styled as Major John Bradford and "Kinsman" he was bequeathed £6.

His widow, Joyce, was named kinswoman [niece] by Charles Carroll, late of Litterlouma, King's County, Ireland, by his will proved Anne Arundel Co. July 28, 1720. Her first husband was James Butler, Gent., who died intestate in Prince George's Co. in 1709, leaving issue and a large estate. It were the Butlers whom the Countess de Auzouer about 1770 enquired in her correspondence with Charles Carroll of Carrollton. Madam Joyce Bradford, as sister, approved the value of the inventory of the estate of Margaret Macnemara, likewise, a niece of Charles Carroll, the Emigrant.

REF: Inventories & Accounts, Liber 30, folio 205; Judgements, Liber 35, folio 174; Wills, Liber 16, folio 176; Liber 18, folio 464.

BRANDT

Marcus Brandt, Charles Co., Gent., July 23, 1705, "Whereas a Coppie of a Will Signed by my Brother Marcus Brandt late of the Island Barbadoes, Gent., deceased, has been transmitted to me which it appears yt there are Some Negroes and Sundry Sums of Money left me"; also referred to gold buttons left him by his grandfather Unnamed.

REF: Wills, Liber 13, folio 506; 1634 Visitation of London, Harleian Soc., Pub., vol. 15, p. 99.

The parentage of Capt. Randolph Brandt of Charles Co., but late of London and the Barbadoes, is listed in the 1634 Visitation of Middlesex and

London as the son of Marcus, late of London and the Barbadoes, who was son of Daniel Brandt of Hamburg, Germany.

REF: Harleian Soc. Pub., vol. 15, p. 99, vol. 90, p. 99; Wills, Liber 13, folio 506.

BRANTHWAYTE

William Branthwayte of Carlingbill, Co. Cumberland, an early Commander of Kent Isle in Maryland, was a grandson of Esquire Calvert of Kiplin. He is listed in the Visitation of Cumberland and Westmoreland as "having died beyond the seas".

REF: Foster's Visitation of Cumberland and Westmoreland, p. 16.

BRASSEUIR

Benojs Brasseuir "late of Virginia and Subject of the Crowne of france" his wife and children on December 4, 1662, were declared "free Dennizen freedome land to him and his heires to purchase". Later orthography Brashear.

REF: Md. Archives, vol. 3, p. 654.

BRATTEN

Thomas Bratten, Somerset Co., Sept. 29, 1712, the residue of his estate was to be "remitted to my father John Bratten of Drumlocher in the parish of Panghloyre near Londonderry, Ireland".

REF: Wills, Liber 13, folio 529.

BRENT

Giles Brent, Fulkes Brent, Mary Brent and Margaret Brent who settled in Maryland about 1640 were issue of Richard Brent, one-time High Sheriff of Gloucestershire, Gent., with proved descent from peers, Magna Carta Barons and ancient royalty.

Giles Brent of Fort Kent Manor, in his will proved in Stafford Co., Va., Feb. 15, 1671/2 made a bequest to "the right heirs of my honoured father Richard Brent, Esq., deceased, anciently Lord of the Manor of Admington and Lark Stoke in the County of Gloucester in England".

REF: The Complete Peerage; Burke's Extinct Peerage; Burke's Peerage; Dugdale's Peerage of England; Will probated Staff. Co., Va.; Judgements, Liber 28, folio 7, Hall of Records, Annapolis.

Elizabeth Brent on July 25, 1684, bound herself to Philip Clarke of Maryland for 4 years.

REF: Ghirelli, folio 10.

BREREWOOD

Thomas Brerewood of My Lady's Manor, Baltimore Co., died 1746, was the husband of the Hon. Charlotte Calvert, daughter of Benedict, 4th Lord Baltimore, and Lady Charlotte Lee who was the daughter of the 1st Earl of Lichfield and granddaughter of Barbara, Duchess of Cleveland, beloved by Charles II.

REF: Wills, Box 7, folder 19; Newman's Heraldic Marylandiana.

BREWEN

Hubbard Brewen, Maryland Merchant, "at present in London bound on a voyage to Maryland" devised his estate to his mother, Ann Brewen of

Brentingly, Co. Leicester, and his sister Ann Beestland wife of Henry Beestland of Market Overton, Rutlandshire.

REF: Glazier 187, Public Record Office, London.

BRICE

John Brice, Anne Arundel Co., Dec. 8, 1713, "I give and bequeath to my Brother John Brice of London Saw Maker the sum of £50 Sterling to be paid him by my Master Benjamin Hattley.... I give and bequeath to John Burcher of London Gunn fforge Eldest son of my Sister Elizabeth Butcher of Goose Grave in Northamptonshire Tenn pounds Sterling. I give and bequeath to Thomas Butcher and also ffrancis Butcher Sons of my aforesaid Sister Tenn pounds Sterling a piece".

REF: Wills, Liber 13, folio 589.

BRISPOE

Anthony Brispoe in 1685 declared that he was "born under the Dominion of the King of Spaine".

REF: Md. Archives, vol. 2, p. 460.

BROGDEN

William Brogden was ordained a Priest of the Church of England at the Chapel Royal at Whitehall, Westminster, 15 August 1735, and assigned to All Hallow's Parish, Anne Arundel Co., 18 July 1739.

REF: Prov. Crt Deeds, Liber EI no. 3, folio 170.

BROOKE

On Aug. 11, 1685, Anne Brooke, aged 20, daughter of Richard Stanford, baker, deceased, was bound to John Payne of Maryland for 4 years.

REF: Ghirelli, folio 11.

Robert Brooke, Esq., who died in Calvert Co., circa 1658 was listed in the 1634 Visitation of Hampshire, England. His maternal grandmother was Elizabeth, the sole-heiress of John Twyne. The Brooke tomb in Whitchurch, Hampshire, contains the Twyne quartering.

REF: Harleian Soc. Pub., vol. 64, pp. 214-15; Newman's Heraldic Marylandiana.

BROOKES

Thomas Brookes of the City of Bristol, Gloucestershire, was transported 1668.

REF: Patents, Liber 11, folio 316.

BROORD

In March 1701/2, the act and fee for the naturalization of James Brood [Broward] and his three sons, James, John and Solomon of Kent Co. came before the Lower House.

REF: Md. Archives, vol. 24, pp. 253, 280.

BROWN, BROWNE

David Brown, Somerset Co., 19 July 1697, "I give and bequeath unto the famous college at Glasgow as a Memoriall and Support of any of my Relations to be educated therein to be paid in Cash or Secured by good exchange to the Visitors or to Mr. James Browne and William Carmichael £100 Sterling".

REF: Wills, Liber 6, folio 150.

Colonel David Brown of Somerset Co., was the great-uncle of George Brown of Edinburgh, Scotland. The mother of the said George Brown was Mary Erskine afterwards Mary Brown, niece of the said Colonel David Brown and George Brown was the only son and heir of his mother.

REF: Prov. Crt Deeds, Liber DD no. 4, (1765-1770) folio 631.

An act of the 1686 Assembly was passed by which Derick Browne was naturalized.

REF: Md. Archives, vol. 13, p. 144.

On August 31, 1685, Elizabeth Brown, daughter of Thomas Brown of London, cornchandler, deceased, was bound to Richard Feverson for 4 years in Maryland; witnessed by Dorothy Brown, her mother.

REF: Ghirelli, folio 12.

Grace Browne, daughter of Richard Browne, of St. Andrew, Holborne, London, was bound to Robert Burman for 5 years in Maryland on July 25, 1685; witnessed by her father and mother Katherine.

REF: Ghirelli, folio 12.

Gustavus Brown, Charles Co. "I was born 10 April 1689 in Dalkeith, Scotland; parents Gustavus Brown son to Mr. Rich'd Brown, Minister of Salton in Scotland in the reign of Charles the first and Jane Mitchelson daughter of George Mitchelson grandson of Middleton". His 1762 last will and testament devised realty in Scotland.

REF: Bible printed Edinburgh 1676; see also Hayden's Virginia Genealogies, p. 147; Md. Wills, Liber 31, folio 633.

John Brown of London in 1690 sold to John Gaither 100 acres of "Freeman's Fancy", a plantation of 300 acres granted originally to John Freeman. In the same year he styled "John Brown of London, Mariner", sold a portion of "Abingdon" to James Finley.

REF: Anne Arundel Co. Deeds, Liber JH no. 2, folios 69, 201.

Capt. John Brown of London, Merchant, Jan. 9, 1700/1, appointed Capt. William Nichols, Mariner of the ship Happy Union, his lawful attorney for all goods, etc...of his son, John, late of London, Mariner, deceased.

The 1634 Visitation of London listed 10 Brownes, all armorial registrants. The merchants were Thomas Browne of Broad Street, originally of Essex, and Thomas Browne of Cripplegate Within, whose background was Gloucestershire — both having a son John.

REF: Anne Arundel Deeds, Liber WY no. 2 (1702-1708), folio 26, Harleian Soc. Pub., vol. 90, folios 110-115.

John Browne "Collector of Customs" at Pocomoke, Somerset Co., June 20, 1727, devised to his wife, Rachel, his estate in Maryland and what he anticipated from the estate of "My Mother Mrs. Margarett Browne of the Kingdom of England, widow".

REF: Wills, Liber 19, folio 751.

Vallentine Brown, Kent Co., Merchant, Jan. 29, 1719/20, declared himself "Late of the Kingdom of Ireland but now of Maryland . . . bequeath to my dear Brother Stephen Brown of the City of Dublin, Gent. except £10 which I bequeath to Mrs. Chivinn of London Goldsmith".

REF: Wills, Liber 17, folio 184.

BRUNE
Lewis De Roch Brune was naturalized in 1694 by an Act of the General Assembly.

REF: Md. Archives, vol. 19, p. 103.

BRYAN
Thomas Bryan, a native of Waterford, Ireland, where he was born Mar. 17, 1741, settled in Maryland and served in the Militia during the Revolutionary War; later settled in Jefferson Co., Ky.

REF: Revolutionary Pension Claims, S3050, National Archives.

BUCHANAN
Isabella, daughter of John Buchanan and Elizabeth his wife, late of the Parish of Clownis in Ireland, buried 18 June 1719.

REF: Original Register of St. Anne's Parish, p. 44.

BUCKLAND
William Buckland, born Oxfordshire, England, was nephew of James Buckland of London under whom he was bound as an apprentice in design and construction, settled in Annapolis, where he was responsible for the beauty of a number of eighteenth century buildings in Annapolis and the surrounding area. Annapolis consequently today has more original eighteenth century dwellings than Williamsburg. He died in 1774 at the age of 40, and left issue.

REF: William Buckland, by Beirne and Scard, pub. 1958.

BULL
Thomas Bull, Aug. 15, 1668, "That my brother-in-law Samuel Lucas of Dover, Baker, and John Marsh of the Same Town to be the executors and to receive estate in England".

REF: Wills, Liber 1, folio 325.

BULLOCK
Francis Bullock July 1, 1669, "And what remains to be sent home for London to be consigned to Mr. William Crouch, an Upholster, Living in Bishopgate Street at Devonshire House for the use of my mother Mrs. Joan Bullock."

REF: Wills, Liber 1, folio 347.

John Bullock, born 1753 in London, England, came to Maryland and served in the Militia of Harford Co., later settled in York Co., Penna.

REF: Revolutionary Pension Claim S22153, National Archives.

BURCH

On Aug. 11, 1685, Solomon Burch, son of John Burch of Guilford, Surrey, clarke, deceased, was bound to John Payne for 13 years in Maryland; witnessed by Elizabeth Burch, his mother.

REF: Ghirelli, folio 13.

BURFORD

Henry Burford, native of London, died Oct. 1818, aged 50.

REF: Congressional Cemetery, Washington, D.C.

BURGESS

Joseph Burges (sic) in will of 23 Oct. 1672, stated, "I Joseph Burges now of Marleborough in the County of Wilts in England, Merchant, but late of the Province of Maryland . . ." appointed his father-in-law John Keynes of Marleborough Afsd, Gent., his executor.

On May 22, 1674, Sir Robert Hanson, Knt, Lord Mayor of London, certified John Keynes of Marlborough, Co. Wilts, Gent., as executor of Joseph Burges, who said Keynes was about to make a voyage to Maryland "if God permits". Thomas Taylor, of Anne Arundel Co., acted as attorney for Keynes.

REF: Wills, Liber 1, folio 615; Testamentary Proceedings, Liber 6, folio 231-3.

BURKE

Martin Burke, born Co. Galloway, Ireland, Nov. 1752, settled in Montgomery Co., Md., where he enlisted in the Maryland Line of the Revolution; later lived in Scott Co., Ky.

REF: Revolutionary Pension Claims, S30298, National Archives.

"Garret Burke a native of Roscommon Co., Ireland, born June 11, 1786, died March 22, 1843".

REF: Stone in Trinity Churchyard, St. Mary's City, Md.

James Burke by will of Aug. 12, 1802, declared himself a "native of Ireland and an inhabitant of Fell's Point, Baltimore".

REF: Wills, Liber 7, folio 36.

BURN

Michael Burn, born in England, substituted for David Ross, in accordance with the "Act to procure Troops for the American Army", passed March Session 1778.

REF: Militia List., Md. Hist. Soc., Balto.

BURNLY

On Aug. 29, 1685, Peter Burnly, aged 21, was bound to George Morris for 4 years in Maryland; witnessed by Enoch Bennister of Canterbury.

REF: Ghirelli, folio 13.

BUTLER

James Butler of Ireland and Prince George's Co., Gent., married Joyce, a niece of Charles Carroll, the Emigrant. He died intestate in 1709 leaving issue (Thomas and Margretta and perhaps others) and an affluent estate. His widow married Major John Bradford of Prince George's County. It was the family of Butlers that the Countess de Auzouer of France enquired in her correspondence with Charles Carroll of Carrollton. In his reply of September 1771, "All the descendants of the House of Butler established in this Province soon after the settlement are extinct or so miserably reduced by proverty as to be unknown".

REF: Md. Hist. Magazine, vol. 39, pp. 203-204; Inventories & Accounts, Liber 30, folio 69; Adm. Accts, Liber 11, folio 173.

Captain John Butler [Boteler], Gent. of the Isle of Kent, in May 1640, deposed that he was 39 years of age and was a native of Roxswell Parish, Co. Essex.

REF: Md. Archives, vol. 4, p. 69, vol. 5, p. 212.

BUTTON
Richard Button, subject of Great Britain, declared himself a Christian on July 26, 1785, and subscribed to the Oath of Allegiance.

REF: Council Proceedings, Md. Archives, vol. 71, p. 39.

BYFIELD
Thomas Byfield, born in England, substituted for James Ringgold, in accordance with the "Act to procure Troops for the American Army", passed March Session 1778.

REF: Militia List, Md. Hist. Soc., Balto.

CADY
John Cady, native of Co. Galway, Ireland, died Feb. 7, 1878, aged 85 years.

REF: Holy Rood Cemetery, Georgetown, D.C.

CAILLE
John Caille of Dorchester Co., who died April 27, 1767, aged 47, was named as a son of John Caile (sic) of Howgate Foot, Co. Westmoreland, England. The will was dated September 27, 1746. The said John Caile by his 1767 will, "I do give to my Brother-in-law James Harmer of England the Money that he owes me upon Bond".

REF: Probate Office, Co. Westmoreland, Eng.; Wills, Liber 35, folio 375.

CALVERT
The ancestry of Leonard Calvert, First Governor of Maryland, and his two brothers who were adventurers on the Ark and the Dove is well documented (one slight error) in The Complete Peerage, 2d ed., vol.

CAMPBELL
Rev. Issac Campbell, born in Scotland, emigrated to Virginia 1748, rector of Trinity Parish, Charles Co., died 1784, aged more than 60 years.

REF: Allen.

James Campbell, born Mar. 16, 1748, the son of John and Jane Campbell of Smithsborough, Co. Monaghan, Ireland, married Jan. 11, 1764, Sarah Rutter.

REF: St. Mary Anne's Parish Register, Cecil Co.

John Campbell of Nottingham, Prince George's Co., on Sept. 28, 1770, made John Weir, Thomas Pringle and William Thompson Smith of the Island of Dominica, West Indies, to settle his one-eighth undivided interest in improved property and negroes on Hope Plantation of the Parish of St. Paul's and to "make over" to the said Thomas Campbell.

REF: Prov. Crt, Liber 12.

Walter Campbell, Dorchester Co., 27 Aug. 1736, "I give and bequeath unto my Uncle William Campbell of Dunbarton in North Britain ...all lands what name or title they are called or in what Country they are scituated".

REF: Wills, Liber 21, folio 870.

CAMPERSON
Leonard Camperson of Talbot Co. was naturalized in 1694 by an Act of the General Assembly.

REF: Md. Archives, vol. 19, p. 211.

CARLOSS
Anna, wife of James Carloss and daughter of Lawrence Gannon, a native of Strokestown, County Roscommon, Ireland, died Cumberland, Md., May 22, 1851, aged 24 years.

REF: St. Peter's and St. Paul's Roman Catholic Cemetery, Cumberland.

CARLYLE
Alexander Carlyle of Hopewell, Somerset Co., Md., Merchant, who had land interest also in Virginia, was father to Adam Carlyle of Britain. On April 22, 1771, Adam Carlyle "late of Lyne Kilno in North Britain, but now of Brampton, Co. Cumberland, Esq.," appointed George Chalmers of Maryland, Esq., and Charles Little of Alexandria, Va., his attorneys to dispose of his father's estate.

REF: Prov. Crt, Liber 12, folio 297.

CARMICHAL
William Carmichal, Queen Anne's Co., Dec. 8, 1768, referred to the last will and testament of his deceased brother, Walter Carmichal of Edinborough.

REF: Wills, Liber 37, folio 130.

CARR
Joseph Carr of Baltimore Town who published the first edition of The Star Spangled Banner was a music publisher of Middle Row, Holborn, Parish of St. Andrews, London, before his settlement in the United States in 1794.

He married Mary Jordon, born c1739, London, according to the register of St. Martin's-in-the-Fields, Trafalgar Square, London. "Joseph Carr of this parish B[achelor] and Mary Jordon Sp[inster], London, were married by license of the Bishop of London this thirtieth day of January 1766 by me R. Dixon, Curator".

REF: Card Index. Parish Registers of St. Martin's in the Fields, London. Society of Genealogists, London.

CARRINGTON

Robert Carrington, late of the Barbadoes, was domiciled in Annapolis June 24, 1731.

REF: Prov. Crt Deeds, Liber PL no 1, folio 1.

CARROLL

Charles Carroll the Barrister who died Anne Arundel Co. 1755 was the son of Charles Carroll Esq. of "Clounlisk in the King's County and Kingdom of Ireland", according to the tombstone of Dorothy (Carroll) Blake at Bennett's Point, Queen Anne's Co., daughter of the Barrister. Charles Carroll of Carrollton acknowledged him as a kinsman, but the relationship was not stated. A secondary source stated that the ancestry of the Barrister was from an "older branch of the Ely O'Carrolls".

The arms used by the Barrister were slightly different from those of Charles Carroll, the Emigrant and Attorney General. Other differences included their religious faith. The Barrister in his will stated that he died in communion with the Church of England.

REF: Newman's Heraldic Marylandiana, pub. 1968; Life & Correspondence of Charles Carroll of Carrollton, by Rowland, pub. Putnam's 1898.

Charles Carroll of Carrollton writing in September 1771, to the Countess de Auzouer, a Carroll, who had married a French nobleman, stated that "Charles my grandfather ye first of our family who settled in the Province was second son of Daniel Carroll of Litterlouna in King's County, in the Kingdom of Ireland, younger brother of Anthony of Lishenboy...He entered the Society of the Inner Temple in London on 6th Mary 1685...the family estate being greatly impaired by the iniquity of the times, which had stripped the most ancient Irish families of their property he resolved to seek his fortune far distant from the scene of such oppression...He arrived in Maryland on ye first of October 1688 with a commission from ye then Lord Baltimore constituting him Attorney General".

REF: From the copybook of Carroll, pub. Md. Hist. Magazine, vol. 39, pp. 203-204.

"Here lyeth Interr'd the Remains of Dorothy Carroll Daughter of Mr. Charles Blake of Wye River in the Province of Maryland & Wife of Charles Carroll son of Charles Carroll Esqr. of Clounlisk in the King's County and Kingdom of Ireland...She departed this life the 8 day of July Anno Domini 1734 Aged Thirty-one Years, Seven Months and Twelve Days".

REF: Tombs at Bennett's Point, Queen's Anne Co.

James Carroll, "Fingaul," All Hallow's Parish, Anne Arundel Co., 12 Febr. 1728/9, "I give to forty such poor mendicants of and in the parish of Eglish and Lorrah in Lower Ormond in the County of Tippernery in the Kingdom of Ireland" each 10 shillings of Irish money.

REF: Wills, Liber 19, folio 791.

CART

Monser Cart, Worcester Co., Mar. 8, 1748/9, declared himself to be late of the Island of St. Domingo.

REF: Wills, 26, folio 27.

CARTER

Edward Carter of Edmonton, Co. Middlesex, England, by will of October 18, 1680, requested that he be buried in the middle isle of St. Dunstan's in the East and near the remains of his former wife, Anne Carter. To his present wife, Elizabeth, he devised land in Virginia and Maryland called "Werton" late in the occupation of William Salisbury.

REF: Public Record Office, London, Cottle 128; Md. Hist. Mag., vol. 5, p. 294.

On July 14, 1684, Henry Carter was bound to Robert Burman for 6 years in Maryland.

REF: Ghirelli, folio 13.

Richard Carter of Maryland, Mercer, who died intestate before Dec. 28, 1708, was born Nov. 30, 1637, son of Thomas Carter and Unika Palisser his wife, of Kirby Wiske, Yorks. He died leaving a widow, Elizabeth, and kinsmen in Yorkshire, Newcastle-upon-Tyne and London.

REF: Provincial Court, Liber PL no. 3, folio 135.

"Here lyes Interr'd the Body of Richard Carter son of Thomas Carter of Kirkly Wisk in the County of York In Great Britain Yeoman who departed this life the 4th Day of March 1708 in the Seventy First Year of his age". His heirs are listed in Provincial Court Deed.

REF: Pleasant Valley Plantation, Talbot Co.; Talbot Co. Deeds, Liber RF no. 11, folio 136 (1710); Prov. Crt Deeds, Liber PL no. 3, folio 135.

CARTWRIGHT

Matthew Cartwright later of St. Mary's Co., declared in 1671 that he was "borne att Middlebourgh in the Province of Zealand under the Domion of the States Generall of the united Provinces".

REF: Md. Archives, vol. 2, p. 282.

CARY

Thomas Cary, of London, Merchant, imigrated to Maryland 1657.

REF: Patents, Liber Q, folio 475.

CASH

John Cash, son of Thomas Cash, of Jamaica Place, was bound to Richard Heath for 7 years in Maryland on July 11, 1684.

REF: Ghirelli, folio 15.

CASTAGNET

Paul Castagnet, a subject of France, on Oct. 22, 1792, declared himself a Christian and subscribed to the Oath of Naturalization. County domicile not stated.

REF: Council Proceedings, Md. Archives, vol. 72, p. 294.

CAUSINE

Ignatius Causine of Causine Manor, Charles Co., Md., on Apr. 7, 1671, stated that he was the "son of Nicholas Causin a Subject of the Crown of France was born at the House of his Father in St. George's River in this Province of an English Mother".

REF: Md. Archives, vol. 2, pp. 256-257.

CAUSSE

Bartholomew Causse "native of the town of Guillac, Department of Hau Languedoc, France", wrote his will on June 1, 1799 at the home of Jean Baptist Chirac, Baltimore Co.

REF: Balto. Co. Wills, Liber 6, folio 189.

CAY

The Rev. Jonathan Cay, a native of Northumberland, and Anglican clergyman, rector of Christ Church Parish, Calvert Co., died testate June 6, 1737.

REF: Rightmeyer's Maryland Established Church.

CEELY

Thomas Ceely styled himself of Cornwall, England, and St. Mary's Co., July 1, 1676.

REF: Wills, Liber 5, folio 53.

CHALMERS

John Chalmers, a Jacobite, captured in 1715 at Preston, Lancashire, and transported to Maryland for seven years of servitude, wrote a protest with keen legality.

REF: Md. Archives, vol. 25, pp. 347-349.

CHALMERS

Robert Chalmers, Gent., late "in Leith North Britain" was granted power of attorney by Thomas Johnston of Glasgow, North Britain, to collect from the heirs of Charles Christie, late Merchant, of Joppa, Baltimore Co., May 7, 1763.

REF: Prov. Crt Deeds, Liber DD no. 3, folio 165.

CHAMBERS

Richard Chambers, of Calvert Co., 1700, mentioned his will already made and left in the possession of Mr. John Ellyston, councilor-at-law, Co., Kent, Eng.

REF: Wills, Liber 11, folio 82.

CHANDLER

Job Chandler of Portobacco, Charles Co., by his will of April 27, 1659, "It is my will and desire if any of my brothers in England shall desire to have any of my children to be sent to them". He is reputed to be the son of a draper of Ware, Herefordshire. One brother is placed as Richard Chandler of London, Merchant, who was granted by Lord Baltimore the Manor of Stratford of 1,000 acres on the Chester River for transporting 20 persons into Maryland to inhabit. The Chaundler family, an armorial, was registrant at the 1634 Visitation of London.

REF: Wills, Liber 1, folio 97; Patents, Liber 6, folio 475; Harleian Soc. Pub., vol. 15, p. 157.

CHAPPELEAR

The Chappelear family of St. Mary's Co., were Huguenots, the progenitor, Isaac Chappelear, Surgeon, died at sea enroute to Maryland with his wife and children. His will made at sea on January 18, 1706/7, was probated at the Prerogativbe Court of Canterbury on May 10, 1707. The aforesaid Isaac Chappelear was a son of the Rev. Louis Chappelier (sic) and his wife, Ann Arnaud, of London, original from Languedoc Province, France.

REF: Register of the Huguenot Churches of London, P.C.C., London; The Chappelear Family, by Nancy Chappelear, pub. Washington, 1963.

CHARLOTTE

"John Charlotte, late of the City of London in the Kingdom of Great Britain now of the City of Annapolis. . .to wife two houses in City of London situate and lying near Cow Crosse", March 10, 1764.

REF: Wills, Liber 32, folio 156.

CHASE

Jeremiah Chase emigrated to Maryland about 1734, after reading at Cambridge University. He was the son of the Rev. Richard Chase of St. Andrews, London, who died 1742.

REF: Md. Diocesan Library, Balto.

The Rev. Thomas Chase married July 19, 1763, Ann Birch, eldest daughter of Thomas Birch, chirurgeon and man-midwife of the town of Warwick, Co. Warwick, England

REF: St. Paul's Parish Register, Baltimore Co.

CHATARD

Pierre Chatard M.D., fled from his father's plantation in Quartier de Plaisance, Santo Domingo in 1794, at the uprising of the blacks; settled in Baltimore.

REF: Hardridge.

CHENEY

Andrew Francis Cheney, chirurgeon, son of James Cheney of Mount Cheney, Co. Cork, Ireland, married July 15, 1755, Mary Day Scott, daughter of Day Scott.

REF: St. Mary Anne's Parish Register, Cecil Co.

CHESELDYNE

Kenelm Chesldyne who emigrated to Maryland in 1669 was son of the Rev. Kenelme Cheselden (sic) and Grace Dryden his wife of Bloxham, Lincolnshire.

REF: Harleian Soc. Pub., vol. 3, p. 21; vol. 73, p. 73, pp. 27-28; vol. 87, p. 66; Heraldic Marylandiana.

CHESHIRE

John Cheshire of Anne Arundel Co., Dec. 31, 1747, bequeathed one-half of his Maryland estate to his cousins, William Cheshire and Richard Pook of Great Britain.

REF: Wills, Liber 25, folio 557.

CHRISTIAN

Lawrence Christian in 1674 upon naturalization declared that he was a native of Germany.

REF: Md. Archives, vol. 2, p. 400.

CHRISTIE

Charles Christie, Baltimore Co., Mar. 17, 1757, ". . . third part with the Real Estate to be converted into money and remitted to my mother Katharine Maniece in Scotland and failing of her to be equally divided between my Brother William Christie and my Sister Mrs. Johnson and Elizabeth Christie".

REF: Wills, Liber 30, folio 279.

Robert Chrystie (Christie) of London, Merchant, was heir in the will of Daniel of St. Thomas Jenifer, probated Annapolis, 1790, as well as "to my relations the Misses Christies in Glasgow". Anne Jenifer, sister of the said Daniel of St. Thomas Jenifer, had married Robert Chrystie by 1734.

REF: Chas. Co. Court Proceedings, Liber R no. 2, folio 484; A.A. Co. Wills, Liber JG no. 1, 194.

CHURCHMAN

John Churchman of Saffron Waldo, Co. Essex, England, in 1696 married Hannah Cerie, daughter of Thomas Curie, late of Oxfordshire.

REF: Nottingham Quaker Monthly Meetings, Cecil Co.

CLAGETT

Thomas Clagett, Calvert Co., July 25, 1701, "I give an bequeath unto my Sonn Edward Clagett and his heirs for Evere all my right title Clayme and interest whatsoever of in and too Severally messuages and Tenements Situate and Being in the Cittie of London in the Kingdom of England formerly belonging too and being part of the estate of my ffather Coll Edward Clagett, deceased, and now in possession of my brothers & sisters or their Assignes".

REF: Wills, Liber 3, folio 8; 1664 Visitation of London, Harleian Soc. Pub., vol. 65, p. 39.

CLARKE

Daniel Clarke, Anne Arundel Co., 2 Oct. 1696, "Whatsoever shall fall at Pennsylvania and what there is in Old England that is my part to my son Thomas by birth".

REF: Wills, Liber 6, folio 97.

George Clarke (1692-1753) settled in St. Mary's Co. and is reputed to have been a refugee from Scotland for his support of the Stuart dynasty.

REF: Family notes.

Richard Clark, Merchant of London, emigrated 1875 on S.S. Maryland.

REF: Patents, Liber 15, folio 332.

Robert Clarke on December 14, 1689, declared himself "now of St. Giles' Parish without Cripple Gate London late of Maryland" devised his entire estate in Maryland to his mother, Jane Clarke, and Brother, John Clarke.

REF: Wills, Liber 3, folio 727.

Sarah Clarke by will of Sept. 26, 1802, declared herself "late of the City of London in the Kingdom of Great Britain but now of Baltimore".

REF: Balto. Co. Wills, Liber 7, folio 69.

CLARLY

George Clarly, aged 52 years, was bound to John Seaman, on July 27, 1685, for 4 years in Maryland.

REF: Ghirelli, folio 17.

CLAUSON

Jacob Clauson "late of Amstell and Subject of the States of Holland" on July 30, 1661, was declared a "free Dennizen".

REF: Md. Archives, vol. 3, p. 430.

CLEMENTS

Andrew Clements in 1674 at the time of his naturalization stated that he was a native of Sweadland [Swedish settlements on the Delaware].

REF: Md. Archives, vol. 2, p. 400.

CLEMENTSON

On July 29, 1661, Andrew Clementson "late of New Amstell and Subject of the Crowne of Sweden" was issued letters of denization.

REF: Md. Archives, vol. 3, pp. 429-430.

CLEMENTZ

On Apr. 23, 1763, Leonard Clementz of Frederick Co. became a naturalized subject after subscribing to the Oath of Abjuration and certifying that he was a German Protestant and had received the sacrament of the Reformed Congregation of Frederick Town.

REF: Prov. Crt Judgements, Liber DD no. 3, folios 130-1.

Valentine Clementz of Frederick Co. after certification that he had received the sacrament of the Reformed Church of Frederick Town took the Oath of Abjuration under the Act of George II (13th year) and thus on Sept. 15th was declared a naturalized subject.

REF: Prov. Crt Judgements, Liber DD no. 2, folios 346-8.

CLINDINING

Thomas Clindining of Baltimore Town Feb. 5, 1762, "I leave and bequeath the Remainder and residue of my Estate to my Natural Son [that is, of the blood] John Clindining of Glasgow if living, but in care he should be Dead then my Will is that the remainder and residue of my Estate be equally divided between my Wife Margaret Clindining Daughter of James Wilson Writer in Glasgow in North Britain and my brother John Clindining, Wiggmaker, in Glasgow to be divided share and share alike".

REF: Wills, Liber 31, folio 570.

CLINTON

Thomas Clinton, born March 25, 1760 of Irish parents, served in Maryland Line during the Revolution, later domiciled in Alleghany Co., Md.

REF: Revolutionary Pension Claim S34693, National Archives.

COBBY

On Aug. 12, 1684, Peter Cobby, son of Robert Cobby of Buckington Town, maltster, deceased, was bound to Thomas Tench of Maryland for 7 years.

REF: Ghirelli, folio 18.

CODD

St. Leger Codd, Cecil Co., Gent., Sept. 9, 1706, "To my son James Codd all my lands in the Parishes of Wateringbury, Lenham and Witchin in the County of Kent in Old England...for want to such heirs (that is James) my will is that all ye mentioned Lands be equally divided between my two sons Berkeley Codd and St. Leger Codd". He was son of William Codd (1604-1653) of County Kent, Engl, and Mary St. Ledger daughter of Sir Warham St. Leger of Warham, Knt., dubbed at Greenwich, June 13, 1608, by James I.

REF: Wills, Liber 12, folio 195; Visitation of Co. Kent, Harleian Soc., vol. 51; Hasted's Kent, vol. 2, pp. 398, 422; Ms. 4108, ff. 63-64, British Museum, London; Heraldic Marylandiana, by Newman.

CODY

William Cody of Charles Co., Taylor, and his children were naturalized in 1711 by an Act of the Assembly.

REF: Md. Archives, vol. 38, p. 143.

COE

On August 6, 1684, Susanna Coe, daughter of Andrew Coe, printer, deceased, was bound to Philip Clarke for 5 years in Maryland.

REF: Ghirelli, folio 18.

COLBERT

John William Colbert, a native of Dublin, Ireland, where he was born in 1759, landed in Baltimore 1773 and served in the Maryland Line during the Revolution; later domiciled in Clermont Co., Ohio.

REF: Revolutionary Pension Claim R2113, National Archives.

COLE

Charles Cole of Annapolis Merchant, Mar. 31, 1753, stated that he made a last will and testament in London.

REF: Wills, Liber 30, folio 511.

Joseph Cole, born in England, substituted for William Spurrier, in accordance with the "Act to procure Troops for the American Army", passed March Session 1778.

REF: Militia List, Md. Hist. Soc., Balto.

Robert Cole of St. Clement's Bay, St. Mary's Co., Yeoman, Apr. 2, 1662, "I give and bequeath all the Estate whatsoever be in Land houses or money that doth any wayes belonging unto me in England or of Right Should belong to me unto my Children in Generall after Death of my Loving Mother Mrs. Jane Cole of Heston in the County of Middlesex"; mentioned his Cousin Mr. Henry Hanks of Holbourn in the City of London.

REF: Wills, Liber 1, folio 182.

COLEBATCH

The Rev. Joseph Colebatch, native of Derbyshire, Anglican clergyman, died 1734 in Maryland.

REF: Rightmeyer's Maryland's Established Church.

COLKE

Oliver Colke in 1674 upon naturalization stated that he was a native of Sweadland [Swedish settlements on the Delaware].

REF: Md. Archives, vol. 2, p. 400.

COLLETT

John Collett by his will, Baltimore Co., 1673, mentioned his uncle, Nicholas Collett of London, and his uncle's daughter, Elizabeth Collett.

REF: Wills, Liber 1, folio 401.

Richard Collett emigrated to Maryland 1650, was son of John Collett, died Mar. 2, 1650, aged 72, of London, and the latter's wife Susan Farrar, daughter of Nicholas Farrar.

REF: Collect Pedigrees in Ryley & Dethick, Visitation of Middlesex, p. 47.

COLLEY

Peter Colley of Talbot Co. was naturalized in 1694 by an Act of the General Assembly.

REF: Md. Archives, vol. 19, p. 211.

COLLICKMAN

In March 1701/2, the act and the fee for the naturalization of Derrick Collickman, Planter of Cecil Co., of Dutch parents came before the Lower House.

REF: Md. Archives, vol. 24, pp. 253, 280.

COLLIER

Mathew Collier, Queen Anne Co., 24 Jan. 1726/7, "I give and bequeath unto my Brother William Collier Living in Rosemary Lane near Little Tower Hill London, Baker, the sum of £20...I give and bequeath to my honored father if Liveing the Sum of £20 Sterling".

REF: Wills, Liber 19, folio 373.

COLLINS

George Collins, Calvert Co., 20 December 1683, "I give to my Daughter Mary in England one hogshead of good tobacco".

REF: Wills, Liber 4, folio 39.

COLMORE

Thomas Colmore of London, Merchant, July 8, 1724, purchased for £370/6/3 from Thomas Bladen of the Parish of St. James within the Liberty of Westminster, Co. Middlesx, England, Fort Kent Manor with Court Baron and Court Leet and all profits of said courts.

REF: Prov. Crt Deeds, Liber PL no. 6, folio 67.

Thomas Colmore, styled late of London, but "now of Calvert Co., Merchant", in 1725 acted as attorney for Benjamin Taylord of London, heir to Joseph Taylor, late of Prince George's Co., deceased. In 1731 when the said Benjamin Taylor of London granted power of attorney to William Govane of Anne Arundel Co., Edmond Colmore of London was one of the witnesses.

REF: Pr. Geo. Co. Deeds, Liber IS no. H, folio 189; Liber IS no. L, folio 141.

COLVIN
Andrew Colvin, born c1798 in Parish of Dramgon, Co. Cavan, Ireland, emigrated to Maryland and died at Hancock, Washington County, on March 14, 1844, aged 46 years.

REF: Headstone in Methodist Cemetery, Hancock.

COLYER
Edward Colyer, Quaker, Aug. 20, 1688, "I give & bequeath all ye remainder of my Estate both real and personal unto my Sister Rebeckak Halbert of London in England".

REF: Wills, Liber 6, folio 28.

COMEGYS
In 1671 Cornelius Comegys made his "humble petition" for the naturalization of himself wife and children, whereby, Cornelius Comegys the "Elder borne in Lexmont belonging to the State of Holland, your Peticoner Millementy Comegys in Barnevelt under the Dominion of the said states your Peticoner Cornelius Comegys the Younger borne in Virginia and your Peticoners Elizabeth, William and Hannah borne within this Province".

REF: Md. Archives, vol. 2, p. 331.

CONELLY
Brian Conelly, Cecil Co., Apr. 16, 1754, "I will and bequeath all my Worldly Goods to my mother Juggy or in Irish Swan Conoley of Grelly near Navin in the County of Merth in the Kingdom of Ireland, but in Case of the Death of my mother I will that my Estate shall descend to my two sisters, vizt Juggy and Jennett equally". He named Mr. James Cusack of Co. Merth the trustee.

REF: Wills, Liber 35, folio 379.

CONN
Hugh Conn, born Macgilligan, Ireland, c1685, studied in Foghanveil (Faughanvale), graduated at University of Glasgow. Emigrated to Maryland, died testate Prince George's County, Md., 1752.

REF: History of the Presbyterian Church in America, pub. by authority of the Presbyterian Hist. Soc., Phila. 1858.

CONNELL
Morgan Connell was among a ship load to Irish servants who were transported in 1678 by Phillip Popleston, "Master of Ship Encrease" of Youghall, Co. Cork, Ireland, and assigned to William Sharpe of Talbot Co.

REF: Patents, Liber 20, folio 184.

CONNER
Arthur Conner, Talbot Co., Dec. 1, 1721, "...unto my two Sisters Sarah and Shely the full one half of my estate after my just debts and Legacies are paid, they live in Lisburn in Ireland".

REF: Wills, Liber 22, folio 103.

CONNOR

Richard Connor, aged 21, was bound to John Paine on Sept. 23, 1685, for 4 years in Maryland.

REF: Ghilleri, folio 19.

CONTEE

Colonel John Contee and his nephew Colonel Alexander Contee of Prince George's Co., were natives of Plymouth, Devonshire, whereas Peter Contee who married Frances Stockett was of Barnstaple, Devonshire. Colonel John Contee, Gent., by his will 1708 "To my Nephew John Contee Son to my Brother Mr. Peter Contee of Barnstaple in the Kingdom of England" £50; "To my Mother Mrs. Grace Contee and my Loving Sister Agnes Berry in the Kingdom of England" land in Charles Co.; "To Brother Mr. Peter Contee living in Barnstaple in the Kingdom of England" a seated plantation in Charles Co. Alexander Contee, aged circa 17, nephew of Colonel John made deposition.

REF: A.A. Co. Deeds, Liber WT no. 2, folio 79; Wills, Liber 12, folio 276.

COODE

John Coode of St. Mary's Co., was born circa 1648 and served as a clergyman of the Church of England at Penryn, Cornwall, from "whence he was turned out", prior to his emigration to Maryland. He was baptized Apr. 3, 1648, in St. Gluveas Parish, son of John and Grace (Robins) Coode.

REF: Visitation of Cornwall by Vivian; Md. Hist. Mag., vol. 70, p. 3; Maryland Archives, vol. 19, p. 469.

COOK, COOKE

Andrew Cook of St. Giles in the Field, Middlesex, Gent., by will of Dec. 31, 1711, devised land called "Cooke's Poynt" at the mouth of the Choptank River in Dorchester Co., to his son Ebenezer Cook and daughter Anne Cook.

REF: Barnes 4, Public Record Office, London.

Francis Cook, Frederick Co., May 12, 1762, "I ordain for each of my Brothers in Germany the third part of my Estate belonging to me from my ffather's Estate there and if any or all of them should come into this part each of them shall have one Shilling".

REF: Wills, Liber 31, folio 629.

George Cook, Rector of Christchurch Parish, Calvert Co., Feb. 28, 1763, "To my son George Cook, to my daughter Jannet Montgomery in Virginia, to the children of my Daughter Elizabeth Cook now Adquick to them and their heirs forever a Bond granted by Dr. Andrew Scott to me Dated at Edinburgh or Commongate in Scotland" 1732.

REF: Wills, Liber 33, folio 374.

Henry Cook, born Hahn, Germany, circa 1753, served in the 4th Regiment, Maryland Line, during the Revolution, and later domiciled in Baltimore Town.

REF: Revolutionary Pension Claim, S8234, National Archives.

On Sept. 4, 1685, Henry Cook, son of John Cooke of St. Giles-in-the-Fields, Middlesex, butcher, deceased, aged 19, was bound to Solomon Niccolls for 4 years in Maryland, witnessed by Elizabeth Cook his sister.

REF: Ghirelli, folio 19.

John Cooke and wife emigrated from London 1660.

REF: Patents, Liber 9, folio 249.

COOPER

Anne Cooper, widow of Peter Cooper, St. Mary's Co., 10 Sept. 1651, "My will and desire is that two of my Said Children be left to the Tuition of my brother John Depotter and the other two to the Tuition of my cousin Richard Bridgman both living in Amsterdam . . . I do desire that my brother William Daynes accompany my Children in their Voyage for Holland . . . loveing brothers William Daynes and Thomas Daynes my Executors".

REF: Wills, Liber 1, folio 29.

Daniel Cooper of Frederick Co., after certification that he had received the sacrament of the Calvinistic Church of Geneve on Aug. 29, 1763, took the Oath of Abjuration under the Act of George II and thus on Sept. 15th became a naturalized subject.

REF: Prv. Crt Judgements, Liber DD no. 2, folios 347-9.

Edward Cooper, Cecil Co., 16 Mar. 1716/7, "Should please God that my Daughter Mary aforesaid Should depart this life before she arrives at age that then my wife Should give unto my Loving sister Margaret Cox wife of Cornelius Cox of Allerster (?) in Warwickshire in the Kingdom of Great Britain, Skinner".

REF: Wills, Liber 14, folio 345.

On July 27, 1685, Margaretta Maria Cooper, spinster, was bound to John and Elizabeth Haines for 4 years in Maryland.

REF: Ghirelli, folio 19.

Patrick Cooper, a Jacobite, captured at Preston, Lancashire, in 1715, and sold in Maryland for 7 years of servitude, petitioned for his freedom on August 3, 1721, which was denied.

REF: Md. Archives, vol. 34, p. 164.

Sampson Cooper of York, England, by will dated Aug. 11, 1659, probated in Maryland Feb. 20, 1659/60, named wife Bridget and sons Samuel and Jonathan devising them estate real and personal in England and Virginia (Maryland).

REF: Md. Wills, Liber 1, folio 209.

On Nov. 25, 1663, Samuel Cooper of St. Mary's Co., son of Sampson Cooper, late of Rippon, Yorks, England, Alderman, appeared at Provincial Court and chose his own guardian.

REF: Md. Archives, vol. 49, p. 94.

Thomas Cooper of Oxford Town, Talbot Co., Dec. 30, 1773, ". . . wife Elizabeth to pay Thomas Cooper [nephew] son of John in the County of Lancaster in the Kingdom of Great Britain £250/7/6 . . . to pay Thomas Hogg son of my sister Elizabeth in the County of Lancaster £250/7/6".

REF: Wills, Liber 39, folio 646.

COPLEY

Lionel Copley, 1st Royal Governor of Maryland, was born 1648, matriculated at Brasenose College, Oxford, July 1655, married Anne, daughter of Sir Philip Boteler of Walton, Woodhulls, Herts; said Lionel was the grandson of Sr. Geoffrey Copley of Sprottsborough created Baronet by Charles II.

Lyonell Copley (sic), by his will of St. Mary's Co., 7 Sept. 1693, "I give and bequeath unto my Son Lyonell Copley Equall part or Share of all my personal estate Except hereafter Excepted and that I am now or in right ought to the possession of in England and Maryland after the other third to be divided equally between my Sonn John Copley and my daughter Ann Copley".

Governor Copley was a native of Wadsworth, York, and son of Lionel Copley of Wadsworth, and Frisalina, daughter of George Ward of Caplesthroen, Cheshire, widow of John Wheeler, of Cripplegate, within, London, apothecary.

REF: Wills, Liber 6, folio 51; Visitation of York, Mss no. 4630, folio 107, British Museum; 1634 Visitation of London, Harliean Soc. vol. 15, p. 341.

CORDEA

Marke Cordea of St. Mary's Co. in 1671 declared that he was a native of Normandy in France. Hester Cordea, his wife, in 1674, when she petitioned for naturalization stated that she was "born att Deepe Normandie".

REF: Md. Archives, vol. 2, pp. 282, 400.

CORE

Elizabeth Core, spinster, aged 17, on July 6, 1685, bound herself to Richard Heath for 4 years in Maryland.

REF: Ghirelli, folio 19.

CORNELISON

On July 29, 1661, Mathias Cornelison "late of New Amstell and Subject of the Crowne of Sweden" was issued letters of denization.

REF: Md. Archives, vol. 3, pp. 429-430.

CORNISH

Major John Cornish, Somerset Co., 20 September 1707, signed himself as "John Cornish Son to Robert Cornish of ye Parish of Thurleston in County of Devon Yeoman".

REF: Wills, Liber 12, folio 201.

CORNWALYS

Captain Thomas Cornwalys, Esq., one of the Gentleman of Fashion on the Ark who held manorial rights on several manors in Maryland was from Co. Norfolk. His lineage was registered at the Herald's Visitation of Norfolk.

REF: Harleian Soc. Pub. vol. 85, p. 66.

COSINS
Bill for the naturalization of John Cosins was introduced in the Assembly in 1683.

REF: Md. Archives, vol. 7, p. 461.

COTTON-BURDITT
Verlinda Cotton, married first Thomas Burditt and secondly Richard Boughton of Charles Co., Md., was born in Accomac Co., Va., and was the daughter and sole-heiress of the Rev. William Cotton who died in Accomac Co. before 1642. The said Rev. Mr. Cotton was the son of Madame Joane Cotton of Bunbury, Cheshire. The Cotton family of Co. Chester was registered in the 1633 Visitation of London as armorial.

REF: Will of William Cotton, probated Northampton Co., Va.; Md. Archives, vol. 60, p. 133; Visitation of London, vol. 1, p. 193, pub. by Harleian Soc. of London 1880.

COUGHLANE
John Coughlane was among a ship load of Irish servants who were transported in 1678 by Phillip Popleston "Master of Ship Encrease" of Youghall, Co. Cork, Ireland, and assigned to William Sharpe of Talbot Co.

REF: Patents, Liber 20, folio 184.

COURTNEY
Thomas Courtney, a native of Armagh Co., Ireland, came to America with British Army, defected and enlisted in the 7th Md. Regt., during the Revolution under the name of John Smith, aged 74 in 1833 and a domicile of Brown Co., Ohio.

REF: Revolutionary Pension Claim, R2371, National Archives.

COUTURIER
M.A.C. Couturier divorcee Lavall in his will dated June 14, 1814, and probated in Baltimore County on December 12, 1825, stated "I was born in the Parish of L'ance a Veaux in the Ward of Missez jurisdiction of Petit Goave, Island and Coast of Saint Domingo in lawful marriage of deceased Matharin Couturier and Ann Pian my father and mother inhabitants of the said Ward of Missez. I was christened in the Parish of St. Ann of L'ance a veaux. I was born the seventh of December One Thousand seven hundred and forty seven. I am Catholic Roman which has been my religion and in which I die". He appointed Mr. Anthony Pontier, Merchant of Baltimore, his executor.

REF: Balto. Co. Wills, Liber 12, folio 201.

COX, COXE
The Rev. Charles Cox, son of Andrew, of Kemberton, Salop, on March 19, 1677, was licensed to preach in Maryland.

REF: Rightmeyer's Maryland's Established Church.

Thomas Coxe, Calvert Co., 22 February 1675/6, "I give and bequeath to my Deare and living wife Ann Coxe of Laycocke in Wiltshire, England, all my estate in Maryland, but if. . .my wife shall be dead before such time as she shall have notice of my death and can be possessed of this my estate, then, my will is that this my whole estate both Reall and personall be equally distributed amongst the children of my sisters".

REF: Wills, Liber 5, folio 28.

William Coxe of Kent Isle, May 26, 1640, aged 35 years deposed that he was born at Scarcliffe, Derbyshire.

REF: Md. Archives, vol. 5, p. 197.

CRABTREE
Samuel Crabtree, Talbot Co., Sept. 10, 1776, bequeathed wearing apparel, silver sleeve buttons, silver shoe buckles, knee buckles, breast and stock buckles to "my son Samuel Crabtree of Old England who did reside in the County of York".

REF: Wills, Liber 41, folio 406.

CRACROFT
John Cracroft [Craycroft] died testate Calvert Co., 1698, was of Hackthorn Parish, Lincolnshire. His plantation carried the name of "Hackthorn Heath".

REF: Visitation of Lincolnshire: Newman's Heraldic Marylandiana.

CRAIG
George Craig, Baltimore Town, 5 January 1816, bequeathed the residue of his estate "to my mother Margaret Craig of Balo Bitt as in the Queens Co., Ireland" in event of her death "to my Sister Sarah who is married to Robert Taylor of Monastereron, Co. of Kildare, Ireland".

REF: Wills, Balto. Co. Liber 10, folio 102.

CRAIK
James Craik, M.D., born 1730 in Dumfiresshire, Scotland, one-time of Port Tobacco, Charles Co., Md., served in the American Revolution, also the French and Indians Wars, later of Fairfax Co., Va.

REF: Sketch of the Life and Character of Dr. James Craik, by J. M. Toner; Appleton Cyclopedia of Amer. Biography.

CRAMER
A.M.C. Cramer, born Oct. 18, 1777, at Dounpatrick County Downs, Ireland, died Cumberland Dec. 29, 1872.

REF: Headstone, Rose Hill Cemetery, Cumberland.

Johann Georg Cramer, born 1730, at Carlsbrunn, Nassau-Saarbrucken, died Sept. 27, 1784, Frederick Co.

REF: Evangelical Lutheran Church, Fred.

Maria wife of George Cramer, born Jan. 17, 1763, in Velcklinger, Nassau-Saarbrucken, daughter of Conrad Volck and Susanna Margreth his wife, died Aug. 26, 1784, Frederick Co.

REF: Evangelical Lutheran Church, Fred.

CRAMLICH
Jacob Cramlich became a naturalized subject on Sept. 10, 1762, after subscribing to the Oath of Abjuration under the Act of George II (13th year)

and certifying that he had received the sacrament of the Church of England at St. Anne's Church, Annapolis on Apr. 14, 1762.

REF: Prov. Crt Judgements, Liber DD no. 2, folios 89-90.

CREAGH

Although tradition in the Maccubin-Creagh branch of the family has the Creagh ancestry as Scotch-Irish, Richard Maccubin who married Elizabeth Creagh in 1772 styled his wife's kinsman, James Creagh, as "late of London".

REF: A.A. Co. Deeds, Liber IB no. 3, folio 320.

CRISALL

John Crisall of Annapolis, 7 Dec. 1785, named his son, Thomas, of Elsworth, Great Britain, son William of London, England, and his daughter Sarah whom he believed lived in Cambridgeshire and whom he was informed to be married and also the son of another daughter unnamed "who is apprenticed to a blacksmith in Cambridgeshire and a married daughter Grace of Huntingdonshire.

REF: A.A. Co. Wills, Liber TG no. 1, folio 322.

CRISMAND

Joseph Crismand of Charles Co., Planter, was naturalized in 1712 by an Act of the Assembly.

REF: Md. Archives, vol. 38, p. 165.

CRISMANDS

Petitions for the naturalization of Charles Crismands of Charles County was read in the Lower House in 1712.

REF: Md. Archives, vol. 27, p. 135.

CROMWELL

Inference is quite strong to place Richard, John, William and Edith, all proved as brothers and sister, as the grandchildren of John Cromwell of Malmesbury, Wilts, and Edith his wife. The latter John Cromwell died testate 1639 and was buried in St. Paul's Churchyard, Malmesbury. It is proved that one or two of his children of the said William and Edith Cromwell settled in New England and left issue. The oft repeated statement that the Maryland Cromwells were descendants of Oliver, the Puritan, is wholly without truth or even a possibility.

REF: Arch Deaconry of Wills, Wiltshire, 7639 no. 23; see also the ancestry and descendants of Oliver, the Puritan, in "Anne Arundel Gentry" 1933 ed, by Newman.

CROSSE

On Sept. 14, 1685, John Crosse, son of Leonard Crosse, of Newgate St., London was assigned to Michael Tawney of Maryland for 9 years; witnessed by Jane Crosse, his mother.

REF: Ghirelli, folio 20.

CROXALL

Joanna Croxall of Baltimore Co. was sister to James Carroll of "Fingual" of All Hallow's Parish, Anne Arundel Co. The said James Carroll by his 1728 will devised his "sister Johanna Croxall" and his cousin Mary Higgins 980 acres of "Park Hall" on Pipe Creek and personalty. Inasmuch as James Carroll bequeathed legacies to 40 mendicants in the parishes of Eglish and Lorrah in Lower Ormond, County of Tipperary, Kingdom of Ireland, it thus proves her Irish birth or ancestry. In 1718 Madam Craxall [Crocksdell] styled "kinswoman" received a legacy in the will of Charles Carroll, the Emigrant. One of the sons of Joanna Croxall was baptized James Carroll Croxall. She died testate in Baltimore Co. during 1756.

REF: Wills, Liber 16, folio 176, Liber 19, folio 791, Liber 25, folio 456, and Liber 30, folio 53.

CULLY

Henry Cully of Kingston, Queen Anne Co., December 8, 1748, ". . . unto my Brother Andrew Cully, Flax Draper in Newbuerg in Barkshire. . . to my Sister Ann James the wife of Thomas Idne, Blacksmith of Marlborough, Wilts. . . to my sister Sarah Horrell of East Smithfield, London".

REF: Wills, Liber 25, folio 571.

CUMMING

Henry Cumming of Parish of St. Botolph Algate, London, Mariner, by will 6 Sept. 1768, "to my Loving Sister Elizabeth Hamilton now living in Maryland the sum of £400 for her own use and not control of her husband". James Hergest, executor of Henry Cumming, appointed James Dick of Annapolis his attorney.

REF: Wills, Liber 38, folio 449.

William Cumming was among 80 Scottish Jacobites who were exiled to Maryland, arriving in August 1717 at Annapolis, and sold into servitude for seven years, as having participated in the Rebellion of 1715 to place James, the Pretender and alleged son of James VII on the throne. He was baptized in Firres Parish, Elginshire, in 1690, the son of David Cuming of an ancient family descended from Scottish peerage and royalty.

REF: Forres Parish Records, Elginshire; Complete Peerage.

CUREY

Robert Curey, Cecil Co., Mason, 2 Jan. 1731/2, "I give and bequeath unto my Well Beloved Brother John Curey in the Kingdom of Ireland my Best Hatt, my best Wigg and my best Briches".

REF: Wills, Liber 21, folio 156.

CURTIS

Michael Curtis of St. Mary's Co., Gent., was naturalized in 1695 by an Act of the General Assembly.

REF: Md. Archives, vol. 19, p. 281.

DAILY

Cornelius Daily, Jan. 15, 1768, Dorchester Co., "Money to be sent Home to Farrell Daily, Brigget Daily, Mary Daily, and Judah Daily my brothers and sisters" living in the County of Math [Merth], near Rills, Ireland.

REF: Wills, Liber 36, folio 343.

DALLEY

Daniel Dalley was among a ship load of Irish servants who were transported in 1678 by Phillip Popleston "Master of Ship Encrease" of Youghall, Co. Cork, Ireland, and assigned to William Sharpe of Talbot Co.

REF: Patents, Liber 20, folio 184.

DALYRIMPLE

Charles Dalyrimple "son of Orangesfields" was at Fort Glasgow on Sept. 1, 1670, preparing to sail for Maryland.

REF: Md. Hist. Soc., vol. 76, no. 1, p. 15.

DANIEL

"Here lyeth the body of John Daniel son of Mr. Joseph Daniel of Warrington in the County of Lancaster; died April 18th 1731, in the 41st year of his age".

REF: Headstone Burying Grounds of Shrewsbury Parish, Kent Co.

DARBY

Deborah Darby on Mar. 20, 1793, produced her certificate to the Baltimore Meeting of Quakers from Coalbrookdale, Shropshire, England.

REF: Md. Hist. Magazine, vol. 4, p. 21.

DARNALL

Philip Darnall of Essendon, Herts, his wife, Mary, and three children Henry, John and Elizabeth emigrated to Maryland prior to 1664. The first wife of Charles, 3d Baron of Baltimore, was likewise a member of this family. Their ancestoral seat was Bird's Place, Essendon, Hertsfordshire.

REF: Clutterbuck's Hist. of Herfordshire, vol. 2, p. 135; Salmon's Herts, p. 28; Md. Hist. Magazine, vols. 21-22.

DARNALL-BOTELER-MYNNE

John, Henry, Phillippe, Ralph, sons of Henry Darnall, were heirs in the will of Anne Boteler (Butler), dated August 24, 1619, of Stapleford, Hertfordshire, also her goddaughter, Anne Darnall, and her "cosens" Susanna and Mary Darnall.

Madame Anne Boteler was the widow of Richard Boteler, Esq. Their tomb is in Watton-at-Stone Parish Church, Herts, Translation from the Latin: "Here lies the bodies of Richard Boteler of Stapleford in the County of Hertfordshire, Esq., who died 5 May 1614, and Anne his wife one of the daughters of John Mynne of Hertingfordbury, Esq., who died 12 October A.D. 1619".

REF: Public Record Office, London, Parker 106.

DAUNTRES

An act was introduced at the 1684 Assembly for the naturalization of Jasper Dauntres.

REF: Md. Archives, vol. 13, p. 126.

DAVEGHE, DE VAGHA

John de Vagha was naturalized in 1694 by Act of the General Assembly.

REF: Md. Archives, vol. 19, pp. 46, 104.

DAVIES

Jonathan Davies, father of Colonel Allan Davies of Charles Co., Gent., emigrated to Maryland from England about 1705 with a young family. He died in Charles Co. in 1766.

REF: Chancery Liber IR no. 7, folio 268 (1747), Hall of Records, Annapolis.

DAVISON

In 1695 an Act passed the Assembly to naturalize Daniel Davison [Dauison] Sr. and Daniel Davison Jr. his son of Calvert Co.

REF: Md. Archives, vol. 19, p. 137.

DAY

John Langley of St. Saviour's Southwalk, Co. Surrey, Phisita, 9 Feb. 1698, bequeathed £40 to his daughter, Mary Day, of Maryland.

REF: Pitt, 26, Public Record Office, London.

DEAKES

Henry Deakes of Lyon Creek, Calvert Co., 20 September 1691, "I give and bequeath unto my well beloved wife [Priscilla]...all my Right title and Interest of all that Deceased ffather's John Deakes Innholder of London in St. Buttols Aldersgate parish that is to say all that my father left me as by his last will and testament may appear and also by Sr Tho: Plaer then Chamberlain of London".

REF: Wills, Liber 2, folio 256.

DEAKINS

William Deakins, born in England circa 1739; enlisted at Harford Co., Md. and served in a Continental Regiment, later domiciled in Williamson Co., Tenn.

REF: Revolutionary Pension Claim S38659, National Archives.

DE BARRETT

Isaac De Barrett in 1669 upon naturalization declared himself a native of Harlem, Holland.

REF: Md. Archives, vol. 2, p. 205.

DE BARRETTE

Barbarah De Barrette wife of Garret van Sweringen, in 1669 declared herself a native of "Valenchene in the Low Countryes Belonging to the King of Spayne".

REF: Md. Archives, vol. 2, 205.

DE BELLEVUE

Louis Sebastian Charles St. Martin de Bellevue, refugee from Isle a Vache, Southern portion of Santo Domingo, settled in Frederick Town, died 1805.

REF: Hartridge.

DEBRULER

By an Act of 1701 of the Assembly John Debruler of Baltimore Co. and his sons, John, William and other sons and daughters (unnamed) were naturalized.

REF: Md. Archives, vol. 24, p. 204.

DE CEAUSE

Leonard de Ceause of Anne Arundel Co., a native of Switzerland, petitioned for naturalization in 1735.

REF: Md. Archives, vol. 39, pp. 175, 181, 236, 241, 244, 251.

DE COURCY

In 1763 it was declared by the coheiresses of Patrick de Courcy, Baron Kinsale, and the sons-in-law that William de Courcy of Wye River, Md. was the rightful heir to the Earldom of Kinsale and Barony of DeCourcy. The descent was through the Salic Law. William de Courcy, however, did not press his claim nor in the correspondence were there any statements as to which Baron the five brothers of Maryland and the two sisters descended. Kinsale was the oldest extant barony in Ireland and Great Britain.

By the deCourcys of Maryland refusing to prove their claim, the barony went to a ropemaker and waterman of Rhode Island, an alleged impostor, according to the daughters of the late baron.

Elizabeth Coursey, Queen Anne's Co., widow, 27 Nov. 1727, "And whereas being Informed that my Mother Mrs. Elizabeth Desmyniers late of the Citty of Dublin in the Kingdom of Ireland Deceased has by her last will and testament Given and bequeathed unto me her Daughter Elizabeth Coursey the sum of £160 Sterling and the one Moyety of the Residue of her fortune not Desposed of by her said Will".

REF: DeCourcy Manuscript and Papers. Manuscript Division, Library of Congress; Lodge's Peerage of Ireland, vol. 6, 1789 ed; The Complete Peerage; Wills, Liber 19, folio 644, Hall of Records, Annapolis.

James de Coursey of Lincoln's Inn, Co. Middlesex, England, possessed land on the Chester River in 1663.

REF: Patents, Liber 10, folio 447.

DEERING

Edmund Deering, Isle of Kent, May 1640 deposed that he was aged 25 and was a native of Somsoin (sic), perhaps Somerton or Somersham, Co. Suffok.

REF: Md. Archive, vol. 5, p. 211.

DEFFOURR

In 1708 an Act for the Naturalization of Benjamin Deffourr "a protestant native of France" was passed by the Assembly.

REF: Md. Archives, vol. 27, pp. 368, 370.

DE GRAFFENRIED

Christopher de Graffenried one-time of Switzerland subscribed to the following; thus he became a subject of the King of Great Britain in Maryland. "These are to Certifie all whom itt may Appear at the s^d Sessions and then and these persuant to the Late Act of Parlim^t made in the Seventh Year of the Present Majesties Reigne Entitled an Act for Naturalization of foreigne protestants Delivered in Court a Certificate of his Taken ye Sacrament of the Lords Supper According to the Directions of s^d Act and made due Proof of the s^d Cert^e so Delivered as aforesaid & took & Subscribe the Oaths and Repeated & Subscribed the Declaration Appointed in & by the S^d Act Given under the Seale of the s^d Sessions aforesaid. Recorded 3d October 1720".

REF: Provincial Court, Liber PL no. 5, folio 123.

DE LA GRANGE

At the 1684 Assembly an act was introduced for the naturalization of Arnoldas De la Grange.

REF: Md. Archives, vol. 13, p. 26.

DE LAPRADE

Anne-Josephine de Laprade, wife of Commander of Artillery and Adjutant General of the Southern District of Santo Domingo, died Baltimore 1799, buried in St. Peter's Churchyard.

REF: Hartridge.

DELARINCENDIERE

E.P.M. Delarincendiere, formerly of the French portion of St. Domingo but "now a resident of Frederick Co.", declared that he imported negroes into Maryland 5 Nov. 1792, for his personal use.

N. Delarincendiere fils declared himself "Proprietor Planter of the French part of St. Domingo now resident of Frederick Town" and that he arrived in Baltimore 25 of Oct. last [1792] by ship "Carolina" Capt. Watson commanding and that he brought a slave for his personal use".

REF: Fred. Co. Deeds, Liber WR no. 11, folio 755.

DE LA VINCENDIERE

Etienne Bellumeau de la Vincendiere, refugee from Santo Domingo, settled in Frederick Co.

REF: Hartridge.

DE LE MAIRE

When John Lemaire [de le Maire] applied in 1674 for naturalization, it was stated that he was "borne att Anjou in the Kingdom of France".

REF: Md. Archives, vol. 2, p. 400.

DE LE ROCHE

Charles De le Roche in 1669 upon his petition for naturalization stated that he was a native of the "kingdom of ffrance". By his will dated Dec. 16, 1675, he bequeathed "Loving brother Peter Delaroche and Mary Burt wife of Burt, Chirygeon Now living in London" his estate at the death of his wife.

REF: St. M. Co., Wills, Liber PC no 1, folio 14; Md. Archives, vol. 2, p. 205.

DE MAGNAN

Marguerite Elisabeth Pauling de Magnan, daughter of Gabriel Michel de Magnan, married Etienne Bellumeau de la Vincendiere. At time of the uprising in St. Domingo she and her two daughters were in France; she later emigrated to Maryland and settled at the Hermitage on the Monocacy near Frederick Town.

REF: Hartridge.

DE MOISNE

Bill for the naturalization of Peter Maide de Moisne was introduced into the Lower House in 1683.

REF: Md. Archives, vol. 7, p. 461.

DEMONDIDIER

Anthony Demondidier Sr., Baltimore Co., 2 Oct. 1693. If children died without issue "the land and plantation or plantations may fall to Elizabeth Horton of London my wife Martha Demondidier one Sister". He appointed Martha Demondidier the executrix but if she died before performance is complete "it is my will and desire that Samuel Smith of Bedeford in England be my attorney. . .". The Horton family was registrants at the 1634 Visitation of London.

REF: Wills, Liber 2, folio 289; Harleian Soc. Pub., vol. 15, p. 395.

DE MONTAGUE

Nicholas de Montague of Cecil Co. was naturalized in 1694 by an Act of the General Assembly.

REF: Md. Archives, vol. 19, pp. 85, 104.

DE MOUDERER

Anthony De Mouderer of Anne Arundel Co. in 1671 declared the Kingdom of France as the country of his nativity.

REF: Md. Archives, vol. 2, p. 282.

DENT

Thomas Dent, Esq., is listed in the 1684 Visitation of Cambridgeshire under his brother's register, Prof. Peter Dent of Cambridge University, as having "ob. in Maryland in the West Indies". The family, however, was an ancient one of Yorkshire.

REF: The Genealogist, vol. 3, p. 242; Original Visitation filed at College of Arms, London; The Maryland Dents, by Newman, 1963.

DENYS

Benjamin Denys Baltimore Co., 20 July 1817, bequeathed to brother "James Denys all claims which I have in France against Martille Sr. of Havore and Cocken & Froplong of Bordeas. . .to my mother widow Michael Denys the portion which I might Inherit from my Cousin James Denys, deceased, at Demquer".

REF: Balto Co. Wills, Liber 10, folio 402.

DE RING

Hans Jacob De Ring of Baltimore Co., upon application for naturalization in 1671 declared himself a native of Holland.

REF: Md. Archives, vol. 2, p. 282.

58

DESJARDINES
John Desjardines in 1674 when he petitioned for naturalization stated he was a native of the "Kingdome of france".
REF: Md. Archives, vol. 2, p. 400.

DESRAMEAUX
Apauline Fournier Martin Desrameaux of Island of St. Lucie now residing in the City of Baltimore by will of May 6, 1803, devised property in the Island of St. Lucie.
REF: Balto Co. Wills, Liber 7, folio 221.

DESSDA
Jean Dessda by will of Dec. 31, 1792, declared himself formerly an "inhabitant of St. Lucie". Witnesses were F. Delaporte, Jauno de Lascaris, August Grenue and Francois de Block.
REF: Wills, Balto. Co., Liber 6, folio 270.

DE VALLON
Marie Pauline Dugas de Vallon, daughter of Madam Bellumeau, settled at the Hermitage, Frederick Co., after residence in Santo Domingo.
REF: Hartridge.

DE YOUNG
Jacob Clause De Young of Baltimore Co. at naturalization in 1671 stated that he was a native of Holland.
REF: Md. Archives, vol. 2, p. 282.

DHYNIOSSA
Alexander Dhyniossa of Foster Island, Talbot Co., and Margretta his wife and Johannes, Peter, Hoanna, Christian and Barbara their children at time of naturalization in 1671 stated that their were "borne in Holland under the Dominion of the States General of the united Provinces".
REF: Md. Archives, vol. 2, p. 282.

DICK
James Dick, of Edinburgh, Scotland, Merchant, Burgess and Guildbrother, son of Thomas Dick, formerly, of said city, Merchant, Bailey and Dean of Guild, came to Maryland about June 1, 1734, and settled as a Merchant in London Town; in 1740 I made a trip to Edinburgh and came again by way of London in 1741, and brought with me my wife, Margaret, and our daughter, Mary, who was born in Edinburgh, Nov. 20, 1732.
REF: Register of All Hallow's Parish, Anne Arundel County.

Peter Dick received the sacrament in accordance to the rites of the Reformed Church of Frederick Town in accordance to the Act of George II, appeared at court on Apr. 16, 1760, subscribed to the Oath of Abjuration and was declared a naturalized subject.
REF: Prv Crt Judgements, Liber DD no. 1, folio 189.

DICKINSON

George Dickinson, born circa 1758 in England and arrived in Maryland when aged 10; enlisted at Gunpowder Falls, Balto. Co., in the Flying Camp in 1776; later domiciled in Tuscaramas Co., Ohio.

REF: Revolutionary Pension Claim S4277, National Archives.

James Dickinson of Talbot on September 16, 1785, devised his nephew John Singleton "my land and Tenement called Leggerton Wood near Sampre in the County of Cumberland in England".

REF: Talbot Co. Wills, Liber JB no. 4, folio 46.

DICKS

John Dicks, a subject of Great Britain, on Apr. 22, 1793, declared himself a Christian and took the Oath of Naturalization. County domiciled not cited.

REF: Council Proceedings, Md. Archives, vol. 72, p. 333.

DIGGES

The Digges family of Maryland and Virginia is directly descended from Sir Dudley Digges of Chilham Castle, Co., Kent, who was knighted on April 29, 1607, during the reign of James I. The ancestry in the direct male line can be traced to the reign of King John (1199-1296) of Magna Carta fame.

REF: Hasted's History of Co. Kent, vol. 3, pp. 126-130; Berry's Kent Pedigrees: Visitation of Kent, Harleian Soc. Pub. vol. 42, p. 64.

DITTON

Thomas Dent, Mar. 21, 1675, certified that William Ditton, Merchant, who came in the Golden Lyon in his voyage from England, died at the plantation of Richard Keene of the Patuxent, on Mar. 21, 1674, and William Ditton and his brother married two sisters and that his wife died and left no issue and made two nieces heirs and that Mrs. Masters, his kinswoman's wife, who came likewise in the Golden Lyon should have £70.

REF: Wills, Liber 2, folio. 49.

DOBBIN

George Dobbin was born Co. Monaghan, Ireland, emigrated to Baltimore in 1798, and died Dec. 3, 1811.

REF: National Intelligencer, D.C.

DONALDSON

James Donaldson of Annapolis, Merchant, by will of February 27, 1737/8, devised land in Dumbartonshire and bequeathed legacies to brother-in-law Colin McLaughlane at Bonnachra, to _____ Leckie of Croy, Scotland, and _____ Leckie of Artmore, husband to the testator's sister, Gresil Donaldson.

REF: Wills, Liber 21, folio 891; Newman's Heraldic Marylandiana.

DONALDSON — LOWRY

James Donaldson Lowry of Baltimore Town changed his name to James Lowry Donaldson on January 7, 1804, in order to inherit from his uncle, John Lowry Donaldson, late of London, England, Esq.

REF: Laws of Maryland, 1803, chapter 81.

DONAUGHE

John Donaughe, born County Galway, Ireland, died September 15, 1852, aged 83; Julia Ann Donaughe, born County Galway, died June 2, 1846, aged 76 years.

REF: Graveyard St. John's Roman Catholic, Carrol Chapel, Montgomery Co.

DONDON

Hanes Dondon, subject of Great Britain, on Nov. 20, 1789, declared himself a Christian and subscribed to the Oath of Naturalization. County domicile not cited.

REF: Council Proceedings, Md. Archives, vol. 72, p. 59.

DORSEY

Considerable research has been conducted professionally in England to prove the parentage of Edward Dorsey of Maryland whose sons gave the peculiar name of "Hockley-in-the-Hole" to their Anne Arundel Plantation. The latest research presents more conclusive evidence that Edward the Emigrant was a grandson of Thomas Darcy of Hornsbye Castle, Yorks, and London who died testate in 1605, leaving a matured son Edward. The Darcys of Hornsbye Castle were a cadet branch of the noble baronage of Darcy, of which Thomas Darcy aforesaid was the great-grandson of Thomas, Lord Darcy, who was executed in 1557 by the decree of the mighty Henry VIII.

REF: Debrett of London, the official authority for British ancestry and publisher of the Ancestry of British Royalty and Nobility.

DOUGLAS, DOUGLASS

The Scottish ancestry of Colonel John Douglass of Cold Spring Manor and Blithewood Plantation, Charles Co., has been placed at Blithewood, now within the town of Glasgow, but once the feudal estate of the Elphinston family in which the Douglases intermarried.

REF: Original research among Scottish parish registers and court records; see also Douglas references listed in Marshall's Guide.

"Erected in Memory of John Douglass of Castle Steuard, Wigtonshire, Scotland, who died here Nov. 2, 1832, Aged 36 years".

REF: Churchyard of Monocacy Chapel, Montgomery Co.

DOWDEE

Peter Dowdee "Borne in the Kingdom of France but now living in Somersett County" was naturalized by act of 1698.

REF: Md. Archives, vol. 20, p. 148.

DOWELL

Nicholas Dowell, Bohemia, Cecil Co., July 19, 1704, "I give and bequeath unto my Cozen Samuel Dowell one....of Tobacco provided he removeth out of the Country of England....I give and bequeath unto my brother's Children in England one-half of" residuary estate. Legacy to wife during life then "to Returne to my said Brother's Children meaning my brother Joseph's Children in Bennetts Cattle [Castle] in London."

REF: Wills, Liber 3, folio 734.

DOWNING

Francis Downing, a native of Yorkshire, England, born Jan. 1, 1746; settled in the Colonies in 1768 and was domiciled in Montgomery Co., Md. when he enlisted at Frederick Town for the Flying Camp and saw service around New York; later lived in Scott Co., Ky.

REF: Revolutionary Pension Claim W8674, National Archives.

DOYNE

The Doyne family was among the Anglican families which settled in County Wexford, Ireland. Robert and Joshua Doyne, brothers, were transported to Maryland about 1670, but returned to Ireland and emigrated in 1680 — Joshua Doyne bringing his wife. Robert Doyne of Wexford received caveat from a public officer in 1645, but the age bracket would indicate that he was of an older generation than the two Maryland colonists.

REF: Professional research conducted for this compiler, but the destruction of records by the Irish revolutionists precludes more definite results.

DRISKOLE

Cornelius Driskole was among a ship load of Irish servants who were transported in 1678 by Phillip Popleston "Master of Ship Encrease" of Youghall, Co. Cork, Ireland; and assigned to William Sharpe of Talbot Co.

REF: Patents, Liber 20, folio 184.

DU CATELS

Edne Germain du Catels, native of Auxere, France, fled from Santo Domingo to Maryland, about 1795.

REF: Hardrige.

DUCHENET

Peter Durant Duchenet by his will of June 20, 1798, declared himself "late of the Island of Currasoo [Curacao] in the West Indies but an inhabitant of Baltimore City.

REF: Balto. Co. Wills, Liber 6, folio 107.

DU FOURR

An Act for the Naturalization of Benjamin Du Four [Deffourr] of Anne Arundel Co., Planter, a Protestant of France, was passed the Assembly Dec. 17, 1708.

REF: Md. Archives, vol. 27, p. 369-370.

DUHATTOWAY

Jacob Duhattoway in 1675 when petition was made for his naturalization it was stated that he was "borne att Dortt Holland under the Dominion of the States Generall of the United Province".

REF: Md. Archives, vol. 2, p. 460.

DUKE

Richard Duke, born in or about 1613, being aged 35 in 1648, was one of the Adventurers on the Ark in 1634. He was absence from the Province between 1642 and 1647 and returned to England in 1653 to bring his wife and children to Maryland. Very strong evidence exists to place him as the Richard Duke of the Parish of Otterburne, Devonshire, son of Richard. A Richard Duke was buried in the churchyard of Otterburne Parish church "27 March 1653".

REF: Otterburne Parish Register; View of Devonshire "by Thomas Wessote, pub. 1845; The Flowering of the Maryland Palatine", by Newman, pub. 1961.

DULANY

The following is from the front page of a Book of Common Prayer and was written by Daniel Dulany 3d: "Of my father's family, my grandfather, Daniel Dulany the Elder, was born in Queen's Co., Ireland, and until 1710 wrote his name Delany and thereafter Dulany. He was a cousin to Dr. Patrick Delany, the friend of Dean Swift, Head Master of Trinity College, Dublin. I have several letters from Dr. Delany to his cousin, my grandfather. The father of my grandfather married a second wife, when my grandfather's home became uneasy to him, and the little aid he received from his father made him quit the university, while yet a youth and leave his country for Maryland, where he arrived almost penniless and would have been indentured for a term of years to pay his passage but for the kind aid of Mr. Plater".

REF: The prayer book had belonged to the mother of the writer who was born a Tasker and who died at Brighton, Eng., 1822, aged 98. Md. Hist. Mag., vol. 13, p. 20

NOTE: For more than 50 years this author has searched diligently for the statement that Daniel Dulany the Elder was an indentured servant which has so often been repeated in print. While many honorable men of aristocratic lineage through circumstances came to the Colonies under indentureship, it was no disgrace. From the phraseology of his grandson, it is concluded that Colonel Plater paid his passage or the difference which was owing and thus *save him from being sold into indenture*.

The inventory of Colonel George Plater, recorded in 1707 in St. Mary's Co., does list Daniel Dulany as his servant — certainly the technicality of the legal contract between master and servant. He became a law clerk to Colonel Plater and when he completed his contract he sailed for London and read law at Gray's Inn.

The two Dulanys "the Elder" and "the Younger" became outstanding authorities of jurisprudence and it was acknowledged that no student of law or member of the King's Bench could surpass the brilliancy of Daniel Dulany the Younger.

The writer of the family history, per prayer book, like many conservative Marylanders was a Tory and consequently settled in England. See also, Inventories and Accounts, Liber 28, folios 20, 32, Hall of Records, Annapolis.

DULIN

Morish Dulin was among a ship load of Irish servants who were transported in 1678 by Phillip Popleston "Master of Ship Encrease" of Youghall, Co. Cork, Ireland, and assigned to William Sharpe of Talbot Co.

REF: Patents, Liber 20, folio 184.

DUNCH

Walter Dunch, formerly of London, Mariner, was domiciled on 500 acres of land in 1668.

REF: Patents, Liber 11, folio 320.

du ROBERET

Francis John Maria du Roberet, born 3 Sept. 1764, at Ploernel Diocese of St. Malo, Bretagne, "formerly Lieutenant of the Navy of his Most Christian Majesty", but then of Baltimore Town, by his will July 15, 1799, bequeathed his only heir "Madam Relagia du Roberet my only sister formerly a Religious in the Convent of the Infant Jesus at Lambese in Bretagne but now residing at Rennes in Bretagne and in her default the Marquis du Roberet and the Countesse de Thergue his sister my first cousin" the portrait of the King and Queen in the little golden chain and "my silver seal". His physician was M. Sourac, and the witnesses to his will were Ann Chefontainer, George de Perrigny, Ch. de la Fillce, De la Ruehe Therandrawn, Ch. M^{dre} De la Fullaye, and Le Ch^r d^e Ustou.

REF: Balto. Co. Wills, Liber 6, folio 198.

DUSSEUIL

Jacques Dusseuil "native of St. Nazaire, District of Toulon, Department of Var now residing in the City of Baltimore" 15 Vendmaire 9th yr. 1801 of the Republic bequeathed property to his father, Jacques Dusseuil, of Toulon.

REF: Balto. Co. Wills, Liber 6, folio 465.

DUTRITEE

Claudius Dutritree was naturalized in 1694 by an Act of the General Assembly.

REF: Md. Archives, vol. 19, pp. 46, 103.

EARECKSON

In 1682 a bill was introduced and passed for the naturalization of Mathew Eareckson of Kent Co.

REF: Md. Archives, vol. 13, pp. 268, 330.

EARLE

"James Earle of Craglethrope, England, settled in Maryland with his family Nov. 1683".

REF: Earle Burying grounds, Queen Anne's Co.

EASBY

William Easby, born Jan. 22, 1791, Stockely, Eng., came to United States with his parents Feb. 1794, died July 29, 1854.

REF: Congressional Cemetery, Washington, D.C.

EBURNATHY

John Eburnathy, Chas. Co., by will 11 March 1733/4, "I give and bequeath to my well beloved father John Eburnathy in or near Arnagh in the Kingdom of Ireland.... devise also to my three brothers Thomas, James and William Eburnathy in or near Arnagh".

On Mar. 12, 1734/5, Thomas and James Eburnathy coheirs of their brother John Eburnathy, deceased, Innkeeper of Chas. Co. by power of attorney from their father John Eburnathy and brother William Eburnathy joint heirs of said John Eburnathy of Arnagh, Parish of Kilmore, Kingdom of Ireland to William and James Middleton of Chas. Co., Gent., portion of "His

Lordship's Favour" as bought by said John Eburnathy of Richard Beale which Ann Aburnathy, relict of John, then possessed.

Oct. 23, 1739, "James Eburnathy late of Co. Arnagh in Kingdom of Ireland but now of Chas. Co. . . . by virtue of power of attorney from William Eburnathy of Co. Arnagh my youngest brother of 13 July 1734" deeded to John Hamill lots in Charles Town formerly in possession of John Eburnathy and "now in possession of Ann Eburnathy".

REF: Wills, Liber 20, folio 608; Chas. Co. Deeds, Liber 0 no. 2, folios 77, 321.

EDELEN

Richard Edelen, the Emigrant, who died 1694 in St. Mary's Co: was of Pinner, Middlesex, but of an ancient family of Hertsfordhsire and the son of the Rev. Philip Edelen who is buried in St. Mary's, Denham, Buckinghamshire, with a memorial to him on the south wall.

REF: Newman's Heraldic Marylandiana.

EDGAR

In 1696 an Act passed the Assembly to naturalize John Edgar of Somerset Co., Gent.

REF: Md. Archives, vol. 19, p. 378.

EGAN

Elinor Egan, Prince George's Co., 21 Sept. 1722, "I give and bequeath unto my Dear Loving Mother Mary Moore of the County of Longford in the Kingdom of Ireland . . . loving father William Moore and Christopher Moore. . . ."

REF: Wills, Liber 18, folio 11.

ELDER

The Roman Catholic branch of the Elder family, according to newspaper clippings, at the time of the installation of Archbishop William Henry Elder in Cincinnati during 1880 stated that the founder of the Maryland family was William Elder who came from Lancashire, England, in 1720.

REF: Undated Cincinnati newspaper clipping in possession of the compiler.

William Elder, native of Co. Kerry, Ireland, died Mar. 31, 1845, aged 70 years.

REF: Congressional Cemetery, Washington, D.C.

ELEXON

John Elexon of Kent Co. in 1671 upon petition for naturalization declared that he was born "under the Dominion of the king of Swedeland [the Swedish settlements on the Delaware].

REF: Md. Archives, vol. 2, p. 282.

ELLERY

Henry Ellery was transported from Tertudos into Maryland by John Goss of St. George's Hundred, St. Mary's Co., who filed landrights in 1663.

REF: Patents, Liber ABH, folio 396.

ELLICOTT

Andrew Ellicott who died 1809 aged 76 and who with his brother, John, founded Ellicott City, now in Howard Co., was the grandson of the emigrant from Falmouth, England, who settled originally in Bucks Co., Penn.

REF: Tombstone at Ellicott City, Md.

Edward Elliott, born in England, substituted for Dennis Shepherd, in accordance with the "Act to procure Troops for the American Army", passed March Session 1778.

REF: Militia List, Md. Hist. Soc., Balto.

ELTONHEAD

William Eltonhead, of Little Eltonhead Manor, Esq., Calvert Co., and his sisters Katherine who married Thomas Mears of Virginia, Jane who married Robert Morson and Cuthbert Fenwick of Maryland, Agatha who married Ralph Wormley of Virginia, Martha who married Edwin Conway of Virginia and Alice who married Rowland Burham and William Henry Corbin of Virginia were all children of Richard Eltonhead, Esq. and Ann Sutton his wife of Lancashire.

Edward Eltonhead who was granted seigniory on Great Eltonhead Manor was an uncle to the aforesaid.

REF: 1664 Visitation of Lancashire; Patents Liber ABH, folio 65.

ELZEY

John Elzey and Peter Elzey of Somerset Co. were sons of Arnold Elzey, merchant, of Southampton and his wife, Joan, the widow _____ Barlowe.

REF: Va. Hist. Magazine, vol. 29, p. 345; Records of Northampton Co., Va., vol. 4, p. 131; vol. 9, pp. 12, 20, 50.

EMACK

William Emack (1770-1833), was born Ardstrain Parish, near town of Omagh, Co. Tyrone, Ireland, intermarried with the Duke family of Calvert Co.

REF: Biographical & Portrait Encyclopedia of Chester Co., Penn., by Samuel F. Wiley, p. 289.

ENLOES

Henry Enloes in 1674 when he petitioned for naturalization, declared that he was born "under the Dominion of the States General of the united Provinces", now the Netherlands.

REF: Md. Archives, vol. 2, p. 400.

ERICKSON

Gunder Erickson stated that he was born out of the British Kingdom but was naturalized in London then a resident of St. Dunstan Stepney in Co. Middlesex, on Nov. 23, 1710, and produced a certificate that he had taken communion of the Christian Church. Recorded at Court on Mar. 4, 1722.

REF: Liber PL no. 5, folio 459, Hall of Records, Annapolis.

EVANS

Evan Evans, D.D. Rector of St. George's Parish, Baltimore Co., May 25, 1721, maintained an estate in Pennsylvania which was to be sold and pro-

ceeds remitted to the Rev. Thomas Lloyd, Clk., of Co. Denbigh who "marryed with my Dear and only Daughter Mary", the Rev. Mr. Lloyd having one time lived in Sutterton, Lincolnshire.
    REF: Wills, Liber 17, folio 297.

Rachel Evans, Stephney Parish, Somerset Co., 20 Apr. 1726, "I give and bequeath unto my two Daughters Anne and Susanna by my first husband, vizt, the Rev. John Howat, Minister, to them and their Heirs and assigns all my right property and Interest of and in two pieces or parcels of Lands lying or being in the Principally of Wales in Monmouth Shire one of them in the parish of Langvihangel Lanternan and the other parcell of Land which came to me by my mother in the parish of Mitchell Troy near the River Tory in Monmouth Shire...my first named Daughter vizt Anne Leaky and Susanna Johnson executrixes.", born 1671 in Wales.
    REF: Wills, Liber 18, folio 510, Rightmeyer's Maryland's Established Church.

EVELYN
Captain George Evelyn, Esq., who had a manorial grant from Lord Baltimore, was a son of Robert Evelyn of Surrey and his wife, Susan Younge. Robert Evelyn Jr., a brother of Captain George Evelyn, was also early associated with Maryland and Virginia.
    REF: Berry's Surrey Pedigress, pp. 74-78.

EVERENDON
Thomas Everendon, Dorchester Co., May 4, 1710, "...unto John Sims and Henry Wilcox of the City of Canterbury in the County of Kent in the Kingdom of Great Britain all that piece or parcel of land in ye parish Commonly Called St. Dunstan's in or near the City of Canterbury of which land was purchased by me...and now and for sometime heretofore used for a burying place for the people called Quakers".
    REF: Wills, Liber 13, folio 56.

EVERSFIELD
The Rev. John Eversfield, rector of St. Paul's Parish, Prince George's Co., by 1734 deed made Moses Eversfield of Southwark, Co. Surrey, Tallow Chandler; Charles Eversfield of Horsham, Co. Sussex, Esq.; and Henry Eversfield, Gent., of Co. Kerry, Kingdom of Ireland, contingent heirs in a deed of gift to his son, John Eversfield. In a deed of gift to his daughter, Eleanor Eversfield, he made Stephen Eversfield of London, Middlesex, the contingent heir.

John Eversfield, Jr., son of the Rev. Mr. Eversfield, took Holy Orders and was rector of a parish in Somersetshire, England, presumably Stoke Gumber. He died in or about 1767 in Somersetshire, leaving a widow in Britain and personalty in Maryland. Among his Maryland property were 6 portraits in frame, 2 coats-of-arms of the Eversfield family, silver seal and violin.

Betty Eversfield of Stoke Gumber, Somersetshire, Widow and Relict of the Rev. John Eversfield, waived all claims to the estate of her late husband in Prince George's Co., and acknowledged the legacy from, Matthew Eversfield and William Eversfield, dated March 5, 1769.

The Rev. John Eversfield, rector of St. Paul's Parish, Prince George's

Co., by his 1781 will named the following kinsmen: Charles Eversfield, Esq., of Horsham, Sussex; Moses Eversfield; daughter-in-law Betty Eversfield and granddaughter Eleanor Eversfield of Stoke Gumber, Somersetshire in South Britain, and willed family portraits and coats-of-arms. The testator also referred to family heirlooms sent him by Charles Eversfield of Horsham, Sussex, and also from "Cozen Moses Eversfield of London".

Matthew Eversfield of John of Prince George's Co. by his will of 1795, referred to Mrs. Eleanor Thomas, a British subject.

REF: Pr. Geo. Co. Wills, Liber T, folio 131; Wills, Liber 1770-1783, folio 413; Pr. Geo. Co. Deeds, Liber T, folios 181, 483; Inventories, Liber 96, folio 16; Adm. Accts., Liber 63, folio 3.

EWING

Thomas Ewing of Baltimore Town, by will of Apr. 11, 1776, named his brother Robert Ewing of Barbadoes, Merchant; sister Elizabeth Poaug of Belfast; brother-in-law Charles Poaug; Thomas Simm "nephew son of my sister Margarey Simm; brother John Ewing of Belfast, Merchant; nephews John, James and Robert Simm sons "of my late sister Margarey Simm"; and niece Jane the wife of Samuel Brown one of the daughters of sister Margarey Simm.

REF: Balto. Co. Wills, Liber 3, folio 402.

EYANS

Richard Eyans by his will dated June 30, 1733, styled himself "late of Euston in Oxfordshire and now of the City of Annapolis", devised his estate to his wife and two children—Jane and Richard.

REF: Wills, Liber 21, folio 276.

EYLES

Samuel Eyles, born Aug. 17, 1745, within 15 miles of Bristol, England, at age 16 his father bound him to sea and at about 18 years of age sailed from England and landed in Baltimore, ran away from the ship; at Church Hill, Queen Anne's Co., Md. enlisted in the 4th Maryland Regiment during the Revolution; name written sometimes as Iles.

REF: Revolutionary Pension Claim R5474, National Archives.

EYRES

John Eyres of Charles Co., Gent., by will of 1702 made his brother, Joseph Eyres of London, his contingent heir, was of an old Yorkshire-Wiltshire family which settled in London. John Eyres is placed as the fifth son of Henry Eyres of London. Arms: "Argent, on a chevron sable three quatrefoils or." Crest: "A leg couped at the thigh quarterly, argent and sable counterchanged, spur or".

The identical arms was basic for James Eyres, created Earl of Newburgh in 1660 by Charles II for his loyalty to the Stuarts.

REF: Wills, Liber 11, folio 362; Visitation of London 1634, Harleian Soc. Pub. vol. 15, p. 261.

FAISOLE

Andre Faisole, subject of the King of Sardonia, on May 27, 1791, declared himself a Christian and subscribed to the Oath of Naturalization. County domicile not cited.

REF: Council Proceedings, Md. Archives, vol. 72, p. 198.

FARMER
Halford Farmer, Chestertown, Kent Co., Apr. 15, 1740, "...to my Daughter Jane a Dwelling house being in and adjacent to the East Gate in the City or Town of Leicester in the County of the same name in the Kingdom of England".
REF: Wills, Liber 22, folio 245.

John Farmer in 1712 brought his certificate of Quakerism from Colester, England, to the Quaker Meeting of West River.
REF: Quaker Notes, by Christopher Johnston, Md. Hist. Soc., p. 127.

FAUBEL
Jacob Faubel, a Hessian soldier of the Revolution, taken prisoner in New Jersey, remained in America after the war, settled in Frederick County, died a Mason, September 10, 1825.
REF: History of Western Maryland, vol. 1, p. 472, by Scharf.

FAVERGE
In 1838 Charles Frederick Louis Faverge's will was recorded in Baltimore County declaring himself a "native of the town of Neuchatel in Switzerland legitimate son of John James and Henrietta Perret".
REF: Balto. Co. Wills, Liber 17, folio 198.

FAWCETT
Thomas Fawcett of Montgomery Co., June 3, 1822, declared himself a subject of Great Britain having been born in Yorkshire, but emigrated to Maryland in June 1820, requested to become a citizen of the United States.
REF: Montg. Co. Deeds, Liber BX no. 1, folio 426.

FEAKINE
John Feakine was among a ship load of Irish servants who were transported in 1678 by Phillip Popleston "Master of Ship Encrease" of Youghall, Co. Cork, Ireland, and assigned to William Sharpe of Talbot Co.
REF: Patents, Liber 20, folio 184.

FELL
Edward Fell, Quaker, Feb. 2, 1738/9, declared himself "of Over Killet in the County of Lancaster, England, having occasion to Travell to London and Over Sea to Maryland". He devised land in Maryland and Great Britain to his daughter, Anne Fell, and the children of his brother, William Fell, if his daughter died without issue.
REF: Wills, Liber 23, folio 150.

FENWICK
Cuthert Fenwick, Gent. who came up from Virginia with the Adventurers on the Ark and who held manorial rights on Fenwick Manor is placed as a scion of the Fenwyke of Co. Northumberland.
REF: Surtees Soc. Pub., vol. 122.

FERDINANDO

Peter Ferdinando of Charles Co., and his children Winifred, Elizabeth, Mary and Ann were naturalized in 1694 by an Act of the General Assembly.

REF: Md. Archives, vol. 19, pp. 85, 103.

FILLINGHAM

Richard Fillingham, Kent Co., July 1, 1676, estate to son Richard Fillingham, but if he died without issue then "unto Samuel Tovey of the Citty of Bristoll".

REF: Wills, Liber 9, folio 35.

FINCH

Capt. William Finch, son of Capt. William Finch Sr., of London, Mariner, owner of the ship "Bradley" died intestate in Prince George's Co., 1742. His widow, Priscilla, married as his first wife, Allen Bowie. On Aug. 14, 1742, Capt. William Finch Sr., of London, made a deed of gift to "my granddaughter Phebe Finch, daughter of my son William Finch" a negro woman called Kizzie. At that time Captain Finch Sr. was in Maryland. By will dated Sept. 8, 1756, probated Feb. 18, 1757, Phebe Finch of London bequeathed her granddaughter, Phebe Finch, "of in Pateucent Maryland" £20.

REF: Public Record Office, London, Herring 48; Adm. Accts., Liber 23, folio 284, Hall of Records; Waters' Gleanings in England; Pr. Geo. Co. Deeds, Liber Y, folio 539.

FINLEY

Jane Finley, Talbott Co., 3 Aug. 1722, "The Remainder of my Estate I leave to my Executor to be sold for Money and that to be remitted to my Sister Jugg Watson living in Old England in Yorkshire at Boughton Neigh Stockley but in Case my Sister be Dead then to my Sister son Bartholemew Watson son of my sister Jugg Watson".

REF: Wills, Liber 19, folio 443.

FITZ

Joh Fitz, Dorchester Co., May 1, ˉ1757, ". . .to my brother John Fitz (sic) in Wiltshire 21 shillings".

REF: Wills, Liber 30, folio 346.

FITZPATRICK

James Fitzpatrick, M.D., was born 1806 at Carbow, County Leinster, Ireland. He came to the United States in 1821 and settled in Alleghany Co., in 1835. He became a distinguished doctor and died at Cumberland, on March 14, 1865.

REF: Gravestone, Roman Catholic Cemetery, Cumberland.

FLEET

Captain Henry Fleet, Gent., who assisted the Adventurers in the early days of the settlement of Maryland and who held the Honour and Manorial Rights on the Manor of West St. Mary's, was of Chatham, Co. Kent. He was furthermore the son of William Fleet, a member of the Virginia Company. His brothers, Edward, Reginold and John Fleet were also in Maryland at one time and attended the 1638 General Assembly.

REF: Berry's Kentish Pedigress; Adventurers of Purse and Persons, by Jester.

FOARY—STEWARD

Martha Foary, daughter of Isaac Foary of Londonderry, Ireland, married William Steward of Washington Co., Md., and died April 8, 1845, aged 70.

REF: St. John's Episcopal graveyard, Hagerstown.

FOOT

Richard Foot, London, Merchant, friend to Lord Baltimore, was granted in 1657 jointly with Nicholas Hayward 2,000 acres of land to be erected into a manor with privileges "usually belonging to manors in England".

REF: Patents, Liber Q, folio 470.

FORBES

Alexander Forbes of Talbot Co. was naturalized in 1695 by an Act of the General Assembly.

REF: Md. Archives, vol. 19, p. 281.

George Forbes, St. Mary's Co., by his will of Oct. 31, 1739, bequeathed "Thomas Forbes in Scotland my brother or the heirs of his body £100 Sterling." To granddaughter, Mary Gordon, £500 of capital stock in the Bank of England in event of her decease before coming of age the four-fifths to "my brothers and sisters in Scotland aforementioned [Robert Forbes, Margaret Forbes, Jane Forbes and Margery Forbes] equally."

REF: Wills, Liber 22, folio 101.

Thomas Forbes emigrated to Maryland from Co. Kildare, Ireland, and served as a recruiting Sergeant under Capt. Lewis during the Revolution.

REF: Revolutionary Pension Claim R14250, National Archives.

FORNERODA

Daniel Forneroda of Anne Arundel Co., a native of Switzerland, petitioned for naturalization in 1735.

REF: Md. Archives, vol. 39, p. 175.

FORTUNE

James Fortune by his will Oct. 17, 1797, probated Balto. Co. named his brother, Anthony Fortune "now residing in Norton St., Marylebone, London; sister Ann Stafford residing in Parish of Tentum, Co. Wexford, Ireland, and brother, Luke Fortune, of Weathersfield, Conn."

REF: Balto. Co. Wills, Liber 6, folio 53.

Willam Fortune, a native of Ireland, born Feb. 20, 1746, served in Maryland Militia during the Revolution; later settled in Simpson Co., Tenn.

REF: Revolutionary Pension Claim S3375, National Archives.

FOSTER

James Foster, born Jan. 16, 1762, in Ireland and brought to Maryland about 1768 by his father; served in the Maryland Line during the Revolution, later lived in Frederick Co., Va.

REF: Revolutionary Pension Claim S8501, National Archives.

FOUEY

Nicholas Fouey of the Parish of St. George in Somershire, England, Mariner, authorized Samuel Gibson to sell his estate in Cecil Co. and to send the proceeds to his wife, Anne. Dated January 9, 1674/5.

REF: Public Record Office, London, Dycer 71.

FOUNTAINE

On July 13, 1665, "Nicholas ffountaine late of Virginia and Subject of the Crowne of france" was granted Dennizacon. Then Nicholas Fountaine of Somerset Co. in 1671 upon petition for naturalization stated that he was a native of France.

REF: Md. Archives, vol. 2, p. 282; vol. 3, p. 529.

FOWKE

The Fowkes of Maryland and Virginia are scions of the armorial family of Gunston Hall, Staffordshire, England. Memorials are found in the Parish Church of Brewood. The will of Roger Fowke, father of Gerard, the American Emigrant, was proved 1649, naming his son, Gerard. The inscription on the tomb of Frances (Fowke) Brown at Dipple, Stafford Co., Va., states that she was descended from "the Fowkes of Gunston Hall in Staffordshire, England".

REF: Breward Parish Register, Prerogative Court of Canterbury; Heraldic Marylandiana.

FOWKE—BROWN

"Here lyeth the body of Frances, wife of Dr. Gustavus Brown of Charles County, Md. By her he had twelve children of whom one son and seven daughters survive her. She was a daughter of Mr. Gerard Fowke, late of Md. and descended from the Fowkes of Gunston Hall in Staffordshire, England. She was born Feb. 2nd 1691 and died much lamented on the 8th of November 1744, in the 54th year of her age".

REF: Burying Grounds at Rose Hill, Charles Co.

FOXCROFT

William Foxcroft, formerly a native of Great Britain, on Jan. 26, 1789, declared himself a follower of the Christian faith and subscribed to the Oath of Naturalization.

REF: Council Proceedings, Md. Archives, vol. 71, p. 322.

FRANCIS

Stephen Francis, a native Italian, became a naturalized subject of Lord Baltimore by act of 1697.

REF: Md. Archives, vol. 19, pp. 547, 570.

Tench Francis, clerk and burgess of Talbot Co., was of the Rev. John Francis, Dean of Linsmore, Ireland, and rector of St. Mary's Church, Dublin. He came to Maryland in 1720 as an attorney for Lord Baltimore. He was later attorney general of Pennsylvania and died in Philadelphia 1788.

REF: Family notes of the Tilghman family.

FRASER

Alexander Fraser, chyrugeon and apothecary, Annapolis, 25 June 1729, "I give and devise unto my Loving Son Stephen Samuel Alexander

ffraser . . . all my Estate . . . in that part of Scotland or North Britain called Frewehie being in the Parish of Faulkland in the Sherifdome of ffife".
REF: Wills, Liber 20, folio 455.

FREEMAN
Henry Freeman in 1674 stated that he was born "in the Kingdom of Sweadland" [Swedish colony on the Delaware].
REF: Md. Archives, vol. 2, p. 400.

Patrick Freeman was among a ship load of Irish servants who were transported in 1678 by Phillip Popleston "Master of Ship Encrease" of Youghall, Co. Cork, and assigned to William Sharpe of Talbot Co.
REF: Patents, Liber 20, folio 184.

FRENCH
Capt. John French, Fell's Point, Baltimore, Oct. 12, 1774, to his daughter Eleanor French whom he placed under the guardianship of a friend in Baltimore Co., the residue of his estate "but in case die before she comes of age or have lawful issue then and in that case I give the same to my nearest relations at King Sale in Ireland".
REF: Wills, Liber 40, folio 173.

FRISBY
James Frisby who died in Cecil Co., Md. 1674, was born in London and married Mary, daughter of John Maddocks [Maddox] of London. James Frisby Jr., the son and heir, on October 24, 1691, instituted action in Chancery for his claims in the estate of his maternal grandfather, "John Maddocks Citizen and Barber Chirurgeon of London in and near the Strand in the Parish of St. Martin in the Fields". It was stated in the lawsuit that James Frisby had "gone beyond the Sea".
On November 10, 1651, Robert Nicholson of London, Merchant, son of Francis Nicholson, willed a legacy to James Frisby and others in Virginia.
REF: Chancery Proceedings Hamilton 120-151, Frisby vs Moore & Bayley; Waters Gleanings in England.

John Frisby of Parish of St. John, Hackney, Co. Middlesex, England, late of the Province of Maryland, was deceased by December 1740.
REF: Prov Crt Deeds, Liber EI no. 3, folio 168.

FUCATE
In 1681 a bill for the naturalization of Peter Fucate [ffowcate] of Baltimore Co. was introduced and passed.
REF: Md. Archives, vol. 7, pp. 149, 216.

FULLWOOD
John Fullwood, aged 33, of Kent Isle, deposed [May 1640] that he was a native of Hope Parish, Herefordshire and had "long lived with a native of Indians called Susquehannoes" and acted as an interpreter to William Claiborne.
REF: Md. Hist. Magazine, vol. 5, p. 231.

FURLY

John Furly Jr., stated 1721 that he was late of London but now of the Province of Maryland.

REF: Provincial Crt, Liber 5, folio 338.

GADDIS

Adam Gaddis, native of Kerry, Co. Down, Ireland, resided in District of Columbia for 17 years, died July 21, 1867, aged 76 years.

REF: Congressional Cemetery, Washington, D.C.

GALE

George Gale of Somerset Co., July 26, 1712, "I do Constitute ordain and appoint my Loving wife Betty and my loving brother Matthew Gale of the Kingdom of Great Britain to be my Executors". The said George Gale was the son of John Gale of Whitehaven (died 1716) and his wife, Mary, daughter of Lancelot Carre.

REF: Wills, Liber 13, folio 438; Probate Crt of Co. Cumberland, Esq.

GALLOWAY

Richard Galloway, the son of Samuell and Ann Galloway, was born in London in the Kingdom of England the 11th 5th day of 1689.

REF: West River Quaker Records, Anne Arundel Co., Md., Md. Hist. Soc, Balto.

GALT

Anne Galt who styled herself "formerly of Colerain [Co. Londonderry] Kingdom of Ireland, but now of Baltimore" by her will of July 22, 1818, mentioned property inherited from the estate of her late father, William Galt, and bequeathed it to her nephew, Richardson Galt. One of the witnesses to the will was Thompson Galt.

REF: Wills Balto Co., Liber 10, folio 537.

GANTT

Thomas Gantt [Gauntt], the emigrant ancestor of the Gantt family of Calvert County was from the Parish of Bulwick, Nottinghamshire. He commemorated his heritage by naming his plantation "Bulwick" and as a commissioner for laying out the port-town on the Patuxent he named it Nottingham. The parent branch was from Leicestershire which borders Nottinghamshire on the south.

Thomas Gantt was named as kinsman by John Bradford of Prince George's County in his will of March 26, 1726.

REF: History of Co. Leicester, by Nichols, vol. 2, p. 303; Dormant & Extinct Baronage, by Banks, vol. 1, p. 313; Wills, Liber 16, folio 176; Liber 18, folio 464.

GARDNER

John Gardner, Baltimore Co., Gent., July 5, 1740, "...unto Robert Godwin of Polsmouth in Hampshire in Old England entire estate".

REF: Wills, Liber 22, folio 524.

Richard Gardner, Calvert Co., 15 January 1693/4, "I give and bequeath unto my two sisters Jane Bennett and Mary Gardner living att William Scott in Oxfordshire £20 each...to be paid out of what money I have in England".

REF: Wills, Liber 2, folio 265.

William Gardner of the Welsh Tract, New Castle on the Delaware, by his will probated Cecil Co., Md., Dec. 12, 1743, named his father William [Gardner] of Kirk and Realock, Co. Antrim, Ireland.

REF: Md. Wills, Liber 23, folio 388.

GAREY

Stephen Garey by his will probated in Dorchester Co. 1675 devised "What land and tenements I have lying and being in ye town of Burroughes of West Rue (alias) Purpeham in ye County of Cornwall and Kingdom of England" to his wife Clare. He furthermore named one of his Maryland plantations "Cornwall". He also devised land in Stafford Co., Va. on the Potomac to his eldest daughter Magdelane.

REF: Wills, Liber 4, folio 202.

GARRETT

Amos Garrett, Anne Arundel Co., Mercht, 4 Sept. 1714, "I Amos Garrett of the City of Annapolis in Anne Arundel County in the Province of Maryland, Merchant, Son of James and Sarah Garrett late of St. Olives Street Southwark then in the Kingdom of England now a part of Great Britain . . . unto my Cousin James Garrett son of Seth Garrett Late of St. Olives Southwark near London . . . I give and bequeath out of my personal estate the sum of £100 Sterling unto my kinsman James Facer Son of Thomas and Martha Facer of the town of Rugby in the Kingdom of Great Britain".

"Here lieth the body of Mr. Amos Garrett of the city of Annapolis in Anne Arundel county in the Province of Maryland, Merchant, son of Mr. James and Mrs. Sarah Garrett late of St. Olive street, Southwark then in the Kingdom of England now a part of Great Britain who departed this life on March the 8th 1727. Aetatis 56".

NOTE: Although he left no issue, his sister Mary married Henry Woodward of Anne Arundel Co., and left a large issue; another sister was Elizabeth Ginn.

REF: St. Anne's Churchyard, Annapolis; Riley's Ancient City, p. 76. Wills, Liber 19, folio 335; Prov. Crt Deeds, Liber DD no. 3, folio 378.

GARRETTS

Rutgerston Garretts of Baltimore Co., a native of Amerfoord, Holland, was naturalized in 1671.

REF: Md. Archives, vol. 2, p. 282.

GASSAWAY-GARRAWAY

Although the parentage of Nicholas Gassaway of St. Margaret's Westminster Parish, London, and Maryland, is well established, there are reasons to assume that the name is a corruption of the distinguished armorial family of Garaway, Garraway. Sir William Garaway, Knt. of London, Merchant who was the son of John Garaway of London and Elizabeth, daughter of Sir John Bridges, one-time Mayor of London, was a registrant at the 1634 Visitation of Middlesex.

Nicholas Gassaway of London Town, Maryland, followed mercantile pursuits and it is not impossible, as one studies the changes and deviation of proper names that the Gassaway and Garraway were once the one and the same. No Gassaway coat-of-arms appears in Burke's Armory, but Garraway is listed. A seal is impressed on the 1739 will of Capt. Thomas Gassaeay, but it is not sufficiently clear for identification. Furthermore, Nicholas Gassaway by his 1793 will bequeathed his "gold seal", all of which indicate that the Gassaways were conscious of their armorial heritage.

REF: Harleian Soc. Pub., vol. 64, p. 92.

GATES
Thomas Gates, English, rector of St. Anne's 1781; St. Peter's, Talbot 1785; removed 1789 to South Carolina.

REF: Allen.

GEIST
A bill for the naturalization of Christian Geist was presented to the Lower House on July 21, 1721, and passed on August 21, 1721, "Christian Geist of the City of Annapolis in Anne Arundel, Gentleman, born under the Dominion of the King of Sweden".

REF: Archives Maryland, vol. 34, pp. 210, 217; vol. 38, p. 288.

George Geist became a naturalized subject under the Act of George II (13th year) by taking the Oath of Abjuration and furnishing certification that he had received the sacrament of the Reformed Congregation of Frederick Town.

REF: Prov. Crt Judgements, Liber BT no. 2, folios 93-4.

GERARD
Thomas Gerard who was granted three manors by Cecilius, Lord Baltimore, emigrated to Maryland in 1638, was of Newhall in Ashton-in-Makerfield, Lancashire. Edward Field aged 74 in 1722 of St. Mary's Co. deposed that he knew Thomas Gerard, Esq., "formerly of New Hall in Lancashire" and heard him say that he "came out of Lancashire".

By his 1673 will he devised his son, Justinian "My whole Right Title and Interest to any land or parcel of land lyeing within the Kingdom of England".

Justinian Gerard, son of Thomas, named his seat on St. Clement's Manor "Bromley". By his will Aug. 4, 1662, he devised his wife, Sarah, "all land & tenements in Lancashire in ye Kingdom of England particularly all y^t dwelling house withal ye Land and appurtentance formerly called by ye name of Newhall in Lancashire in ye Kingdom of England aforesaid being late in ye possession of one Mr. Landre.

Robert Gerard, Esq., a kinsman of Thomas, the Emigrant, was one of the Gentlemen of Fashion who arrived in Maryland during 1634 on the Ark, but returned later to England.

REF: Chancery, Liber PL no. 4, folio 754; Wills, Liber 1, folio 567; Wills, Liber 6, folio 43; Newman's Heraldic Marylandiana; The Flowering of the Maryland Palatinate.

GERRALD
Margaret Gerrald was among a shipload of Irish servants who were transported in 1678 by Phillip Popleston "Master of the Ship Express" of Youghall, Co. Cork, Ireland, and assigned to William Sharpe of Talbot Co.

REF: Patents, Liber 20, folio 184.

GERY

Oliver Gery, one-time Merchant of London, in 1668 was granted land in Maryland.

REF: Patents, Liber 11, folio 316.

GHISELIN

Caesar Ghiselin of Prince George's Co., Md. "who was born beyond the seas" became a naturalized subject of the Crown of England at London on Oct. 12, 1698, as certified by Henry Smith, notary of London.

REF: Provincial Crt, Liber PL no. 5, folio 284.

GIBBS, GIBS

Abraham Gibbs became a naturalized subject of Britain after receiving the Sacrament of the Lutheran Church, Frederick, July 13, 1760, and taking the Oath of Abjuration in court in accordance to the Act of George II.

REF: Prov. Crt Judgements, Liber DD no. 1, folio 191.

Abrahan Gibs born 1724 in the Grafschaft Grumbach in vicinity of Grumbach, Kreis Birkenfeld, lived with his wife who died before him 31 years in matrimony, died of a stroke the 29th March 1784.

REF: Evangelical Lutheran Church, Frederick.

Patrick Gilleece, a native of Dremrigan Parish, County Cavan, Ireland, settled in Washington Co., Md., died December 4, 1863, aged 56 years.

REF: Hancock Cemetery, Washington Co.

GILLESPIE

John Gillespie, Frederick Co., Sept. 26, 1768, "I give and bequeath unto my Brother Thomas Gillespie in Ireland in the Parish of Clougher and County Tyrone the full sum of £30 Pennsylvania Currency...I give and Bequeath the first born Son of only Brother William Gillespie in Carolina the remainder of my Estate".

REF: Wills, Liber 36, folio 673.

GILLMYER

Francis Gillmyer, "born Germany 1753, died Apr. 22, 1816".

REF: St. Joseph's Catholic Churchyard, Emmitsburg, Md.

GILLY

Thomas Gilly, Calvert Co., Dec. 6, 1720. "...unto my Loveing wife Clarane and my two sonns Robert Gilly and William Gilly all the Remainder of my Estate as well in England".

REF: Wills, Liber 16, folio 264.

GITHINS

Philip, John and Mary Githins by the will of their aunt, Mary Hoskins of Richmond, Co. Surrey, England, widow, dated July 30, 1678, probated Dec. 28, 1678, bequeathed £10 each "to the three children of my late deceased brother John Githins in Meriland" and made her brother, William Githins, Gent., her executors.

REF: Waters' Gleanings, p. 27.

GLANVILL

William Glanvill, Mariner, died intestate in Somerset Co. prior to Oct. 1672. His Maryland estate was in the possession of Randall Revell who sailed for England regarding the differences between him and Alice Glanvill, of Ratcliff, Co. Middlesex, England, the administratrix of the estate, jointly with Edward Peirce. He was granted land 1668 in Maryland.

REF: Prov. Crt, Liber JJ no. 4, folio 425; Patents, Liber 11, folio 351.

GODLINGTON

Thomas Godlington of London, Merchant, emigrated 1659.

REF: Patents, Liber 4, folio 198.

GOETZ

Dr. John Goetz of Baltimore, by will 30 Nov. 1816, bequeathed one-third of his estate to "my Dear Brother Sebastian Goetz of the City of Maintz on the River Rhine in Germany".

REF: Balto Wills, Liber 10, folio 269.

GOLDSBOROUGH

My father, Nicholas Gouldesburgh or Goldsborough, was a younger brother, he was born at Malcolm Regis, near Waymouth, in the County of Dorset, in or about 1640 or 1641.

My mother was the sole daughter of Abraham Howes, the son of William Howes of Newberry, in the County of Burks [Berks].

My father marryed my Mother in the year 1659 at Blandford, in the County of Dorset, where myself was born the beginning of December 1660. My father went from England to Barbadoes in 1669, from thence he came to New England, & from thence to Maryland. In the beginning of the year 1670, he died on Kent Island & was there buried on Tobies Wells' plantation.

I came into Maryland in the beginning of the year 1678. I was marryed to Elizabeth Greenbury Sep. 2nd 1697. My Mother came into Maryland in or about the year 1670. She here intermarried with George Robins.

(signed) Robert Goldsborough
August 20th 1722.

REF: Old document found among the papers of the Goldsborough family. See also The Maryland Original Research Society, bulletin no. 1, pub. 1906.

GOLLEY

Peter Golley of Talbot Co. was naturalized in 1694 by an Act of the General Assembly.

REF: Md. Archives, vol. 19, p. 211.

GOODMAN

William Goodman received the sacrament of the Reformed Congregation at Frederick Town on Apr. 13, 1761, as prescribed by the Act of George II (13th year) before taking the Oath of Abjuration and becoming a British subject.

REF: Prov. Crt Judgements, Liber DD no. 1, folios 186-7.

GOODWIN

Lyonel Lyde and Edward Cooper of Bristol, Eng. on May 13, 1741, made Lyde Goodwin of Bristol, Merchant, their attorney to collect all debts due them in Maryland.

REF: Prov. Crt Deeds, Liber EI no. 3, folio 256.

GORDON

Charles Gordon, emigrated from England in 1750 and settled in Cecil Co., Loyalist during the Revolution.

REF: Md. Hist. Mag., vol. 72, p. 373.

The Rev. John Gordon, Anglican clergyman, with charges in Anne Arundel and Talbot Counties, was born 1717 in Aberdeem, Scotland, son of Dr. John Gordon, also a clergyman. He died 1790 in Talbot County leaving no issue but several nephews in Maryland.

REF: Records of Queen's College, Oxford; Talbot Co. Wills, Liber JP no. 6, folio 341.

GORMLEY

James Gormley, a native of "Ireland County of Terone, Parish of Astraw and for several years past a resident of the United States" mentioned his brother, Michael Gormley of Ireland, in his will of January 21, 1839.

REF: Balto. Co. Wills, Liber 17, folio 205.

GORSUCH

Anne, wife of John Gorsuch, Rector of Walkorne, Hertfordshire, as a widow with her children emigrated to Virginia and ultimately settled in Maryland is listed in the 1633 Visitation of London as domiciled in Bishopgate Ward. The family was originally from Lancashire and bore the arms of the Hillson family.

REF: Harleian Soc. Pub., 1880, vol. 15, folio 327; Heraldic Marylandiana, by Newman.

GOSFRIGHT

Charles Gosfright by his will probated Calvert Co., 1678, bequeathed his father, George Gosfright, his entire estate in Maryland and Virginia.

REF: Wills, Liber 9, folio 51.

GOSIDGE

Charles Gosidge of Baltimore Co., son of John and Ann Gosidge of the Kingdom of England, married Mar. 15, 1690, Ann Hawkings.

REF: Quaker Notes, West River, by Christopher Johnston, Md. Hist. Soc., p. 9.

GOSLIN

Agnes Goslin in 1728 brought her certificate from Sedsberg, Yorks, to the Quaker Meeting at West River, Anne Arundel Co.

REF: Quaker Notes, Christopher Johnston, Md. Hist. Soc.

GOSS, GOSSE

John Goss of St. George's Hundred, St. Mary's Co., emigrated from Tertudos with his wife, Frances, and unnamed daughter; claimed landrights in 1663.

REF: Patents, Liber ABH, folio 396.

"Dennis Gosse born in the Parish of Black Point of the Island of Guadaloupe the ninth Day of October one thousand seven hundred and fifty three" then of Baltimore referred to his friend, Nicholas Loigerot, a refugee from St. Domingo in his will of May 22, 1805.

REF: Balto Co. Wills, Liber 7, folio 413.

GOTTEE

John Gottee and Margaret his wife of Dorchester Co., in 1671 at time of naturalization declared themselves as natives of the Kingdom of France.

REF: Md. Archives, vol. 2, p. 270.

GOUGH

Benjamin Gough by his will of August 6, 1810, declared himself "a native of England but now of Baltimore" bequeathed his "brother William Gough of Bradford in Wiltshire, England", his entire estate.

Thomas Gough of Baltimore Co. who was in Maryland as early as 1725, was of Perry Hall, Staffordshire.

REF: Balto Co. Wills, Liber 9, folio 31; Heraldic Marylandiana, by Newman.

The Gough family of Baltimore Co. was in some manner allied with the Bongough family of Bristol, England. James Carroll, born Maccubin, by his 1832 will referred to his grandfather Gough and the said James Carroll bequeathed his grandson, Harry Dorsey Gough Carroll "legacy left the family by Henry Bongough of Bristol, England."

REF: Baltimore Co. Wills, Liber 14, folio 128.

GOUNDRIL

Rev. George Goundril, rector of St. Andrew's Parish, St. Mary's Co., came to Maryland May 1770; had been vicar of Kilusea and curate of Essington; was son of the Rev. George Goundril, rector of Sproutley, Yorkshire, near Hull; married Hannah Simpson of Dartington.

REF: Register of St. Andrew's Parish.

GOUTEE

Joseph Goutee and his sons Joseph and John of Talbot Co. were naturalized in 1694 by an Act of the General Assembly.

REF: Md. Archives, vol. 19, p. 211.

GOVER

John Gover, Quaker, later of Calvert Co., then of Tiverton, Devonshire, Eng., on Feb. 23, 1750, indentured himself for 5 years to serve as a taylor in Maryland.

REF: Guildhall Libery, Record Office, London; Immigrants to America, by Kaminhow.

GRAHAM

John Graham, Talbot Co., April 18, 1759, ". . .to my dearly beloved Father Francis Graham living in Cavanallee near Straban in the County of Tyrone in the Kingdom of Ireland" residuary estate.

REF: Wills, Liber 30, folio 732.

Martha, daughter of Moses Graham and Alice his wife, late of ye Parish Clownis in Ireland, buried 8 June 1719.

Moses Graham late of the Kingdom of Ireland was buried 30 Oct. 1719.

REF: Original register of St. Anne's Parish, Anne Arundel Co., p. 46.

GRAHAME

Samuel Grahame of Charles and St. Mary's Co., son of "Mr. Samuel Grahame, Tenant at Dunsre" was an apprentice to John Briscoe of Chaptico. Writing on July 3, 1773, to his father in care of "Messrs Muire and Rilsland, Merchts, in the Street above the Cross of Glasgow" stated that the "people here seem all very discreet and there are a great number of Scothmen round me that I shall have acquaint of...My Master here is a very vivl young gentleman and has himself a very good education and is connected with the best in the country, has a good Estate here and lives a genteely and comfortable as if he has in Scotland an Estate of five hundred yeo...the winters here are very cold more cold and chill then I ever felt at home, but the winter is not generally longer than two or three months". He furthermore cautioned his brother, James, to save "as expence was great coming over and that if he came to remain a while", and that it took him ten weeks to make the crossing. He gave his address incare of Mr. John Briscoe, Mercht, at Chaptico. He ultimately married a daughter of the Piles of Sarum and died in 1787 possessed of a considerable estate.

REF: Chancery, Liber 26, folio 75.

GRAY

John Westcott, apothecary of London, in his will 11 April 1694, mentioned a bill due from his "sister Mary Gray of Maryland in Virginia".

REF: Bond 236, Public Record Office, London.

GREEN

Gerard Green, a German Protestant, took the sacrament in St. Anne's Church and on September 24, 1765, became a British subject.

REF: Prov. Crt Judgements, Liber DD no. 9, folio 30.

Henry Green of Talbot Co. in 1674 stated that he was "borne in holland under the Dominion of the States General of the United Provinces".

REF: Md. Archives, vol. 2, p. 403.

Thomas Green, Esq., one of the Gentlemen of Fashion on the Ark and 2d Governor of Maryland, was the second son of Sir Thomas Green, Knt whose great-grandfather received the Rectory of Bobbing from Henry VIII upon the dissolution of the monasteries. Robert Green, brother to Thomas, the Adventurer, came to Maryland, but returned to England. When Lord Baltimore granted Governor Thomas Green a manor with court baron, he named it "Bobbing" after his ancestoral estate.

REF: Halsted's Co. Kent, vol. 2, pp. 543-544, 635-639; Berry's Kent Pedigress, p. 302; 1530 Visitation of Kent; The Flowering of the Maryland Palatinate by Newman.

GREENFIELD

Entries of the ancestry of Thomas Greenfield, Gent., who settled in Southern Maryland are found in the Parish Register of Godling, Nottinghamshire. Thomas Greenfield, by his will proved in Prince George's Co., August

17, 1715, "...but for want of heirs Male then to the poor of the Town of Godling in Great Britain the place of my Nativity". Beside "Godling" he named other plantations after his native shire, that is, "Stoke", "Stoke Bardolph" and "Woodborough", all Nottingham parishes.

REF: Godling Parish Register (1558-1654), vol. 1; Wills, Liber 14, folio 89.

GREENING

Albert Greening of Anne Arundel, "born under the Dominon of the Emperour of Germany" was naturalized in 1721/2 by an act of the Assembly.

Albert Greening, Anne Arundel Co., Mar. 1, 1721/2, "I give and Bequeath to my Deceased Brother Alereld Greening's youngest child named Albert Liveing in the City of Bremen in Germany".

REF: Wills, Liber 17, folio 263; Md. Archives, vol. 38, p. 288.

GROOME

Richard Groome of St. Clement's Danes, London, on Nov. 10, 1697, apprenticed himself to Thomas Robinson of St. Mary's Whitechappell, Plaisterer, and in the presence of his mother and with the consent of his wife, Susan, to serve Thomas Robinson in the "plantation of Maryland beyond the seas". Richard Groome was then 26 years of age and contracted to serve four years. Robinson was to transport him to Maryland and provide him with cloathes, meat, drink, washing and lodging. The witnesses were Margaret Groome and Thomas Bell.

REF: Pr. Geo. Co. Deeds, Liber A, folio 132.

Samuel Groome of London, Merchant, by his will of Apr. 27, 1697, devised his son, Samuel, land and houses in Aiot, Hertfordshire, Mansfell St., Goodman's Fields, Middlesex, and also land in Maryland.

REF: P.C.C. Lort 57.

William Groome of Mt. Calvert Manor, Calvert Co., in 1677 made the following devise: "I give unto William my eldest Son a Certaine farme in old England once in the tenure & occupation of one Steevens wh is at present is in Controversie in Law my brother Robert Groome defending my right therein at a place called Ivengoe in the County of Berks it being worth by Estimation fifty or sixty pounds per annun Rent".

REF: Wills, Liber 5, folio 191.

The will of Daniel Grome [Groome] probated London 1697 devised land in Maryland to which he was entitled by the will of his father, Samuel Groome, and referred to cousins, Daniel and Samuel Groome, sons of Daniel Groome.

The said Daniel Groome married Margaret Carter of the Parish of St. Martin in the Fields, Middlesex, who was the daughter of Francis Carter who by will bequeathed a legacy to Daniel Groome and "my dafter Margaret his wife".

REF: Public Record Office, London. Scroope 110.

GROSH, GROSCH

Johann Conrad Grosh, born May 18, 1712, in Eichloch in Rhein-grafischen Hernschaft, now Rommershein, Alzer, died June 22, 1794, in Frederick Co.

Maria Sophia, wife of Johann Conrad Grosch, elder of the congregation; she was born Apr. 11, 1717, in Woellstein Wollstein Alzey), parents were Johann Nicol Gutenberger and wife Sophia; she died Apr. 1785.

REF: Evangelical Lutheran Church, Frederick.

GUICHARD

Samuel Guichard of Anne Arundel, Planter, in 1712 petitioned for naturalization.

REF: Md. Archives, vol. 38, p. 165.

GUIDE

Peter Guide, subject of the King of Sardonia, on May 21, 1791, declared himself a Christian and subscribed to the Oath of Naturalization. County domicile not cited.

REF: Council Proceedings, Md. Archives, vol. 72, p. 196.

GUYBERT

Joshua Guybert in 1678 petitioned the Assembly for naturalization having been "borne in the Citty of Rheines in high Brittany in the Kingdom of France" and came to dwell "within this Province by and upon Confidence of your Lordship's fathers Declaration" of 2 July 1649.

REF: Md. Archives, vol. 7, p. 78.

HACK

Anna Hack upon her application for naturalization in 1666 stated that she was "borne at Amsterdam in Holland" and that her sons George and Peter were born at Accomacke in Virginia and for "many yeares inhabited within this Province".

REF: Md. Archives, vol. 2, p. 144.

HACKEMAN

Hermann Henry Hackeman, Baltimore Town, 12 Jan. 1814, "I Give and Bequeath to my sister-in-law Apeline Cornelia Hackeman of Bergen, Norway" interest on $10,000.00 "at her death that Sum or principal is to devolve to the children of my three deceased Sisters living at or near Drint-wedo about 4 or 5 German Miles from Bremen in the Borough of Barnstorff Countship of Dispholz belonging to the Territory or Dominion Hanover".

REF: Balto Co. Wills, Liber 10, folio 46.

HADDICK

Benjamin Haddick, Prince George's Co., Feb. 24, 1702/3, provided for his estate to be sold and proceeds "be remitted home to England to my Dear and Loving Wife Elizabeth Haddick Liveing in the Lower End of Queen Street near Ratliff Cross in London".

REF: Wills, Liber 11, folio 335.

HAILES

Thomas Hailes of Kent Isle, May 1640, deposed that he was aged 34 and a native of Waddington Parish, Lincolnshire.

REF: Md. Archives, vol. 5, p. 189.

HALDIMAND

Peter Haldimand, Gent., "a Foreigner of the Portestant or reformed Religion" was naturalized in 1769.

REF: Md. Archives, vol. 62, p. 120.

HALES

Spencer Hales, Gent., of Calvert Co., Md., 1675 devised his sister, Ann Hales, all land in England and Maryland.

REF: Wills, Liber 2, folio 409.

HALL

The Rev. Henry Hall, first rector of St. James' Parish, Anne Arundel Co., who died 1722, was a native of North and South Bersted, Co. Essex, England. After his marriage in Maryland, he had it recorded in the register of St. Mary Magdelen Church, South Bersted, Essex, as well as the birth of his son and heir, styling himself as "Henry Hall minister of the parish church of St. James in Maryland in the West Indies".

REF: Register Book 1670-1773, St. Mary Magdalene, South Bersted, Co. Essex; Newman's Heraldic Marylandiana.

Simon Hall, St. Mary's Co., 1725, "I give to my Cousin Margarett Brown that house messuage or Tenement to her Heirs or Assigns for Ever in South Shield and in the County of Durham".

REF: Wills, Liber 18, folio 417.

William Hall of Charles Co., by his will of Apr. 6, 1697, styled himself "Chirurgeon borne in ye Citty of Chichester in ye County of Sussex in the Kingdom of England Second son of William Hall of the said Citty & Kingdom of England, Glazier". He bequeathed his wife house and gardens in Chichester on North Street.

REF: Wills, Liber 7, folio 261.

HALLOWES

John Hallowes, an Adventurer on the Ark, later Major of the Virginia Militia, was born in Lancashire. He died after 1657. Some years later his nephew, Samuel Hallows, who declared himself a "nephew to Major John Hallowes late of Rachedale, County Palatine of Lancaster, England, who in Virginia beyond the seas, instituted action in the Virginia courts and later Great Britain for 2400 acres of land which his uncle died seized on in Westmoreland Co., Va. The nephew was the son and heir of Mathew Hallowes who was the eldest brother of the said Major John Hallowes.

REF: Va. Colonial Decisions, vol. 1, p. 26; Tyler's Magazine, vol. 1, p. 26; William & Mary Quarterly (1st ser.), vol. 15, p. 190.

HAMILTON

Alexander Hamilton, wealthy merchat of Bladensburg, declared himself in 1799 will probated in Prince George's Co., to be the "Eldest son of

John Hamilton of Kypewriter in Marechlineshire of Ayr in Scotland and his heir-at-law and residuary legatee". He willed gold watch and seal to Margaret Reed, his Scottish niece. His inventory listed one riding chair.

REF: Pr. Geo. Co. Wills, Liber T no. 1, folio 430.

"John Hamilton late of the Kingdom of Ireland but now of Charles Town in the County of Cecil and Province of Maryland in America Rector of St. Mary Anne Parish in said County". He devised his sons "all my Estate in Land called Killeterre situate, lying and being in Tyrone in the Kingdom of Ireland", and said sons were to be placed under the guardianship of "my two brothers Sir Patrick Hamilton and Thomas Hamilton in the Kingdom of Ireland". 1 Aug. 1764.

REF: Wills, Liber 39, folio 373.

The Rev. John Hamilton, late of Strabane, Co. Tyrone, Ireland, married Sept. 7, 1757, Jane, daughter of Benjamin Peck of New York and widow of the Rev. Richard Currer.

REF: St. Mary Anne's Parish Register, Cecil Co.

Thomas Hamilton declared himself Apr. 15, 1805, "Citizen of the United States America, Merchant of the City of Baltimore State of Maryland, at present on board the Schooner Ann Eliza, Capt. Wm. N. Williams of Baltimore on voyage from Baltimore to Havana". He bequeathed legacies to his family of Leith, Scotland, and arranged for grave stones to be placed on his parents' remains in High West Church yard, Leith.

REF: Balto Wills, Liber 7, folio 451.

HAMMOND

John Hammond of Frederick Co. after certification that he had received the sacrament of the Church of England at St. Anne's Church, Annapolis on Sept. 14, 1762, subscribed to the Oath of Abjuration under the Act of George II (13th year) and on Sept. 15th was acknowledged a naturalized subject.

REF: Prov. Crt Judgements, Liber DD no. 2, folio 347.

Under the Act of George II (13th year) John George Hammond, John Hammond, Andrew Hammond and Mathew Hammond of Anne Arundel Co., after having received the sacrament according to the Church of England, as certified by the rector of St. Anne's Parish, subscribed to the Oath of Abjuration and became on Sept. 8, 1761, naturalized subjects, country of origin not stated.

REF: Prov. Crt Judgements, Liber DD no. 1, folio 493.

Leonard Hammond of Queenhythe, grandson of Leonard Hammond of Royaton, Hertfordshire, registered his quartered arms at the Visitation of London showing in the first and fourth quarters the arms used by Philip Hammond, of Maryland, Esq., ie "Three demi-lions passant guardant".

REF: Visitation of London 1633, Harleian Soc. Pub., vol. 15, p. 344;

Thomas Hammond of Deal, Co Kent, England, Mariner, Commander of the Ship Neptune, his will probated in Maryland Mar. 2, 1761.

REF: Wills, 31, folio 178.

HAMPTON

John Hampton, a so-called Scotch-Irish, was Presbyterian preacher of the Snow Hill Congregation and died testate June 1721/2, Somerset Co. He bequeathed one-third of his estate in America, London and elsewhere to his wife Mary, and made his brother, Robert Hampton of Londonderry, Ireland, his executor of his European estates. Furthermore, he bequeathed legacies to his sisters Marjory and Frances, presumably domiciled in Ireland. Legacies were also willed to his cousins James and William Round of Somerset County.

REF: Wills, Liber 17, folio 121.

HANNA

Robert Hanna, born 1755 in Ireland, settled in Harford Co., where he served in the Flying Camp in 1776, then in the Militia; later domiciled in Fayette Co., Penn.

REF: Revolutionary Pension Claim S22823, National Archives.

HANSLAP

"Henry Hanslap transported himself into the Province of Maryland the 7th Day of October 1676, pp the Shipp Crowne Malaga whereof Thomas Applewaite was then Command^r". He was baptized at the parish church of Aynho, Northamptonshire, Nov. 9, 1635. The coat-of-arms impressed on his 1695 will conforms to the arms on tombs and memorials in St. Michael's Church, Aynho.

In February 1679, he claimed 600 acres of land for his own emigration and eleven other persons which he purchased from Phineas Hyde of Limehouse, Co. Middlesex, Eng., all of whom came in the "Hound of London".

REF: Patents, Liber WC no. 2, folio 172, Hall of Records; English lineage certified by the College of Arms, London, as stated by the late Hester Dorsey Richardson of Baltimore.

HANSON

Considerable legend has been written about the royal and Swedish ancestry of the Hon. John Hanson, a prominent emigrant of Charles County, who died testate in 1714, all of which lacks logic and documentation. Unfortunately, the coat-of-arms impressed on the 1740 original will of his son, Samuel, has been cut from the document and thus has erased all evidence of armorial heritage and ancestry.

While evidence is insufficient to prove a direct connection from local sources, there are clues to assume that the Hansons of Charles County are descended from an old English family of Berkshire. Thomas Hanson of Blewburry, Berks, was the father of Sir Robert Hanson, Knt., Alderman, High Sheriff, and Lord Mayor of London (1672-73), who lived in Bow Lane in Aldermary Parish in London and was buried in St. Mary at Hill Church, London. As High Sheriff he was knighted on February 1, 1665/6, by Charles II.

If Christian names are clues, the names of the Charles County Hansons fit perfectly into this branch as well as the age brackets. John Hanson whose son and heir was Robert had settled in Charles County by 1672.

REF: 1664 Visitation of London, Harl. Soc. Pub. vol. 92, p. 73; Visitation of Berks, Harl Soc. Pub. vol. 57, p. 137; Charles County Gentry, by Newman, pub. 1940; Heraldic Marylandiana, by Newman, pub. 1968.

Hans Hanson in 1671 when he petitioned for naturalization stated that he "was borne in Delaware Bay of Swedish parents".

REF: Md. Archives, vol. 2, p. 331.

HARDWICH

Joseph Hardwich one-time of St. Mary's Co., Md., later of Westmoreland Co., Va., was "late of Prestbury in Southampton, England, but now in residence in Virginia or Maryland", statement dated Sept. 25, 1675.

REF: Westmoreland Co. Records Liber 1665-1677, folio 310.

HARGATE

Peter Hargate Frederick Co., on Sept. 4, 1762, in court subscribed to the Oath of Abjuration in order to become a naturalized subject under the Act of George II (13th year), after having received the sacrament of the Reformed Congregation.

REF: Prov. Crt Judgements, Liber DD no. 2, folio 353.

HARGROVE

Thomas Hargrove of Baltimore City, Innholder, bequeathed property to his two sons living in Ireland.

REF: Balto. Co. Wills, Liber 7, folio 327.

HARMER

On July 29, 1661, Gothofrid Harmer "late of New Amstell and Subject to the Crowne of Sweden" was issued letters of denization.

REF: Md. Archives, vol. 3, pp. 429-430.

HARRANT

Peter Harrant of Charles Co., a Frenchman, petitioned for naturalization in 1733.

REF: Md. Archives, vol. 39, p. 145.

HARRENT

Joseph Harrent, Balto. 27 November 1817 "a native of France but a citizen of Baltimore" bequeathed to his nearest relatives in France all property in France and to his "beloved friend Mr. John Tessier now residing in Baltimore".

REF: Balto. Co. Wills, Liber 10, folio 477.

HARRINGTON

John Harrington who emigrated to Maryland in 1659 was the brother-in-law of John Norwood of Anne Arundel Co., and was the son of Sir James Harrington of Merton, Oxon, who was knighted at Whitehall, December 23, 1628.

REF: Professional English research commissioned 1761 by Norwood descendant.

HARRIS

John Harris, Charles Co., June 22, 1751, "I give and Bequeath to my Loving Brother Thomas Harris of Brudford in the County of Wilts all the residue of my Estate".

REF: Wills, Liber 28, folio 295.

John Harris, London, Merchant, on Dec. 19, 1657, was granted by Lord Baltimore 1,000 acres of land to be erected into a manor with privileges "usually belonging to manors in England". John Harris son of Josias was listed in the 1633 Visitation of London.

REF: Patents, Liber Q, folio 463; Harleian Soc. Pub. vol. 15, p. 351.

Richard Harris, born 1759 at Horley near Banbury, Oxon, settled in Baltimore where he enlisted in the 4th Maryland Regiment during the Revolution; then served in the Maryland Navy; later settled in Grantham District of Upper Canada.

REF: Revolutionary Pension Claim R4671.

Thomas Harris by his will proved Mar. 29, 1727, in Prince George's Co., devised his estate to his wife, Mary and her heirs. Allen Lock who was one of the witnesses soon married the widow. At settlement on Apr.26, 1727, it was stated "The Heirs if any are In England. The deceased being an Englishman Born".

REF: Wills, Liber 10, folio 107; Ad. Accts, Liber 9, folio 208.

William Harris, Sept. 20, 1669, "Then I give unto my Sister Bird in England £5 Sterling,,,, And to my own Sister Alis Curtis I give one pr. of Cordivant Gloves Living at the Signe of the Sugar Loafe at the end of Clement Lane without Temple Bar".

REF: Wills, Liber 1, folio 382.

William Harris, Anne Arundel Co., 13 Jan. 1732/3, "My will further is that my Executors hereafter named pay and deliver unto my Said Wife [Margaret] on her arrival here into this Province from the Kingdom of Ireland all my Whole Estate....but in case my wife and family should not come into this Province....that Money to be Remitted to my family in Ireland".

REF: Wills, Liber 20, folio 580.

HARRISON

Robert Harrison who died in Dorchester Co., Md. 1802, was the son of Christopher Harrison and Mary Caile his wife, and was born November 5, 1740, at Appleby, Co. Cumberland. The tomb of his father is in St. Lawrence Church, Appleby. He arrived in Maryland 1755 bearing letters to Governor Sharpe recommending him for an office "on account of his alliance". His coat-of-arms which he used and which is reputed to have been brought to Maryland by him was confirmed in 1634 by the College of Arms by the registrant of William Harrison of Tower Ward, London. A lenthy pedigree of his family appears in the 1634 Visitation of London.

REF: Harleian Soc. Pub. vol. 40, p. 355; Md. Hist. Mag., vol. 10, p. 376.

William Harrison, of Whitehavenm Co. Cumberland, England, Mariner, June 29, 1751, named his brother John Harrison and sister Elizabeth Harrison, and appointed his uncle, Charles Dickinson of Dorset Co., William Goldsborough of Talbot Co., Gent., and John Fisher of Whitehaven, Merchant, executors of estate.

REF: Wills, Liber 28, folio 416.

HARTWAKE

On Apr. 4, 1762, George Hartwake received the sacrament of the Church of England at St. Anne's, Annapolis, and on Sept. 10, 1762, at court he subscribed to the Oath of Abjuration under the Act of George II (13th year) in order to become a naturalized subject.

REF: Prov. Crt Judgements, Liber D.D. no. 2, folios 89, 91.

HARVEY

Thomas Harvey of Calvert Co., a Frenchman, and his children were naturalized in 1715.

REF: Md. Archives, vol. 38, p. 182.

HARWOOD

Capt. Thomas Harwood, Mariner, of London and Streatley, Berks, was granted a manor in Maryland by the Lord Proprietary. In 1701 he made a deed of gift to his son, Richard, of Anne Arundel Co., plantations in Anne Arundel and Baltimore Counties.

By his will, dated Apr. 22, 1704, probated Mar. 1712/3, he bequeathed his son, Richard £1000 and "all my plantations in Maryland in America" and to all the children of his son Richard "which shall be living at my death £90 at 21 years".

REF: Md. Patents, Liber WT no. 1, folio 27; P.C.C. Canterbury, Public Records Office, London, Leeds 61.

HARWOOD—BACON

Risdon Bozman Harwood of Anne Arundel Co., 29 July 1790, conveyed his rights "which I have either in my one Right or in Right of my Wife Rachel Harwood under or in Virtue of will of Anthony Bacon, late of the City of London, deceased, which said Anthony Bacon was the brother of the Rev. Thomas Bacon of Frederick Co., father of the said Rachel Harwood".

REF: Prov. Crt Deeds, Liber JG no. 1, folio 650.

HATTON

Sir Christopher Hatton, Knt., married Alice, daughter of Sir Thomas Fanshaw of Essex Knt. (knighted 1624). Sir Christopher Hatton, Knt. (knighted 1625), son and heir; Sir Robert Hatton, Knt. (1617), 2d son; Sir Thomas Hatton, Knt. (1616), 3d son were all listed in the 1633 Visitation of London as the sons of John Hatton of Hogginton in County Cambridge, by Jane, daughter of Robert Shute, Justice of the King's Bench, Cambridge.

REF: Visitation of London, Harleian Soc. Pub. vol. 16, pp. 264, 390.

Elizabeth Hatton, widow of Richard Hatton late of London, and brother of Thomas Hatton, Secretary of Maryland, emigrated with her five children, prior to April 23, 1654.

REF: Patents, Liber ABH, folio 422.

John Hatton, Dec. 14, 1654, "I John Hatton of London, Salter...but intending a long voyage by Sea and that nothing is more certain than death....I give, will and devise unto my brother Thomas Hatton all such Lands as were left me by my late ffather John Hatton, deceased, by his last will and testament...I give and bequeath to Robert Lewellin of London,

Salter, the sum of 40 shillings to buy a ring". He also mentioned his sisters Sarah, Susan and Hanna and brothers Henry and Samuel.

The abovementioned, John Hatton, died in Maryland without issue in 1663 possessed of extensive plantations on both the Western and Eastern Shores. His brother, "Thomas Hatton of Tewkesbury in the Cty of Glocester in the Kingdom of England Brother and heir of Jn⁰ Hatton formerly of London and late of this province [Maryland] merchant, deceased" petitioned Charles Calvert, Governor of Maryland. The Council directed the Chancellor on Apr. 15, 1671, to form a jury to enquire of what land John Hatton died seized.

Samuel Hatton, presumably, brother of Thomas and John, was in Maryland in 1663, when he was ordered by Cecilius, to appear at St. Mary's City relative to the estate of John Hatton. A Samuel Hatton of Talbott Co. emigrated in 1667.

REF: Wills, Liber 1, folio 519; Md. Archives, vol. 51, pp. 101-103; Patents, Liber 17, folio 483.

Mary Hatton, widow, Prince George's Co., 6 Sept. 1730, "I give to my Sister Sarah Copping of St. Mary's Parish in Norwich and to my Cuson Abraham Alley of St. Lawrence Parish to Each Thirty Shillings Sterling".

REF: Wills, Liber 20, folio 249.

Thomas Hatton, son of Mathew, was baptized 25 Oct. 1601, at St. Margaret's Westminster; Richard Hatton, son of Mathew, was baptized 25 Aug. 1605. While the baptizm would correspond perfectly with the generation of Thomas Hatton of Maryland and his brother William whose widow and children emigrated to Maryland, the absence of the Christian name of Mathew among the Maryland generations may leave some doubts for the antiquarian.

REF: Register of St. Margaret's Westminster, folios 66, 71, Society of Genealogists, London.

HAUER

Daniel Hauer, born Lothringen, Germany, March 24, 1748, left London August 24, 1769, arrived Philadelphia January 1770, and to Frederick Co., Md. about 1771. He died August 18, 1831.

REF: Diary of Jacob Engelbrech, Md. Hist. Mag, vol. 10, p. 81.

HAUSIL

The Rev. Bernhardt Michael Hausil, Lutheran, married at Rotterdam, Holland, Sybilla Margaretha Mayer, born Ulm, Wurtenberg, Aug. 4, 1733, emigrated to Maryland in 1752.

REF: Md. Hist. Mag., vol. 10, p. 57.

HAWKINS

Elizabeth Hawkins, Charles Co., widow, June 12, 1716, ". . . unto my three Grand Children ffrancis Wine, Elizabeth Wine and Mary Wine Son and Daughters of Henry Wine late of the Kingdom of Great Britain. . . . . to my Daughter Elizabeth Lewis wife of _____ Lewis of Great Britain five shillings".

REF: Wills, Liber 14, folio 510.

HAWLEY

Jerome Hawley, one of the three original Councilors for the Province and a Gentleman of Fashion on the Ark, was a son of James Hawley of Boston near Brentford, Co. Middlesex, England, and step-son of Sir William Courtney of Newhouse, Wilts, Bart. He died in Virginia 1638.

Capt. William Hawley, brother to Jerome, was likewise in Maryland, and was granted in 1648 5700 acres known as St. Jerome's Manor, later to be called Hawley's Manor.

REF: Archives of Maryland, vol. 4, pp. 40, 41, 45; vol. 10, p. 444; The Flowering of the Maryland Palatinate, by Newman; Harleian Soc. Pub. vol. 15, p. 370.

HAYWARD

Nicholas Hayward, London, Merchant, friend of Lord Baltimore, was granted Dec. 19, 1657, jointly with Richard Foot 2,000 acres of land to be erected into a manor with privileges "usually belonging to manors in England".

REF: Patents, Liber Q, folio 470; Liber 4, folio 544.

Stephen Hayward one-time Merchant of London emigrated in 1657 and received land grant.

REF: Patents, Liber 4, folio 186.

HEALY

Caleb Healy, Anne Arundel Co., June 17, 1784, declared himself to be the "son of Andrew Healy of Parish of Hansworth near New Inn in Staffordshire in Old England".

REF: A.A. Co. Wills, Liber TG no. 1, folio 190.

HEATH

In 1684 Mr. James Heath was styled "late of London and now of the Province of Maryland".

REF: Prov Crt, Liber TL no. 2, folio 76.

HEATHCOTT

The estate of Nathaniel Heathcott of Anne Arundel Co., Gent., who died prior to 1685 descended to his nephew "Samuel Heathcott of Derby in the County of Derby in the Kingdom of England, Gent."

REF: A.A. Co. Deeds, Liber WH no. 4, folio 25; Newman's Heraldic Marylandiana.

HELITAS

Marie Magdaline Cavaros Helitas, Widow of Francois Helitas, possessed a plantation in the Parish of St. Louis, Island of St. Domingo, according to her will written in Baltimore, May 26, 1805, at 2 o'clock in the afternoon.

REF: Balto. Co. Wills, Liber 7, folio 42.

HENDERSON

Henry Henderson in 1674 upon naturalization stated that he was a native of Sweadland [Swedish settlements on the Delaware].

REF: Md. Archives, vol. 2, p. 400.

The Rev. Jacob Henderson, Prince George's Co., Queen Anne's Parish, to my "Six nephews and two nieces Children of Thomas Thompson by my sister Mary.....and to my half brother and two half sisters in Ireland" Sons and Daughters of my mother by John Harrison". Will probated 1751.

REF: Wills, Liber 28, folio 185.

"On the Nineteenth day of November A.D. Seventeen hundred & Sixty one, Mr. Richard Henderson of Bladensburgh in Prince Georges County, Merchant, the third Son of the Reverend Mr. Richard Henderson, Minister, of the Parish of Blantyre In the Shire of Lanark in Scotland by Janet Cleland his wife was married to Sarah Brice the Second Daughter of John Brice, Esq., of the City of Annapolis".

REF: Register of St. John's Piscataway Parish, transcript of, Md. Hist. Soc., Balto.

HENRICKSON
On July 29, 1661, Bartholomew Henrickson "late of New Amstell and Subject of the Crowne of Sweden" was issued letters of denization.

REF: Md. Archives, vol. 3, pp. 429-430.

John Hendrickson of Kent Co., a native of Rotterdam, Holland, and his children John, Samuel, Rachel, Mary, Mildred, Margaret, Martha, Rebecca, Hannah and Ruth applied for naturalization in 1730.

REF: Md. Archives, vol. 37, p. 21.

HENRY
John Henry, Pocomoke, Somerset Co., 1 Oct. 1715, "I give and bequeath to my Dear Brother Hugh Henry and Loving Sisters Jennet and Hellen Henry fifteen pounds Sterling which I will be quickly after my Decease paid in the hands of the Rev. Mr. Alexander Sinclare in Plunket Street, Dublin".

REF: Wills, Liber 14, folio 408.

HENSTONE
Under the Act of George II (13th year) Mathais Henstone of Frederick Co., received the sacrament in accordance with the liturgy of the Church of England, as certified by the rector of St. Anne's Parish, Annapolis, and on September 8, 1761, became a naturalized subject. country of origin not stated.

REF: Prv. Crt Judgements, Liber DD no. 1, folio 493.

HERMAN
In 1666 Augustine Herman applied for naturalization by which he "Humbly sheweth" that he "was borne at Prague in Bohemia" and that his children Ephraim Georgius Casparus Anna, Margarita, Judith and ffrancina were "born at New York out of the Limitte of this Province". He made the famous map of Maryland and received seigniorial rights on Bohemia and St. Augustine Manors in Cecil Co. His wife was Jenetie Varlett, daughter of Caper Varlett of Utrecht, Holland.

REF: Md. Archives, vol. 2, p. 144; Augustine Herrman, by Earl L.W. Beck, pub. 1941.

HESSELIUS
Gustavus Hesselius of Prince George's Co., Limner, "born under the Dominions of the King of Sweden" and his daughter, Mary, born in the Province, were naturalized by an Act of the Assembly in 1721.

REF: Md. Archives, vol. 38, p. 288.

HESTER

Farel Hester, a native of Co. Roscommon, Ireland, came to the Colonies in 1774, born 1750, settled in Frederick Co., Md. where he served in the Militia; later domiciled in Edgar Co., Ill.

REF: Revolutionary Pension Claim S32315.

HEUISLEY

Max Heuisley, subject of the Elector of Bavaria, on June 10, 1791, declared himself a member of the Christian faith and subscribed to the Oath of Naturalization. County domicile not noted.

REF: Council Proceedings, Md. Archives, vol. 72, p. 203.

HICKS

John Hicks, St. Mary's Co., May 21, 1749, "Whereas my Daughter Elizabeth in England being married to one Mr. Hall and is well provided for by a settlement from her said husband before marriage....she have no part of my personal estate"; said to be of Whitehaven, Co. Cumberland, Eng.

REF: Wills, Liber 28, folio 517.

HIGGINBOTHAM

The Rev. Ralph Higginbotham, native of Waterford, Ireland and graduate of Trinity, Dublin, was rector of St. Anne's Parish, Annapolis, and Vice President of St. John's College; died Anne Arundel Co. 1813.

REF: Rightmeyer's Maryland's Established Church.

HIGGINSON

John Taillor of London, Merchant, 22 of the 10th mo. 1738, directed his grandson, Tailler Higginson, of the North Branch of the Patuxent River in Maryland to sell certain property in Maryland.

REF: Prov. Crt Deeds, Liber EI no. 3, folio 259, 271.

HILL

Adam Hill, Talbot Co., Mar. 2, 1767, "I give and bequeath...unto my loving mother Margaret Ramsay in the Town of Ayr in North Britain...£500 Sterling annually during life....son Adam Hill in City of London annual interest on £200 Sterling during minority...to loving sister Elizabeth Donaldson of the Town of Ayr..."

REF: Wills, Liber 35, folio 253; Secker III, Public Record Office, London.

James Hill, born Aug. 12, 1764, in Ireland, brought to Maryland by an early age by his father and settled in Cecil Co., where he served in the Militia during the Revolution; later domiciled in Fairfield Co., Ohio.

REF: Revolutionary Pension Claim S9579, National Archives.

James Hill, a Jacobite, captured at Preston, Lancashire, in 1715, and sold in Maryland for seven years of servitude, petitioned for his freedom August 3, 1721, which was denied.

REF: Md. Archives, vol. 34, p. 164.

John Hill, Kent Co., Aug. 1, 1771, "I give and bequeath unto my brother Thomas Hill the son of Sarah Hill of the Parish of Pitney in Somersetshire in England" the residue of his estate, but if his brother were deceased then to Michael Bartlett of the same county and parish (no stated relationship).

REF: Wills, Liber 39, folio 38.

Joseph Hill of Anne Arundel Co., Feb. 24, 1703/4, residue to "be Sent by my Executors to my father in England but particularly my Gold ring I desire may be Sent to my Father".

REF: Wills, Liber 3, folio 147.

Richard Hill, Anne Arundel Co., 20 Octo. 1700, "I give and bequeath to Mrs. Mary Young £20 Sterling to her proper use and behoofe to my Sister Abigail Parr in Worstershire near Sturbridge".

REF: Wills, Liber 6, folio 394.

HODGES
John Hodges of Anne Arundel Co., in 1711 was late mariner of Bristol, Eng.

REF: Prov. Crt Deeds, Liber TP no. 4, folio 84.

HODGSHON
William Hodgshon, Calvert Co., M.D., 3 February 1734/5, "It is my will that Immediately after my Decease my said Ex^S or either of them take my son Ezra unto their Guardianship and as soon as may be send him to the Port of Liverpool in England and some good and trusty Person who shall Conduct him unto the Care and possession of my Brother Robert Hodgshon now an Inhabitant of Darlington in the Bishopric of Durham".

REF: Wills, Liber 21, folio 277.

HODGSON
The tomb of John Hodgson at Tusculum, the plantation of the Gale family in Somerset Co., states that he was "Late of Whitehaven" which is in Co. Cumberland.

REF: Newman's Heraldic Marylandiana.

HOLDSWORTH
John Holdsworth of Calvert Co., Gent., by his will dated Apr. 8, 1709, and probated 1712, made the unnamed children of his sister in England contingent heirs to his real and personal estate.

REF: Wills, Liber 33, folio; 448; Foster's Yorkshire Pedigrees.

HOLIDAY
Thomas Holiday, born Nov. 26, 1774, was a native of Dungannon, co. Tyrone, Ireland; died Nov. 29, 1829.

REF: Headstone, Congressional Cem., Washington, D.C.

HOLLAND
John Francis Holland "Baltemore County by birth a German" was naturalized by Act of Assembly in 1707.

REF: Md. Archives, vol. 27, p. 152.

HOLLIS
John Hollis, a native of Manchester, England, emigrated to Baltimore about 1785, and married in the Smith family. Their son, Commodore George

Nicholas Hollis, was a distinguished officer in the United States Navy, but won greater distinction in the Confederate Navy.

REF: Md. Hist. Mag., vol. 34, p. 242.

HOLLYFIELD

Joseph Hollyfield, Pr. Geo. Co., Feb. 4, 1763, "Give and bequeath unto my Eldest son Joseph Hollyfield all my real and personal estate purchased by my grandfather Thomas Hollyfield lying and being in Warwickshire in Great Britain in the town of Birmingham."

REF: Wills, Liber 32, folio 334.

HOLT

John De Bert Holt, of Queen Anne's Co., Surgeon, Apr. 3, 1755, declared himself "formerly a native of Germany born in Heildersburg in the Palatinate and devised his brother Philip his claims in the estate of their father.

REF: Wills, Liber 29, folio 367.

HONORE

John Anthony Honore, a subject of France, on July 7, 1781, declared himself a Christian, and subscribed to the Oath of Allegiance.

REF: Council Proceedings, Md. Archives, vol. 71, p. 178.

HOPKINS

William Hopkins of Biddeford, Co. Devon, Mariner, devised "all that my house Lott and Wharves with all singular the appurtenances thereunto belonging lying at Chestertown in Kent Co. in Maryland unto my two sons James Hopkins and Wm Hopkins . . . . . Tenement called addipit in Buckland Brewer in the County of Devon to daughter Judith Hopkins during life and then to my son William. Wife Elizabeth to be executrix and guardian of children during their minories. Dated May 19, 1743.

REF: Deeds, Liber JJ no. 18, folio 155, Hall of Records.

HOPPER

William Hopper, Queen Anne's Co., 12 Apr. 1711, "give and bequeath unto my son William Hopper my houses, lands and tenment . . . . and for want of such issue to my Daughter Jane whom I had by my present wife, , , and for want of such Issue to my Daughter Jane Hopper whom I had by a former wife Dorothy in the Bishoprick of Durham in England".

REF: Wills, Liber 13, folio 240.

HOUGH

Edmond Hough of Worcester Co., Sept. 14, 1760, devised land to "Elizabeth Copeland Jr., of Linley, Yorkshire in the Kingdom of England" in the event that his daughters and granddaughters died without issue.

REF: Wills, Liber 31, folio 850.

HOULDCRAFT

George Houldcraft, St. Mary's Co., Chirurgeon, Sept. 21, 1662, Legacies to wife then "unto my brothers which by name are Called Michael Houldcraft and Valentine Houldcraft . . . . . which are in England".

REF: Wills, Liber 1, folio 237.

HOW

Obediah How of Calvert Co., by will of 1686, referred to his uncle, Joseph How, to whom he devised his entire estate in England and Maryland.

REF: Wills, Liber 4, folio 286.

HOWARD

Edmund Howard, Charles Co., Gent., Dec. 3, 1709, "I give and bequeath unto my Dear and well beloved Brother Mr. Rich[d] Eyton, Merchant, in London and to his wife and also to my Dear and only Sister Mrs. Hester Tyndale wife to Mr. Athelstand Tydale upholster in Bristoll and to her husband I give each of them 30 shillings to buy a mourning ring".

REF: Wills, Liber 13, folio 632.

Mathew Howard who died c1658 in Anne Arundel Co., was the son of Philip Howard and Joan Marriott and great-grandson of Lady Margaret Douglas by her first marriage to Lord Thomas Howard; said Lady Margaret married secondly, Mathew, Earl of Lennox.

REF: Providence Ye Lost Towne at Severn, by James E. Moss, pub. 1976, p. 454.

NOTE: Meticulous English research by the author.

Michael Howard, Talbot Co., Gent., 1 Febr. 1734/5, bequeathed a legacy "to my Honored Father and Mother the sum of £10 a piece to be remitted to my Brother Adam or Francis Howard". He furthermore named "nephew Michael William Howard now with me the son of my Brother Matthew Howard late of the City of Dublin, deceased". The nephew was to be educated at Westminster School and King's College in Cambridge until he shall arrive at the age of 21, and mentioned his "sister-in-law Sarah Howard the Relict of my said Brother" and for the use the said brother's daughter Elizabeth. To the "two eldest sons of my Brother Mr. Adam Howard of the County of West Meath in the Kingdom of Ireland". Said Michael Howard was late of Gray's Inn.

REF: Wills, Liber 21, folio 779.

HOWE

Robert Howe, Dorchester Co., Oct. 5, 1764, "I give and bequeath to my beloved Brother Thomas Howe of Carrick on Sure in the Co. of Tipperary and Kingdom of Ireland £200 Sterling to be paid to my Trusty friend Mr. Robert Goldsborough Son of Charles in eight months after my Decease to be by him remitted to my Said Brother".

REF: Wills, Liber 34, folio 114.

HUBBS

Jacob Hubbs, born Oct. 30, 1762, Halifax, Nova Scotia, while living on the Maryland frontier served in the Militia during the Revolution; later lived in Bullock Co., Ky.

REF: Revolutionary Pension Claim S16421, National Archives.

HUETT

John Huett, son of the Rev. John Hewitt, English orthography, was born in England and was the first Anglican minister for Somerset Co. and rector of Stepney Parish. His father, born Sept. 1614, was of Pembroke College

1633, Cambridge, and D.D. Oxford 1643. He was chaplain to Charles I and the Earl of Lindsey and also rector of St. George's by St. Paul's, London. He was executed June 8, 1658, on Tower Hill by the Puritans for complicity in a royalish plot. The grandfather of the Maryland emigrant was Thomas Hewitt, a clothmaker, of Eccles, Lancashire. The Rev. John Huett died in Somerset Co. June 24, 1658.

REF: Directory of Cambridge Men; Old Somerset, by Torrence.

HUFF

Peter Huff, born on Isle of Guernsey, and was brought to the Colonies by his parents, when he was aged 9, born in or about 1754; from Federick Co., Md. he served in the Maryland Militia during the Revolution; later domiciled in Turnbull Co., Ohio.

REF: Revolutionary Pension Claim S9597, National Archives.

HUMPHREYS

Francis Humphreys, Talbot Co., Miller & Innkeeper, Dec. 30, 1770, devised his nephew Thomas Humphreys of Kingdom of Ireland the dwelling-plantation and mill at decease of the testator's widow, Martha.

REF: Wills, Liber 38, folio 289.

"John Humphreys late Rector of this Parish was born in the City of Limerick in the Province of Munster in Ireland and aged this year of Grace 1739 53 years in which he dyed. His parents were persons of repute and figure. His father being a practitioner in Physick eminent for his skill and practice, born in Leicestershire in England and married to a Daughter of the North family of Roper. He lost his parents very Early never having known his father nor had he at the age of twelve Years one relative living in the Kingdom nor has he Seen one Since except one Hoddilow by proffession a Dry Salter. Had lived in Maryland 16 years." His widow, Theodosia, married Philip Key, Esq., of St. Mary's Co., as his second wife.

REF: St. Anne's Parish Register, transcript Md. Hist. Soc., Balto.; Historic Notes of St. Anne's Parish, by Rev. Ethan Allen, pub. 1857.

HUNTER

Samuel Hunter, Frederick Co., Sept. 18, 1758, ". . . unto my Brother James Hunter of the Kingdom of Ireland" estate, if his children died young and without issue.

REF: Wills, Liber 30, folio 702.

HUSBAND

Richard Husband, London, Merchant, friend of Lord Baltimore, in 1658 who was granted seignorial rights at Elk Pointe on Kent Isle for 1,000 acres, was of Wapping, Middlesex.

REF: Patents, Liber Q, folio 472; Md. Archives, vol. 10, 351.

HUSSEY

In 1656 Thomas Hussey of Charles Co., Mercht, held a note of £200 on his father "John Hussey of Harby in ye County of Lincoln Clarke. . . . to Thomas Hussey Mercht Sonne of ye sd John".

REF: Md. Archives, vol. 65, p. 673.

HUTCHISON

William Hutchison died testate in Prince George's Co. 1711, and devised his son and heir, John, "Sangwhaire" in Ayreshire, North Britain, as descended to him by the will of his father, Mr. John Hutchison. To his brother, George Hutchison, a legacy which was to be sent him in Scotland. It is reputed that the testator owner over 6,000 acres of land in Maryland.

REF: Wills, Liber 13, folio 317.

HYDE

Henry Hyde who died testate in St. Mary's Co., will dated Oct. 29, 1675, was a registrant at the 1683 Visitation of Cheshire, whose ancient seat was Norbury.

REF: Harleian Soc. Pub., vol. 93, pp. 18, 59; vol. 18, vol. 59.

HYNDERSON

Robert Hynderson, a Jacobite, captured in 1715 at Preston, Lancashire, and sold in Maryland for seven years of servitude, petitioned for his freedom on August 3, 1721, which was denied.

REF: Md. Archives, vol. 34, p. 164.

ICON

John Icon, May 29, 1672, "I do hereby Give and bequeath unto Mathias De Costa all and Singular my Estate that now I possessed in the Province of Maryland. . .unto me in England and more particularly Three houses in the City of Bristoll Scituated in Temple Street which my Uncle Thomas Ward gave unto me by his will and testament which will my ffather Griffin Icon caused to be recorded in London before my departure out of England".

REF: Wills, Liber 1, folio 498.

IIAMS

NOTE: The origin of this distinctive family has been the subject of much and varied contention. Claims of Dutch, Flemish, Scottish and Welsh have all been suggested. The progenitor, William Iiams, was a native Britisher, as no record exists of his naturalization in Maryland. A descendant after extensive travel and research in Britain has revealed the fact that it is Cornish and the Maryland orthography is a corruption of the ancient I'ans of County Cornwall.

The family I'ans was seated in the time of Henry VIII in the Parish of Stratton, Cornwall. Arms were issued to Robert I'ans of Whitstone by Elizabeth, her Master of Ordance and Her Majesty's Privy Council in Ireland. The family pedigree in the County Record Office of Cornwall for the most part goes back only to February 1640, using the orthography I'ans and Ians. The last of the line in Cornwall seems to have been Colonel Wrey I'ans of Whitstone House, Cornwall, who died in 1816, although he left married daughters who did not carry down the name. Colonel I'ans served as His Majesty's Justice of the Peace for Cornwall and Devon.

The 13th century accounts of the Earldom of Cornwall contain such family names as Ian, Ians, Iane, Iannes, etc. The Maryland family always pronounced their name as one syllable.

REF: "Remembered in this Land", privately printed 1978, by Lois Ijams Hartman, Pasadena, Calif.; Burke's Armory.

IMBERT

Andrew Imbert was naturalized in 1694 by Act of the General Assembly.

REF: Md. Archives, vol. 19, pp. 46, 103.

INCH

John Inch, Kent Co., 7 Mar. 1734/5, devised his dwelling-plantation to his son, Benjamin, but if he died before the age of 21, "I give and devise the aforesaid Land and Plantation to my Brother William Inch in Woster in Kidemuster.

REF: Wills, Liber 21, folio 415.

INGRAM

Thomas Ingram, Kent Co., Gent., Sept. 13, 1669, "I give unto the said William Vaughan £36 Sterling money which is in the hands of my brother Anthony Ingram of the City of London, Gentl".

REF: Wills, Liber 1, folio 407.

IRELAND

Edward Ireland by will 30 June 1814, declared himself a "Native of the Island of Barbados and for nearly 30 years past a Citizen of the State of Maryland".

REF: Balto Co. Wills, Liber 10, folio 202.

IRVINE

Mark H. Irvine, formerly a subject of Great Britain, on Jan. 10, 1789, declared himself a Christian and subscribed to the Oath of Naturalization.

REF: Council Proceedings, Md. Archives, vol. 71, p. 318.

ISRAEL

On Oct. 19, 1701, John Israel of Anne Arundel Co., Merchant, declared himself to be late of the town of London.

REF: A.A. Co. Deeds, Liber WT no. 1, folio 200.

IUYER

William Iuyer of Dartmouth, Eng., Esq., arrived in Maryland 1684, and died the following year. William Elliott of Dartmouth, Mariner, reported his death.

REF: Testamentary Proceedings, Liber 13, folio 266.

JACKSON

Henry Jackson by will probated Balto. 15 July 1817, declared himself "formerly of Church Street in the City of Dublin now residing in Lombard Street in the City of Baltimore...I do bequeath to my beloved Daughter Eleanor Bond, widow of Oliver Bond, formerly of Bridge Street in the City of Dublin".

REF: Balto Co. Wills, Liber 10, folio 334.

James Jackson, "formerly a subject of Great Britain" on Oct. 2, 1789, took the Oath of abjuration and declared himself a member of the Christian faith. County domicile not cited.

REF: Council Proceedings, Md. Archives, vol. 72, p. 50.

Nicholas Jackson of London, Merchant, in 1657 was about to emigrate to Maryland.

REF: Md. Archives, vol. 4, p. 214.

JACOBSON

On July 29, 1661, Peter Jacobson "late of New Amstell and Subject of the Crowne of Sweden" was issued letters of denization.

REF: Md. Archives, vol. 3, p. 429-30.

JACQUES

Lancelot Jacques by his will probated in Washington Co., Md., 1791, referred to his great age and bequeathed his brother, Jeffrey Jacques, of Cumberland, Eng., an annuity of £20 Sterling during his life and that of his wife, Anne. Legacy was left to his nephew, Arthur Jacques, of Hutton Bushel, Yorks. Other bequests were willed to his kinsmen in Maryland.

REF: Wills, Wash. Co., Md., Liber A no. 2, folio 92.

JAQUET

John Daniel Jaquet, native of Germany, emigrated to Maryland and served in the German Regiment during the Revolution; later domiciled in Carbon Co., Penn.

REF: Revolutionary Pension Claim W27879½, National Archives.

JARBOE

Lieut. Col. John Jarboe was born about 1619 at Dijon, Dukedom of Burgundy, Kingdom of France, Deposing to be 40 years of age in 1659. In January 1646/7, being a non-British subject, he took the Oath of Fealty to Lord Baltimore. At a session of the Upper House in 1666 it was shown that "John Jarbo of Dijon in the realm of ffrance. . . .was borne att Dijon in ffrance".

REF: Md. Archives, vol. 2, p. 144.

JENIFER

Daniel of St. Thomas Jenifer by his will April 15, 1790, Anne Arundel Co., bequeathed a legacy to his "relations the Miss Christies in Glasgow" and also to Robert Christie of London, Merchant.

REF: A.A. Co. Wills, Liber JG no. 1, folio 194.

JENKINS

Austin Jenkins, aged 27 years, sailed for Maryland from England "for employment".

REF: Emigrants from England 1773-1776, by Gerald Fothergill, p. 35.

John Jenkins, born in Wales, substituted for John Henry Maccubin, in accordance with the "Act to procure Troops for the American Army", passed March Session 1778.

REF: Militia List, Md. Hist. Soc., Balto.

Richard Jenkins, Baltimore Co., 17 Nov. 1734, "I give and bequeath unto my Brother John Jenkins living in Derbyshire near York in England or elsewhere my plantation. . . .residue to my brother John Jenkins, Brother Thomas Jenkins and my sister Mary Jenkins".

REF: Wills, Liber 21, folio 318.

JENNINGS

Edmund Jennings, Deputy Secretary of Maryland, 1732-1740, was the grandson of Sir Edmund Jennings of Ripon, Yorks, Knt. and the great-grandson of Sir Edward Barkham of Co. Norfolk, Bart.

REF: Harleian Soc. Pub. vol. 15, p. 50; The Genealogist n.s., vol. 17, pp. 259-261.

Edmund Jennings, in the County of York, Esq., Mar. 10, 1756, bequeathed a legacy to James Buchanan, of London, Merchant; nephew Edmund Jennings of North America a plantation in the Fork of the Patuxent; and an estate to his son Edmund Jennings.

REF: Wills, Liber 30, folio 85.

Richard Jennings of London, Merchant in 1657 expressed his intentions to emigrate to Maryland.

REF: Patents, Liber 4, folio 190.

JERMINGHAM

Henry Jermingham of St. Mary Co., Esq., by will Nov. 19, 1772, was seized of property on Cannon Hill in Surry which he owned jointly with his uncle, Sir George Jermingham of Cossey Hall, Co. Norfolk, England, Bart.

REF: Wills, Liber 39, folio 143.

JOHNS

Descendants of Richard Johns who emigrated to Calvert Co. in 1670 are lead to believe that their ancestor was the son of Sir Thomas who was son of Sir Henry son of Sir Thomas, according to Francis Culver, late genealogist. Unfortunately, Culver had the bad habit of not documenting some of his work. No knighthood was ever conferred upon a Johns, per Shaw's Knights of England.

Richard Johns became "convinced" of the righteous pecularities of Quakerism, but from the inventory of his estate at this death in 1717, it would indicate that he did not pursue the abstemious life of the brethren. His cellar contained 1,070 gallons of cyder (presumably unfermented), *but* 20 gallons of brandy. His personal estate was valued at £2i67/16/11. While Quakers were noted for hard bargaining and great wealth which consisted in land, grain, livestock and at times in slave traffic they refused to spend their resources on luxuries, Richard Johns was an exception.

He did not confine himself to the plain, austere black garb of the sect, as his clothing was appraised at £23/18/10. His silver plate was valued at £45, so his table was not set with the plain accessories of his pious friends. His education was not neglected, for his library was appraised at £6/15/—. He furthermore assumed the life of a patrician at his plantation with 44 negro slaves.

It is a matter of public record that he contributed heavily to the Monthly Meetings, perhaps a motive for his exemption from the rigidities of the sect.

REF: See, Hopkins-Baldwin Chart, Gift Collection, Hall of Records, Annapolis.

JOHNSON

In 1682 a bill was introduced and passed for the naturalization of Albert Johnson of Talbot Co.

REF: Md. Archives, vol. 7, pp. 268, 330.

Bernard Johnson of Calvert Co., Cooper, stated in 1671 at the time of naturalization that he was "borne in Holland and Under the Dominion of the States General of the united Province".

REF: Md. Archives, vol. 2, p. 270.

Cornelius Johnson in 1674 when he petitioned for naturalization stated that he was born "att ffiacena under the same Dominons", that is, the States General of the United Provinces, now The Netherlands.

REF: Md. Archives, vol. 2, p. 400.

George Johnson, Somerset Co., 23 November 1680, "I give and bequeath the one Moytie of a house lyeing and being in the City of Canterbury in the County of Kent in England unto the oldest child of my brother John Johnson living in Woburn in new England. . .I give and bequeath unto the Eldest child of my sister Susan Johnson that shall be Living att the time of this my Last will and testament is performed four Pounds Left me by my dear and Loving ffather and a bill of 16 lb. Money Sterling due from my Brother Edward Johnson in New England. . . .I give and bequeath to my Brother William Johnson in New England his Eldest Child that shall be Living att the time of my Decease One house Lying and being in Canterbury, Kent County, Old England and in a parish Called Alfidge over against the Bishop's Pallace that was left me by my ffather Edward Johnson after the decease of my grandfather William John. . . .give undo my Sister formerly Called Susanna Prentice alias Johnson".

REF: Wills, Liber 2, folio 189.

"By Order from the Honble Charles Calvert Esqr the after Written pautent of Dennizacon was Granted to Hendrick Johnson". 15 December 1668. "Whereas Hendrick Johnson late of Amsterdam belonging to the States of Holland" on 26 February 1668/9, was granted a "ffre Dennizen".

REF: Md. Archives, vol. 5, pp. 35-36.

John Johnson of Talbot Co. in 1674 stated that he was "borne in holland under the Dominion of the States General of the United Provinces".

REF: Md. Archives, vol. 2, p. 403.

On July 29, 1661, Paule Johnson "late of New Amstell and Subject to the Crowne of Sweden" was issued letters of denization.

REF: Md. Archives, vol. 3, pp. 429-430.

Peter Johnson in 1669 upon his application for naturalization stated that he was born in the "kingdome of Sweadland" [Swedish settlements on the Delaware].

REF: Md. Archives, vol. 2, p. 205.

An Act for the naturalization of Simon Johnson and his children past the Lower House in 1683.

REF: Md. Archives, vol. 7, p. 487, 489.

Statement made by Mrs. Ann G. Ross, late of Frederick, granddaughter of Governor Thomas Johnson (1732-1819) that Thomas Johnson the Elder, her great-grandfather, was of Porte Head, Yarmouth, England. He was a barrister and had a brother who was with the Department of Foreign Affairs under Queen Anne. He eloped with a chancery ward and sailed for Maryland under the protection of her father, Captain Roger Baker, who commanded the vessel.

NOTE: Conflict of interest. If her father were living, why was she a ward of the Court of Chancery.

REF: Biographical Sketches of Distinguished Marylanders, by Boyle, p. 73, pub. 1877.

JONATHAN

John Jonathan, subject of Great Britain, proved himself a Christian and subscribed to the Oath of Naturalization on Dec. 28, 1789.

REF: Council Proceedings, Md. Archives, vol. 72, p. 70.

JONES

Henry Jones, a native of Wales, Great Britain, settled in Washington Co., Md. and died at Hancock on May 31, 1851, aged 65 years.

REF: Headstone, Hancock Cemetery.

Rev. Hugh Jones, of Christ Church Parish, Calvert Co., 3 Jan. 1701/2, "I give and bequeath to my eldest brother Mr. Richard Jones late minister of Laackrath in the Isle of Anglice", residue of estate but if he is dead then I give and bequeath the Same to my youngest brother Mr. John Jones and in case neither of them be liveing I give and bequeath the above portion of my Estate to my said Eldest Brother's Children".

REF: Wills, Liber 11, folio 151.

John Jones was transported into Maryland during 1678 from the Kingdom of Ireland.

REF: Patents, Liber 20, folio 184.

Richard Jones, a subject of Great Britain, on July 1, 1785, declared himself a Christian and subscribed to the Oath of Naturalization.

REF: Proceedings of the Council, Md. Archives, vol. 71, p. 36.

Thomas Jones, son of Capt. Thomas Jones of Liverpool, married Oct. 15, 1751, Elizabeth Guibert, daughter of Joshua Guibert of St. Mary's Co.

REF: Somerset Parish Register, Somerset Co.

JONSTON

"Francis Jonston, Anglican, of Devonshire, son of Francis, Minister of Evangelic truth. He was secluded in a life often afflected and was buried in 1679".

REF: Stone at Poplar Hill Churchyard, St. Mary's Co.; see also Bulletin 3 of Maryland Original Research Society of Balto., pub. 1913, p. 60.

JORDAN

John Morton Jordan, of Annapolis and late of London, Merchant, by will June 6, 1771, possessed land in Antigua and Virginia; named his half-sister Mary Sydenham, widow, of Jonathan Sydenham, late of London, Merchant, and his half-brothers Joseph and George Morton and half-sister Frances Merriweather; executors Michael McNamarra of Great George St., Westminster, London, and Edmund Jennings late of Maryland but then of London.

REF: Wills, Liber 38, folio 473.

JOURDAIN

Captain Jean Jourdain, later styled Gordon, 22 Mar. 1662/3, as "John Jourdaen stated that he was late of the Island of Barbados belonging to the Crowne of England and Subject of the Crowne of ffrance". At naturalization in 1669 he declared himself to be a native of "Rouan", in the kindome of ffrance".

REF: Md. Archives, vol. 2, p. 205; vol. 3, p. 562.

JOURDAN

John Jourdan native of Ireland, enlisted in the 3th Maryland Regiment during the Revolutionary War.

REF: Revolutionary Pension Claim S34945, National Archives.

JOURDEAN

"patent Denizacon mutatis ut est fol 277 John Jourdean". 17 July 1667.

REF: Md. Archives, vol. 5, p. 11.

JOWLES

Henry Jowles, Attorney, Calvert Co., 19 Sept. 1693, "I give and bequeath unto my son John Jowles now living in the Kingdom of England all that Tract or parcel of land called Gillingham lyeing upon Bush River in Baltimore County". Henry Jowles was late of Gray's Inn, London.

REF: Wills, Liber 6, folio 399, Bond's Maryland Court of Appeals, vol. 1, p. xxii.

JUBB

Robert Jubb, Anne Arundel Co., 5 Apr. 1723, "I give and bequeath to my Sister Mary Jackson now living in Great Britain and her children £15 Sterling to be paid on demand".

REF: Wills, Liber 19, folio 811.

KEARNEY

John A. Kearney, born Ireland, June 24, 1798, died Aug. 27, 1818.

REF: Congressional Cemetery, Washington, D.C.

KEATING

Henry Semple Keating of Baltimore and George Keating of Frederick Co. the sons of Thomas and Elizabeth (Semple) Keating were heirs in 1811 in the estate of John Semple, Ironmonger, one time of Dublin, Ireland, [Annapolis], Md., and Prince William Co., Va.

REF: Chancery, Liber 46, folios 161-268, Hall of Records, Annapolis.

KEENE

Richard Keene, Calvert Co., 1 April 1672, "I do give and bequeath unto my dear ffather Henry Keene of Wordstowne [Worplesdon] in Surry in the Kingdom of England the Sum of twenty pounds Lawfull Money of England".

REF: Wills, Liber 2, folio 384. Pedigree furnished by the College of Arms for an American descendant; Newman's Heraldic Marylandiana.

KEENER

Meliker Keener and John Keener became naturalized subjects on Sept. 10, 1762, after subscribing to the Oath of Abjuration under the Act of George

II (13th year) and certifying that they had taken the sacrament of the Church of England at St. Anne's Church, Annapolis, on Apr. 14, 1762.

REF: Prv. Crt Judgements, Liber DD no. 2, folio 89-91.

Melcher Keener, born 1720, Saarbrucken, Alsace, emigrated to York Co., Penn., settled in Baltimore and died Aug. 27, 1798.

KEITING
Nicholas Keiting, Apr. 20, 1657, "I bequeath all Estate I have in Ireland or Elsewhere unto my Sonne Thomas".

REF: Wills, Liber 1, folio 150.

KEMP
The Rev. James Kemp, born 1764 at Keith Hall and Kinkell Parish, Aberdeenshire, Scotland, emigrated to Maryland 1787 and settled in Dorchester Co., later elected Anglican Bishop of Maryland, died 1827, aged 62.

REF: Obituaries, Md. Hist. Soc., Balto.

Nicholas Kemp of Frederick Co., after furnishing certification that he had taken the sacrament of the Protestant Calvinistic Church of Geneve subscribed to the Oath of Abjuration under George II whereby on Sept. 15 1762, he became a naturalized subject.

REF: Prov. Crt Judgements, Liber DD no. 2, folios 347-9.

KENNEDY
George Scott Kennedy was born in Malinie, Scotland, in 1700, came to Maryland in 1730, and in 1758 was appointed High Sheriff for Frederick Co.

REF: Williams' Hist. of Washington Co., Md., vol. 2, p. 1189, pub. 1906.

KENNER
William Kenner of White Haven, Co. Cumberland, England, Mariner, devised property to his cousin, Richard Kenner of Northumberland Co., Va.; to "my sister-in-law Mrs. Elizabeth Hall all my deceased wife's wearing apparel now under the care and possession of her brother Mr. William Hicks of Maryland, Merchant; children of his brothers and sisters Matthew Kenner, Frances Kenner, Elizabeth and Mary; son William Hicks Kenner were to be placed under the guardianship of friend, Mrs. Sarah Hicks of White Haven, widow and said son to be placed in an English school; will dated Dec. 11, 1758.

REF: Wills, Liber 31, folio 976.

KENSLEY
Benjamin Kensley, native of Lincolnshire, England, died Oct. 6, 1845, aged 62.

REF: Congressional Cemetery, Washington, D.C.

KEUNDLER
Adam Gottlieb Raal of Baltimore Town was appointed attorney by the heirs of Michael Keundler, late of York Co., Penn., the said heirs being domiciled in Mittelsin, Duchy of Hanau, Germany.

REF: Wills of Raal, proved Baltimore Co., Nov. 20, 1813, Liber 9, folio 375.

KEY

"I Philip Key of St. Mary's County in Maryland, son of Richard and Mary Key, born in the Parish of St. Paul's Covent Garden in London ye 21st March 1696", his will dated March 10, 1764.

His will contained other interesting genealogical facts such as "Steel Seal with "my Coat of Arms", picture of the Royal family, "my family pictures drawn in England" and the family pictures painted by Heselius and Rose, also gold rings which had been ordered from England.

REF: Wills, Liber 32, folio 208.

William Key, Kent Co., Apr. 20, 1679, "I give and bequeath a parcell of land what I have at Langford Bay called Langford unto my loving brother Randall Key of ye Citty of Bristoll".

REF: Wills, Liber 10, folio 79.

KEYN

Nicholas Keyn, a native of Ireland, was transported in 1641.

REF: Patents, Liber ABH, folio 102.

KIERSTEDE

Jochen Kierstede and Hans Kierstede, both styled chyrungions, native of North Europe were domiciled and land owners in Calvert Co., prior to Nov. 1708.

REF: Provincial Crt, Liber TL no. 3, folio 115.

KILM

In August 1729 a bill was introduced in the Upper House for naturalization of Conrade Kilm of Annapolis, Cooper, Anna Maria his wife and John his son.

REF: Md. Archives, vol. 36, p. 381.

KINKEE

Herman Kinkee "Dutchman born in Holland" and his children were naturalized in 1720 by an Act of the Assembly.

REF: Md. Archives, vol. 38, p. 261.

KIRKWOOD

David Kirkwood, native of Dumbean Parish, Ireland; came to the Colonies in 1772 when about 36 years of age; enlisted at Hagerstown, Md., and served throughout the Revolution; later a domicile of Harrison Township, Champagne Co., Ohio.

REF: Revolutionary Pension Claim W29916½, National Archives.

KITCHIN

An Act for the naturalization of Justus Englehard Kitchin, of Anne Arundal Co., Painter, a native of Germany, was passed the Assembly in December 1708.

REF: Md. Archives, vol. 27, pp. 369-370.

LACAZE

"I William Lacaze a native of Tarbu in the Kingdom of France, but at the age of 5 years removed with my parents to Dax where I have resided and where my family still remains. I am son of John Lacaze and Magdeline Sumalieu of the said Dax, and now residing in Baltimore on Charles Street", according to his will Dec. 24, 1800. The witnesses were Michael Barou, Joseph Bertouin and Louis Barbarin.

REF: Balto. Co. Wills, Liber 6, folio 352.

LAMEE

John Lamee [Larne] of Dorchester Co., weaver, and his children "born under the Dominion of the Most Christian King [Sweden ?] were naturalized in 1713 by an Act of the Assembly.

REF: Md. Archives, vol. 38, p. 181.

LAMORE

Thomas Lamore and Peter Lamore of French descent were granted circa 1663 "Pattents of Dennizacon".

REF: Md. Archives, vol. 3, p. 489.

LANDRETH

John Landreth, son of William and Margaret (Brown) Landreth, was born in Parish of Slitchill, Berwickshire, Scotland, married March 25, 1765, Margaret Gillis, widow of Levin Gillis, and daughter of William and Sarah (Eccleston) Nutter.

REF: Stephen Parish Records, Wicomico Co.

LANE

John Lane, Somerset Co., 4 May 1712, "My land at the sea side and my land in Nuswadding Neck I do order my well beloved brother Walter Lane to dispose of. . . . and to send the produce thereof to my Wife and family in England".

REF: Wills, Liber 13, folio 530.

Samuel Lane who settled in St. James' Parish, Anne Arundel Co., was the son of Richard Lane and Alice Carter his wife of Herefordshire and London, England. Samuel Lane by his will Jan. 18, 1681/2, stated that if his sons died without issue before coming of age, then "I give the Same to my nephew Thomas Lane of the Kingdom of Ireland".

REF: Wills, Liber 2, folio 185; Article by A. Russell Slagle, Md. Hist. Magazine, vol. 71, no. 4 (1976).

LANGWORTH

James [Johannes] Langworth, one-time Surveyor General of Maryland, who died testate Chas. Co., 1660 was of County Kent, England, and declared himself a cousin of Governor Thomas Green, likewise, of County Kent.

REF: Visitation of Kent 1663-1668, by Howard & Hovenden, pub. 1887.

LAW

William Law in 1785 declared himself "formerly of the City of London in the Kingdom of Great Britain but now of Prince George's County in the State of Maryland", when he granted power of attorney.

REF: Montg. Co. Deeds, Liber B, folio 167.

LAWRENCE

"28 of Aug. 1749. On this day Mr. John Lawrence late of Liverpool in Lancashire England and Miss Mary Plafay of Piscataway" were married.

REF: Register of St. John's Piscataway Parish, Pr. Geo. Co., transcript of, Md. Hist. Soc., folio 288.

John Lawrence by his will of Baltimore Town dated Sept. 28, 1797, declared himself formerly of Great Britain.

REF: Balto. Co. Wills, Liber 6, folio 126.

The lineage of Sir Thomas Lawrence of Chelsea, Middlesex, Bart, Secretary of Maryland, President of the Council and Acting Chief Executor, may be found in the The Complete Baronetage as well as his son, Thomas, who was clerk of the court for Talbot County.

REF: Newman's Heraldic Marylandiana; The Complete Baronetage.

LAWSON

James Lawson of Glasgow, Scotland, Merchant, resided in Charles Co., Md., became the mortagee of extensive property in Western Maryland in 1769 possessed by John Semple, Ironmonger, originally of Dublin, Ireland, late of Maryland and Prince William Co., Va. In 1801 a lenghty lawsuit developed in Chancery among the heirs. While James Lawson returned to Glasgow, some of his children remained in Charles Co.

On Jan. 1798, Robert Lawson of Chas. Co., Md. referred by will to his father in Scotland and to the slaves then in his possession mortgaged to his father and which had not been sold in 1788 by the commissioners of the late John Semple and thus requested that they be sent to his father or assigned.

The said Robert Lawson devised his dwelling-plantation and land in Fairfax Co., Va. to his sister, Mary Lawson, of Maryland and to his sister Agnes Lawson of Glasgow, Scotland, personalty. He named his sister Mary Lawson, Alexander Hamilton of Prince George's Co. and Robert Ferguson and Mathew Blair of Charles Co. his executors. At probation on June 26, 1798, Mary Lawson was Mary Jenkins.

His will was probated in Fairfax Co., Va. in 1798, when George Jenkins and Mary his wife, late Mary Lawson, certified to the instrument.

REF: Chancery, Liber 46, folios 161-228, Hall of Records.

LAZEAR

Joseph Lazear of Prince George's Co., Planter, "born under the Dominion of the Emperour of Germany" and his children Joseph, Thomas, John, Elizabeth, Mary and Deborah born in the province were naturalized in 1721 by an Act of the Assembly.

REF: Md. Archives, vol. 38, p. 288.

LEAFF

Francis Leaff of Calvert Co., by his will of 1698 requested his "Cousin Nicholas Gassaway of Anne Arundel Co." to see that the money and his estate in England be recovered for the benefit of "my children".

REF: Wills, Liber 6, folio 194.

LE COMPTE, LACOUMTE

"Anthony LeCompte of the Parish of Mackeneere Callis in France and Esther Dottante of Deepe in France were Mared" June 11, 1661.

On February 22, 1664/5, the Lieutenant Generall ordered that Antoine LaCompte, his wife and children be issued "Patent of Dennizacon". In 1674 the following was recorded at a session of the Assembly: "John Lacounte Moses Lacounte Philip Lacounte Anthony Lacount all the sons of Anthony Lacounte borne att Picardie in the kingdom of france Hester Lacount Katherine Lacount Daughters to the said Anthony Lacount and both sonns & daughters borne within your Lordshipps Prouince of Maryland and your Peticoners borne elce where being now Removed into the Province haue for fivers yeares therein inhabitted being invited to come and dwell within this Prouince by and uppon Confidence of your Lordships declarcon of The Second of July 1649 . . . . . . And Bee itt ordeined & Enacted by the Right Hon[ble] the Lord Prop[ry] of this Prouince by and with the aduice & Consent of the upper & Lower houses of this present Generall Assembly that your Lordshipps humble Peticoners. . .John Lacount Moses Lecount. Philip Lecount, Anthony Lecount, Hester Lecount, Katherine Lecount, they and every of them as nature all borne people of this Prouince of Maryland".

REF: St. Hellen's Parish Register, Bishopgate, London, folio 156; Md. Archives, vol. 3, p. 513.

LEDERER

John Lederer of Calvert Co. upon naturalization in 1671 stated that he was born under the Dominion of the Emperor of Germany.

REF: Md. Archives, vol. 2, p. 282.

LEE

Robert Lee, St. Mary's Co., December 28, 1687, "Whereas there is due to me from Coll. Diggs 6226 lbs. tob. I desire that my Executors will shipp off that tobacco and consigne to one Mr. Nicholas FitzGerald, Merchant, in London who knowes my relacons in Watterford and whom I entrust to convey what I shall leave behind to my father (Michael Lee) and mother (Christian) and relacons in Watterford".

REF: Wills, Liber 4, folio 280.

LEIGH

Joanna Leigh, daughter of John and Amelia Leigh of North Court, Isle of Wight, married Captain Richard Bennett Lloyd, son of Colonel Ann (Rousby) Lloyd, of Wye House. At the outbreak of the Revolutionary War Captain Lloyd resigned his commission in the Colestream Guards and returned to Maryland. He died and was buried at Wye House; born August 13, 1750, died Sept. 22, 1787.

REF: Md. Hist. Mag., vol. 17, p. 29.

LEMMON

Richard Lemmon by his will, dated Aug. 11, 1796, probated in Baltimore Co., declared himself as "late of Ireland now of Baltimore Town", and devised his entire estate to his brothers Jacob Lemmon and John Lemmon.

REF: Balto. Co. Wills, Liber 5, folio 392.

LEROI
Le Mauguen Widdow Leroi, by will July 29, 1799, willed property on the Island of St. Domingo. Her witnesses were Mouchet, John Lominio and John Pradere.
REF: Balto. Co. Wills, Liber 6, folio 207.

LE VACHER DE VAUBRUN
John Levacher de Vaubrun, born in France and commissioned a lieutenant in the Maryland Line during the Revolution, married Anne Howard, daughter of Judge Samuel Harvey Howard of Annapolis, en route to France in 1782, the ship was lost at sea.
REF: Revolutionary Pension Claim W10010, National Archives.

LEVET
Arthur Levet, Talbot Co., "late of Sussex Co., England, Sept. 7, 1700, devised dwelling on North Street of Petworth, Sussex, England, commonly called "Dowings", and also named uncle Benjamin Shove of Sowthwark Burrough, London.
REF: Wills, Liber 11, folio 96.

Elizabeth Levett, Prince George's Co., Widow, 22 Sept. 1725, "I give and bequeath unto my son Robert Lovett all my right title and claime Interest and demand of in and to every part or parcel of the Estate in Beverley in Yorkshire which may be due to me as Relict of my late husband Robert Levett, deceased".
REF: Wills, Liber 18, folio 416.

LEWGER
John Lewger, late of London, Gent., first Secretary of State for Maryland and Lord of St. Barbara and St. Anne's Manors, was of the Lewger family of Essex with ancient branches in Suffolk and Norfolk. Although he returned to London where he died of the plague in 1665, he left descendants in Maryland.
REF: Foster's Alumni Oxonienses; Harleian Soc. Pub., vol. 32, p. 188; Heraldic Marylandiana, by Newman.

LEWIS
Richard Lewis of Baltimore Co., son of Richard and Elizabeth Lewis, late of England, married June 15, 1723, Betty Giles.
REF: Quaker Notes, by Christopher Johnston, Md. Hist. Soc., p. 18.

LIVERS
On May 1, 1704, a bill was endorsed for the naturalization of Arnold Livers, a Taylor, native of Holland.
REF: Md. Archives, vol. 24, pp. 402, 410.

LLOYD
Minchin Lloyd who settled in Charles Co. about 1798 was son of Edward Lloyd and Abigail Minchin of Cos. Limerick and Tipperary, Kingdom of Ireland. Lineage certified by Chief Herald of Arms of Ireland and correct coat-of-arms of the family confirmed.
REF: The Lloyds of Southern Maryland, by Daniel B. Lloyd, pub. 1971, Washington.

Thomas Lloyd of St. James Parish, Anne Arundel Co., Sept. 18, 1748, bequeathed legacy to his daughter, Mary, the wife of Captain Warren Burney, of Wapping Parish, Hermitage St., London.

REF: Wills, Liber 25, folio 438.

LOCKWOOD

Oct. 14, 1704, "I Robert Lockwood of the County of Anne Arundel in the Province of Maryland Son of Robert and Elizabeth Lockwood of Aberford in Yorkshire the Kingdom of England...I give and bequeath unto the children of my Sister Ann Laws wife of Robert Laws of Abersford in Yorkshire ...£100 Sterling".

Robert Lockwood late of Anne Arundel Co., was brother to Thomas Lockwood, deceased, whose son and heir was Thomas Lockwood of Aberford, Co. Yorks, Wheelright.

REF: Wills, Liber 12 pt. 2, folio 75a; Prov. Crt Deeds, Liber TP (1709-1719), folio 493.

LOGAN

Thomas Logan, born Aberdeen, Scotland, married February 13, 1774, Susanna Daly, late of Dublin, Ireland.

REF: St. Paul's Parish Records, Balto Co.

LOMAS

John Lomas of Annapolis, Md., "but now of the City of Glasgow in North Britain, Gent., by will of October 22, 1754, bequeathed to Walter Johnson, John Mill & George Spence of London, Merchants, his entire "estate in Great Britain and all interest elsewhere and in the estate of my deceased brother, Henry Lomas, by agreement between my sister, Mary Roson, and her husband John Roson.

REF: Public Record, Office, London, Herring 331.

LOOCKERMAN

Jacob Lockerman petitioned the Assembly in 1678 for naturalization having been born under "the Jurisdiction of the States of Holland". He was baptized at New Amsterdam March 17, 1652, the son of Govert Lockerman, born at Turnhout, now in Belgium, and his second wife Marritje Jans, and immigrated to New Amsterdam [New York] April 1633.

REF: Md. Archives, vol. 7, p. 79; Md. Hist. Mag., vol. 11, pp. 193-195; N.Y. History & Biographical Register, vol. 8.

LOOTON

Bill for the naturalization of "Jacob Looton an Alien" of St. Mary's Co., was introduced in the Lower House in 1682.

REF: Md. Archives, vol. 7, pp. 291, 314.

LOTHIAN

Alexander Lothian, St. Mary's Co., Dec. 2, 1768, bequeathed his silver mill for carrying snuff to his friend and relative, Alexander Ferguson, Advocate, Esq., son of James Ferguson, of Craigderrock, Edinburgh, Esq. and his pistols and holster to relative the eldest son of Robert Ferguson of Cork; his two seals to Mr. Archibald Campbell of Leonardtown.

REF: Wills, Liber 37, folio 254.

LOVELACE

Madame Anne (Lovelace) Gorsuch, consort of the Rev. John Gorsuch, who was prosecuted by the Puritan divines, appears in the 1633-35 Visitation of London, as the daughter of Sir William Lovelace, Knt. She and her Gorsuch children later settled in Maryland via Virginia.

REF: Harleian Soc. Pub., vol. 90, p. 327; vol. 42, p. 126.

LOW

Abraham Low, a Jacobite, captured at Preston, Lancashire, in 1715, and sold in Maryland for 7 years of servitude petitioned for his freedom on August 3, 1721, which was denied.

REF: Md. Archives, vol. 34, p. 164.

LOWE

Vincent Lowe of Great Choptank Island, Gent., 14 Dec. 1691, "And as for the Land Lying in Old England in the Parish of Denby in the County of Derby Left me by my Mother Anne Lowe by her last will and testament & fifty pounds Sterling Allsoe left me by my Said Mother I...give it to my brother Nicholas Lowe to him and his heirs for ever In consideration of Debt I owe unto him'.

REF: Wills, Liber 6, folio 7a.

LOWES

Henry Lowes, Somerset Co., June 26, 1761. "I leave my House in Chapple Street, Whitehaven, to be rented out at yearly Rent for three Years from this Time, the said Rent to be applyed as after mentioned...if in that Time there be no certain account of my son Tubman, being living, in that Case I leave my said House in Chapple Street Whitehaven...but if my Son Tubman be not living then after the said Term of three years aforesaid Give and Bequath to my son Henry Lowes the above said House".

REF: Wills, Liber 35, folio 348.

LOWNDES

Christopher Lowndes, the emigrant to Maryland, was the 5th son of Richard Lowndes, of Bostick House in Hassall, Cheshire, England, and Margaret Poole his wife. He was baptized at Sandbach 19 June 1713, and was made an heir in his father's will in 1743.

REF: Earwaker's History of Sandbach, pp. 122-128; Md. Hist. Mag., vol. 2, p. 276.

LUMBROZA

Jacob alias Lumbroza "late of Lisbone in the Kingdom of Portugall" on September 10, 1663, was granted patent for denization.

REF: Md. Archives, vol. 4, p. 488.

LUSKIE

John Luskie, Charles Co., Mar. 29, 1769, Son Charles "to have all right and title to all my Estate Real or personal lying in the Kingdom of Scotland".

REF: Wills, Liber 38, folio 446.

LUTHER

George Luther, born Mar. 1, 1754, at Strasburg, Germany, came to Virginia with his parents and settled near Alexandria, Va. In Frederick Co., Md., enlisted in the Maryland Line during the Revolution, later domiciled in Randolph Co., N.C.

REF: Revolutionary Pension Claim W10207, National Archives.

Michael Luther, native of Strasburg, Germany, born Mar. 7, 1751, came to the Colonies in 1759 and settled near Alexandria, Va.; served in the Maryland Line during the Revolution, and later was domiciled in Randolph Co., N.C.

REF: Revolutionary Pension Claim W4721, National Archives.

LUX

Darby Lux who died testate in Baltimore Co. 1750, was a scion of the family of Kenton Parish, Devonshire.

REF: Parish Register of Kenton Parish, Devon.

LUXFORD

George Luxford, Annapolis, Scrivener, Dec. 31, 1753, styled himself the son and heir of George Luxford, late of Linfield, Co. Sussex, Gent., deceased, and referred to the marriage contract of his father and Mary Wyatt of Co. Sussex, Gentlewoman, and also legacies due him by the death of his aunt.

REF: Wills, Liber 29, folio 520.

LYNCH

Hugh Lynch born in Ireland about 1745, emigrated to America in 1770 and settled in Baltimore County where he enlisted in 1776 in the Flying Camp and saw service around New York in the early days of the Revolution; living in Baltimore in 1818.

REF: Revolutionary Pension Claim, S34968, National Archives.

LYON

William Lyon, M.D., born 1715 in Scotland, died 1794 in Baltimore Co., was the son of a Presbyterian minister, arriving in Maryland about 1785.

REF: Rev. Ethan Allan, notes on the clergy in Maryland.

McBEAN

John McBean, a Jacobite, captured at Preston, Lancashire, in 1715, and sold in Maryland for seven years of servitude, petitioned for his freedom on August 3, 1721, which was denied.

REF: Md. Archives, vol. 34, p. 164.

McCALL

William McCall, a native of England, substituted for Colonel Edward Lloyd, in accordance with the "Act to procure Troops for the American Army", passed March Session 1778.

REF: Militia List, Md. Hist. Soc., Balto.

McCORMICK

John McCormick born Sept. 22, 1750, emigrated from Ireland with parents and settled in Kent Co., from Washington Co., Md. served in the Militia during the Revolution; removed later to Richland Co., Ohio.

REF: Revolutionary Pension Claim R6651, National Archives.

McAVOY

Thomas McAvoy, a native of Parish of Clary, Queen's County, Ireland, settled in Washington Co., Md. and died March 29, 1850, aged 55 years.

REF: Gravestone, Methodist Cemetary, Hancock, Md.

McCULLOCH

David McCulloch of Joppa, Balto. Co., Merchant, was second son of John McCulloch of Torhouseky, Shire of Galloway, Scotland.

REF: Register of All Hallow's Parish, Anne Arundel Co., Transcript Md. Hist. Soc., folio 145.

McDERMOTT

John McDermott, Frederick Town, Cecil Co., July 19, 1755, "I order and direct if any either or all of my three brothers now supposed to be in Ireland should come into this Province before aforementioned two years or before my personal estate shall be devised", then his executors were to pay each £60 current money of Pennsylvania.

REF: Wills, Liber 29, folio 554.

McDONALD

Alexander McDonald, for 31 years the honest and diligent English schoolmaster in Fredericktown, born 1742 in Edinburgh, Scotland, married the daughter of Lorentz Hoff and his wife Susanna with whom he had one son and two daughters, died of a high fever and jaundice with whom he was bedfast 10 days, died the 3d at 1,30 aged 53 years, 1795.

REF: Evangelical Lutheran Church, Fred.

McDONALL

John McDonall, Anne Arundel Co., Dec. 1, 1772, "I give and devise all my real estate to Samuel McDonall son of my brother James McDonall of Atrim and to Elizabeth McDonall daughter of my brother Andrew McDonall of Belfast in the Kingdom of Ireland.

REF: Wills, Liber 39, folio 251.

McDONNELL

Patrick McDonnell, a native of County Longford, Parish of Templemuhal, Ireland, died September 8, 1823, in his 48th year.

REF: Gravestone, Cemetary, Hancock, Md.

McELHINEY

Rev. George McElhiney, native of Ireland and rector of St. Anne's Parish, Annapolis, died May 1841, aged 42.

REF: Historical Notice of St. Anne's Parish, by Rev. Ethan Allen, pub. 1857.

McGHEE

Andrew McGhee, Dochester Co., Feb. 25, 1773. To "nephews Samuel and John McGhee sons of John McGhee living in North Carolina Guilford Co.

all lands. . .on condition that the aforesaid Samuel and John McGhee do pay
unto my brother William McGhee of Ireland the sum of £50 Sterling also to
my brother Alexander McGhee of Ireland £25, also to Isabell and Mary
daughters of John McGhee of Ireland £25, and also John McGhee of North
Carolina £25".
REF: Wills, Liber 39, folio 541.

MacGIFFIN

Alexander Macgiffin, a Jacobite, who was transported to Maryland
after the battle of Preston in 1715, ran away after his arrival, believed to New
York.
REF: Md. Archives, vol. 25, pp. 347-349.

McHENRY

James McHenry who emigrated to Baltimore Co. in 1771 was born
Nov. 16, 1753, at Ballymena, Co. Antrim, Ireland, and was the son of Daniel
McHenry of the same place, who was born in 1725.
REF: Dictionary of American Biography; Bookplate of John McHenry, Md. Hist. Soc., Balto.

MACKIE

Ebenezar Mackie, a subject of Great Britain, on November 30, 1782,
subscribed to his belief in the Christian religion and took the oath of
naturalization "as a subject of this State [Maryland]".
REF: Md. Archives, vol. 48, p. 311.

McKIM

The background of the McKim family is old Scotland via a branch
which settled in County Londonderry, Ireland, and which in the last century
was known as Scotch-Irish. The father of the emigrant was John McKim.
Merchant, of Londonderry, whose son Thomas McKim around 1735 settled
on the Delaware at New Castle. His descendants or kinsmen came to
Baltimore Town and as merchant-shippers established a financial empire
which brought great wealth to the family. The marriage with Margaret Duncan brought the Christian name of Duncan into the family.
REF: Md. Hist. Soc., Balto.

McLACHLAN

James McLachlan, Kent Co., June 29, 1768, bequeathed legacy to his
brother, Archibald McLachlan of the Shire of Dumbarton in North Britain
and referred to his deceased brother, Collins.
REF: Wills, Liber 37, folio 148.

McLEOD

William McCleod emigrated in 1774 from Scotland to Queen Anne's
County and indentured himself to Charles Crookshanks, a Merchant, cer-
tainly of Scottish ancestry. He was born about 1747, the son of Hugh
McLeod, Esq., of Geanies of County Ross.
REF: Letters to Scottish kinsmen, Md. Hist. Soc., Mag., vol. 76, no. 1, pp. 45-61.

McLEROY

William McLeroy of Baltimore Town on September 4, 1802, bequeathed legacies to his father Daniel McLeroy and Nancy...in Co. Antrim in the Kingdom of Ireland.

REF: Balto. Co. Wills, Liber 7, folio 64.

MacMANUS

John MacManus, Cecil Co., Attorney, 1 Feb. 1737/8, "I bequeath to my Wife the full use and benefit of my Estate real and personal in the Kingdom of Ireland belonging to me either by Inheritance or Legacy till my Daughter Eleanor shall arrive at 21, particularly my houses in the Town and Corporation of Carrish fergus in the County of Amtrim and my lands and Tenements calle Arrearages...also clock and some plate left me by my brother-in-law John Eagleson, Curate of the Parish of Dunboo in the County of Londonderry in the said Kingdom at my departure from the said Kingdom together with the thirds of the Estate of my father Brian MacManus, deceased".

REF: Wills, Liber 21, folio 854.

MacNEMARA

Margaret, wife of the Hon. Thomas Macnemara of Annapolis (died 1720) was niece of Charles Carroll, the Emigrant, late of King's County, Ireland, and sister to Joyce (Carroll) Butler-Bradford. She and her husband were styled kinsmen in the will of Charles Carroll, the Emigrant, of Anne Arundel Co., dated 1 December 1718.

When the Countess de Auzouer of France writing to Charles Carroll of Carollton about 1770 relative to her Macnemara kinsmen, the Said Charles Carroll replied that one was a Surgeon's Mate on board a Russian battleship in the Mediterranean and the other in partnership in iron works in Maryland.

REF: Wills, Liber 16, folio 176; Judgements, Liber 35, folio 175; Copybook of Charles Carroll, pub. Md. Hist. Magazine, vol. 39, pp. 203-204.

Aug. 30, 1771, Thomas Macnemara, late of the City of Annapolis, Surgeon on Ship "Metronmena" in the service of the Empress of Russia, was eldest son and heir of Michael Macnemara, late of Annapolis, Gent., deceased.

REF: Prov Crt Deeds, Liber DD no. 5, folio 270.

McPHERSON

Donald McPherson of Charles Co., Md. writing to his father, dated "Portobago, Md., 2 June 1717,...the poorish planter here lives almost as well as the Lairds of Colloden". He was born near the House of Colloden where his father lived and as a young lad was sent to Virginia with Capt. Toline in 1715 on account of his participation in the "Cause of the King". He was indentured to "Shon Baynes". The letter was directed to "Shames Makaferson heir to Lairt of Collottin's House neir Inerness in de Nort of Skotlan". He signed as Tonal Makaferson.

REF: Md. Hist. Mag., vol. 1, pp. 347-348.

Rev. John McPherson, came to Maryland after 1751; Scottish; rector of St. Anne's in Annapolis and William and Mary in Charles Co.; died 1785, nearly 60 years of age.

REF: Allen.

McSHERRY

The McSherrys of Baltimore are descendants of Patrick McSherry and his wife Catharine Gartland of Armagh, Ireland, who emigrated originally to Pennsylvania prior to the Revolution.

REF: Scharf's History of Western Maryland, vol. 1, p. 412.

MAGOWAN

Walter Magowan, born in Ireland, rector of St. James Parish, Anne Arundel Co., 1769; died Anne Arundel 1786, more than 50 years of age.

REF: Allen.

MADIERE

Theresa Madiere formerly of St. Domingo at present resident of Baltimore willed a slave to M. Counges formerly of St. Domingo now of Baltimore and bequeathed her property in St. Domingo to her two sons, Jean Baptist Chambeiland and Charles Chambeiland [Chamberland], circa 1817.

REF: Balto Co. Wills, Liber 10, folio 323.

MAHER

Patrick Maher served in the Revolution, enlisted in Frederick Town, native of Ireland, born March 17, 1753; later of Rockbridge Co., Va.

REF: Revolutionary Pension Claim R6831, National Archives.

MAIDWELL

Thomas Maidwell, 27 Oct. 1651, "...bequeath unto my loving Wife Margaret Maidwell living in Petticote Lane near Bishopgate, London, all my Estate...in case my wife be dead before this my last will be proved I doe make my two Sonnes Nicholas and Thomas my lawful executors".

REF: Wills, Liber 1, folio 35.

MAKEMIE

Francis Makemie who brought Presbyterianism to Somerset Co. was born circa 1658 at Rameldon, Co. Donegal, Ireland, educated at the University of Glasgow, and emigrated to Maryland in 1683. He died 1708 Accomac Co., Va.

REF: Monument to his memory, Accomac Co., Va.; see also Whitelaw's Virginia Eastern Shore, vol. 2, p. 1285.

MAINWARING-BROOKE

Madame Mary Brooke, second wife of Robert Brooke, of Brooke Place Manor, Esq., was a daughter of the Rt. Rev. Roger Mainwaring, Bishop of St. David, the ancient seat of the family being in Cheshire.

REF: Ormerod's History of Cheshire; Visitation of Shropshire, Harleian Soc. Pub., vol. 29, pp. 347, 426; Newman's Heraldic Marylandiana.

MANADOE

Peter Manadoe, a Frenchman, of Cecil Co., "born under the Dominion of the French King", and his children were naturalized in 1720 by an Act of the Assembly.

REF: Md. Archives, vol. 38, p. 201.

MANNERING

George Mannering of London, Gent., received a special warrant for 600 acres of land from Lord Baltimore October 9, 1688.

REF: Patents, Liber 11, folio 579.

MANSELL

Robert Mansell, St. Mary's Co., Taylor, 16 Apr. 1716, "I give all the rest of my estate to my Cozan Robert Mansell and his sister Grace of Hatherly, Devonshire".

REF: Wills, Liber 14, folio 403.

MANWARING

John Manwaring "late of City of London but now of the town of Baltimore" by his will of August 8, 1707, named his wife "Mary late Whitechurch, son William Whitechurch Manwaring living with wife, and two sons, Jacob and George Henry Manwaring by his wife Eleanor Hill.

REF: Balto Co. Wills, Liber 6, folio 11.

MARCH

John March, Kent Co., M.D., 23 Oct. 1723, "I give unto my Aunt Elizabeth Quick of Lime House in London the Sum of three pounds Sterling".

REF: Wills, Liber 18, folio 219.

MARCHEGAY

Bennitt Marchegay, a Frenchman, on October 7, 1665, was issued letters of denization.

REF: Md. Archives, vol. 3, p. 533.

MARDEN

James Marden, subject of Great Britain, on Sept. 23, 1791, declared himself a Christian and subscribed to the Oath of Naturalization. County domicile not cited.

REF: Council Proceedings, Md. Archives, vol. 72, p. 221.

MARKLAND

Charles Markland, Esq., who died intestate in Talbot Co., 1740, was born in Childwall, Lancashire, and educated at Oxford. His coat-of-arms was impressed on the 1729 will of George Lane of Talbot Co.

REF: Talbot Co. Wills, Box 15, folder 54; Markland Family, by Frank Bradley, The Genealogist (American), vol. 1, no. 1, 1980.

MARLER

Jonathan Marler, Charles Co., 29 July 1673, named his plantation "Manchester" "...unto John Marler of Manchester brother to the said Jonathan Marler 100 acres leased to John Gimbro in event he came into the Province, if not to Thomas Wakefield...I give and bequeath unto my Brother John Marler and Samuel all the Effects of Land and houseing within the bounds of England".

REF: Wills, Liber 1, folio 561.

MARSHALL

Richard Marshall, son of Lawrence Marshall of Mangottis Field, County Gloucester, was in Maryland prior to 1644, and at his death about

1646 left a daughter, Agnes. On 11 Feb. 1647/8, Hugh Donne, of Co. Devon, administrator of the estate of Richard Marshall, delivered to William Marshall and John Hatch several heads of cattle from the estate of the said Richard Marshall.

REF: Md. Archives, vol. 4, pp. 362-3, 374.

MARSHAM

Richard Marsham who became one of the husbands of Anne Calvert, granddaughter of George, 1st Baron of Baltimore, is placed as a younger son of Thomas Marsham, of London, registrant at the 1633-35 Visitation of London.

REF: Harleian Soc. Pub., vol. 17.

MARTIN

"Whereas Abdelo Martin Subject to the Crowne of Spaine haveing transported himselfe and Children into this province here to inhabite" was granted letters of denization. 17 march 1667/7.

REF: Md. Archives, vol. 5, p. 25.

"Here lyeth ye body of Elizabeth Martin borne in Hertfordshire late wife of Thomas Martin, who departed this life in the year 1676, aged 40 years".

REF: Burying grounds at Hampden, Talbot Co.

Joseph Martin, born Kilnirnie, Ayreshire, Scotland, c1808, settled in Allegany Co., died May 11, 1875.

REF: Headstone, Methodist Cemetary, Allegany Co.

MARTY

Stephen Marty, St. Mary's Co., 18 April 1684, "I give and bequeath unto Elizabeth my wife now in Waterford in Ireland...".

REF: Wills, Liber 4, folio 41.

MASON

Thomas Mason of Cecil Co., by will of November 4, 1731, bequeathed his sister, Mary, all estate real and personal including £150 Ster" bequeathed me by Amy Lee of Eaton near Windsor in that part of Great Britain called England".

REF: Bedford 171, Public Record Office, London.

MASSEY

Henry Massey, formerly of Liverpool but later of Maryland, Merchant, by his will and the settlement of his estate prove that his brother was Roger Whichcot Massey, late of Preston, Lancashire, Gent., and brother to John Massey, late of Rosthern, Cheshire, Esq., also brother to Samuel Massey of Wisbeck, St. Peter's in the Isle of Ely, Co. Cambridge, Doctor of Physick. The latter on October 31, 1768, appointed William Lydebotham of Piscataway, Prince George's Co., Merchant, his attorney to receive all his rights and interest in the estate of his brother, Henry Massey, deceased.

REF: Pr. Geo. Co., Deeds, Liber AA, folio 27.

119

The Rev. Leigh Massey, son of James Massey, of Oxmanton, near Dublin, Ireland, was rector of William and Mary Parish, Charles Co.; died Jan. 10, 1732/3, aged 29.

REF: Rightmeyer's Maryland's Established Church.

MASTER

The book-plate of Legh Master of Frederick Co., who died on March 22, 1796, aged 79, states that he was "of Newhall in the County of Lancaster, Esqr."

REF: Newman's Heraldic Marylandiana, see particularly the reproduction of his original book-plate.

MATHEWS

Henry Mathews in 1674 at the time of his naturalization stated that he was a native of Sweadland [Swedish colony on the Delaware].

REF: Md. Archives, vol. 2, p. 400.

MATTHEWS

Martha Matthews was transported into Maryland from Tertudos by William Stephenson who claimed landrights in 1654.

REF: Patents, Liber ABH, folio 396.

MATHIASON

On July 29, 1661, Hendrick Mathiason "late of New Amstell and Subject to the Crowne of Sweden" was issued letters of denization.

REF: Md. Archives, vol. 3, pp. 429-430.

Mathias Mathiason als Freeman of Cecil Co. was naturalized in 1695 by an Act of the General Assembly.

REF: Md. Archives, vol. 19, p. 211.

MATTSON

Bill for the naturalization of Andrew Mattson was introduced in the Lower House in 1683.

REF: Md. Archives, vol. 7, p. 461.

MAYNADIER

In October 1727 petition for the naturalization of "Daniell Maynadier of the Parish of St. Peter's in Talbott County Clerk" and his children was introduced in the Lower House. "born under the Domionin of the King of France" and his children already born Daniel and Jane."

REF: Md. Archives, vol. 36, pp. 16, 25; vol. 38, p. 404.

MEAGER

James Meager, formerly a subject of Great Britain, on Jan. 10, 1789, declared himself a Christian, and subscribed to the Oath of Naturalization.

REF: Council Proceedings, Md. Archives, vol. 71, p. 318.

MEDAIRY [MADORI]

Hans Jacob Madori with wife Hester and two children emigrated from Lauden, Canton of Basel, Switzerland, in 1739 and landed in Philadelphia, thence to Baltimore Co.

REF: The Medairy Family of Maryland 1565-1971, by Bernard John Mediary Jr., pub. Balto. 1972.

MEDLEY
John Medley, by will circa 1661, "I do Desire that these my trustees will be pleased to use their Endeavour for the recovery of £500 in Money that was my late Wife's porcon and it lyes in Lancashire in one Mr. Thomas Gerratt's hands who lives in the house called Gotto".
REF: Wills, Liber 1, folio 147.

MEESE
Lieut-Col. Henry Meese, one-time Merchant of London, resided in Maryland and Virginia where he served in the Virginia House of Burgesses. Lord Baltimore 1658 conferred seignorial honours on him by the grant of Worton Manor. He returned to Great Britain where he died, believing that he left issue in Virginia.
REF: Newman's Heraldic Marylandiana.

MEIN
Andrew Mein, Talbot Co., Aug. 2, 1770, "I given and Devise to my Cousin Andrew Mein son of William Mein, Merchant, in Edinburgh 50 Guineas...to my wife Ann Mein all that tract or parcel of land belonging to me and lying in or about Newstead near Edinburgh in Scotland".
REF: Wills, Liber 39, folio 388.

MERCER
The Mercer family of Maryland had its beginning in Virginia. John Francis Mercer Governor of Maryland 1801-1803 was the grandson of John Mercer of Dublin, Ireland, who settled in Virginia during 1720, and Grace Fenton his wife of the Cheshire family.
REF: Md. Hist. Mag., vol. 2, p. 191.

MERRIKEN
The Merrikin family of Anne Arundel Co., was identified with "Ratcliffe in the Parish of St. Dunstan's Stepney als Stebonheath, Co. Middlesex, England". Hugh Merriken, son of John and Emigrant, returned to England with his family, where he died intestate, and his widow of Co. Middlesex administered on his estate. Their son and heir, Joshua Merriken, returned to Maryland and claimed his inheritance from his Maryland kinsmen.
REF: Md. Archives, vol. 20, p. 541; vol. 23, p. 20; Newman's Mareen Duvall of Middle Plantation.

MERRITT
William Merritt, Blacksmith, Anne Arundel Co., 12 Mar. 1784, referred to his eldest son, William Merritt, born in Tukesbury, Old England, and if son, Henry, died without issue then his legacies were to "descend to my Brother Thomas and son William Merritt in Tukesbury, Glostershire".
REF: A.A. Co. Wills, Liber TG no. 1, folio 180.

MERTONS
Anna F. Mertons, born July 14, 1798, Hamburg, Germany, died Cumberland June 8, 1876.
REF: Headstone Rose Hill Cemetary, Cumberland.

MESSENGER

Mary Daughter of the Revd Joseph Messenger late Minister of the Episcopal Congregation at Dumfries in North Brittain and now rector of Saint John's Parish in Prince Georges Co., Md., and Mary his wife, was born on the 14th Day of January 1776.

REF: Register of St. John's Piscataway Parish, transcript of, folio 415, Md. Hist. Soc., Balto.

Rev. Joseph Messenger, English, rector of St. Andrews 1775, coming from Virginia; also rector of William and Mary Parish in Charles Co. and St. John's in Pr. Geo. Co.; died 1810, more than 63 years of age.

REF: Allen.

METCALFE

Francis Metcalfe, St. Mary's Co., Aug. 5, 1773, "I give unto my dear Father William Metcalfe of Spowford in the County of York what ever remains of my goods".

REF: Wills, Liber 39, folio 354.

MEYOR

Peter Meyor "late of New Amstell and Subject of the Crowne of Sweden haveing transported himself, wife and Children" was declared on July 22, 1661, "free Dennizen".

REF: Md. Archives, vol. 3, p. 430.

MICHEL

Nicolas Francois Just Michel, native of Fontainbleau "late Notary General of the Western Part of Santo Domingo", died at Fell's Point, Aug. 1795.

REF: Hartdrige.

MICHAELSON

On July 29, 1661, Clement Michaelson "late of New Amstell and Subject of the Crowne of Sweden" was issued letters of denization.

REF: Md. Archives, vol. 3, pp. 439-430.

MILBURN

William Milburn, Kent Co., February 20, 1722/3, ". . . unto my Relations that shall happen to Come out of England by my father's side and shall prove themselves to be such in blood" the whole estate, ". . . in case that none of my father formerly Should come and prove their birth right to belonging to the family of John Milburn and born at Newcastle in Old England that they my Said Estate both real and personal shall fall to John Patterson my mother's brother he proving himself to be soe". if none arrive to claim then to Samuel Milburn of Cecil Co.

REF: Wills, Liber 18, folio 68.

MILHAW

Michael Milhaw by his will dated 25 May 1802, declared himself "a native of Capte Francois, aged 39 years, a son of James Milhaw, deceased, formerly a planter at Marmelode dependency of the Northern part of St. Domingo, and Mary Magdelene Coulard".

REF: Balto. Co. Wills, Liber 10, 123.

MILLER

Charles Miller, native of England, died Oct. 8, 1862, aged 65 years.

REF: Congressional Cemetery, Washington, D.C.

MILLS

On July 12, 1672, letters of denization were issued under the Great Seal unto Mary Mills daughter of Peter Mills of St. Mary's Co.

REF: Md. Archives, vol. 5, p. 112.

"Whereas Peter Mills Late ***** Belonging to the States of holland and Subject of the Nation aforesaid haveing transported himselfe and Children into this province" he was granted leave to inhabit as a free Dennizen, 23 March 1668/9.

REF: Md. Archives, vol. 5, p. 37.

MINNHANE

John Minnhane in 1678 was transported from the Kingdom of Ireland.

REF: Patents, Liber 20, folio 184.

MISSELLS, WESSELLS

Gerardus Missells and James his son were naturalized in 1694 by Act of the General Assembly.

REF: Md. Archives, vol. 19, p. 46, 103.

MITCHELL

Abel Mitchell, a native of London, England, born Sept. 30, 1750, arrived 1769 in Baltimore, and served in the Maryland Navy during the Revolution; later removed to Philadelphia.

REF: Revolutionary Pension Claim R7264, National Archives.

Hugh Mitchell of City of Glasgow in North Britain, Gent. who bought lots in Charlestown, Charles Co. 1760 and 1762 was brother to John Mitchell, late of Glasgow, but afterwards, Merchant of Charles Co.

REF: Chas. Co. Deeds, Liber G no. 3, folio 435; Liber L no. 3, folio 536.

MITFORD

William Mitford, Talbot Co., 8 Oct. 1716, "I leave a legacy to my Sister Margaret Mittford liveing in North Allerton Yorkshire......I bequeath the sum of ninety odd pounds Currency which is for the use of the College of Virginia".

REF: Wills, Liber 14, folio 395.

MOALE

"Mr. John Moale, son of Richard and Elizabeth Moale, born in Kenton Parish, Devonshire, England, Oct. 30th 1697, emigrated to America 1719, married Rachel, daughter of Genl John Hammond of Severn River April 17th, 1723, died March 10th 1740, and was interred in the family burying grounds on Moale's Point, from whence his remains were removed to St. Thomas' by his descendants Sept. 2nd 1826".

REF: Churchyard St. Thomas' Garrison, Baltimore Co.

MONDEL

William Mondel of Baltimore Town by his will of December 27, 1817, bequeathed "to my Honoured Father Mr. John Mondel of the Town of

Whitehaven in the Co. of Cumberland in the Kingdom of Great Britain $2000.00 Spanish mill dollars". Other legacies were bequeathed to his brother, Captain William Mondel of Whitehaven; brother Richard Mondel of Whitehaven; sister Jannet Mondel of London; sister Margaret wife of Samuel Thompson of Ayreshire, Scotland; sister Ann Smith of Co. Cumberland.

REF: Balto. Co. Wills, Liber 10, folio 600.

MONK

"In memory of John Clarke Monk a native of Bristol, Gloucestershire, England, who departed this life Dec. 1 A.D. 1827, aged 67 years, 9 months 14 days".

REF: Spesutia Churchyard, Perryman, Baltimore Co.

Mary Monk, daughter of Rinaldo Monk, late of London, England, by his wife Rachel, widow of Edward Riston of Rangers' Forest, Baltimore Co., married July 19, 1772, William Jacob, the fifth son of Zachariah Jacob of Anne Arundel Co.

REF: St. Paul's Parish Register, Balto. Co.

MONPOEY

Pierre Monpoey, subject of France, declared himself a Christian and subscribed on Sept. 17, 1793 to the Oath of Naturalization; county domicile not cited.

REF: Council Proceedings, Md. Archives, vol. 72, p. 350.

MONTGOMERY

Peter Montgomery of Charles Co., Planter, "a native of France" and his children already born, that is, Francis and John Baptish Montgomery, were naturalized by an Act of the Assembly in 1727.

REF: Md. Archives, vol. 38, p. 415.

MONTSON

On July 29, 1661, Peter Montson "late of New Amsetil and Subject of the Crowne of Sweden" was issued letters of denization.

REF: Md. Archives, vol. 3, pp. 429-430.

MOORE

Francis Moore, Borough of Southwark, Distiller, London, by will April 5, 1698, bequeathed his son, Francis, £10 "wh is gon on a venture to Maryland and my largest silver tankard".

REF: Public Record Office, London, Pett 26.

James Moore, native of Co. Tyrone, Ireland, died Sept. 25, 1853, aged 73 years, 3 mos. 1 day.

REF: Congressional Cemetery, Washington, D.C.

Josias Moor Dorchester Co., Dec. 18, 1766. "I give and bequeath unto my nephew Patrick Moor son of Mathew Moor late of the Town of Rothsay in the Isle of Bute North Britain all the remaining part of my Real and Personal Estate. . . . to pay unto my Loving Brother Archibald Moor During his life yearly the sum of Fifty Shillings Ster. . . . if any of Patrick Moor's Sons come here before they arrive at the age of Twenty one they shall be under the Guardian ship of Robert Stevens".

REF: Wills, Liner 36, folio 596.

MORAN

In 1728 petition was submitted for the naturalization of Gabriel Moran of Charles Co.

REF: Md. Archives, vol. 36, pp. 110, 190.

MORANGES

Etienne Moranges "born at Clermont formerly the Capital of Auvergne now the Chief place of the Department of the Paye de Dome aged fifty two years and Eight months", according to will dated Dec. 25, 1803.

REF: Balto. Co. Wills, Liber 7, folio 270.

MORELAND

Lieut. Col. Jacob Moreland was heir and joint-executor of the will of John Stanley of Prince George's Co., Gent., who died testate 1705. Thus, Jacob Moreland of Capplethewaite Hall in "ye Parish of Kirkly Lonsdale in the County of Westmoreland" granted power of attorney to William Hodgson, Doctor of Physick, to receive land willed him by Mr. John Stanley on Swanson Creek and Patuxent River and a plantation on the Eastern Shore.

REF: Wills, Liber 12, folio 19; Prov. Crt Deeds, Liber PL no. 6, folio 260.

MORELL

Nathaniel Morell, Charles Co., 19 Oct. 1745, ". . .my brother the Rev. Dr. Thomas Morell of Cue Green near London my silver watch, Gold buttons and such of my papers as the Rev. Mr. Theophilus Swift shall think proper to send him and also my picture be carefully sent to my brother . . . . . . to my Sister Ann Daughter of my mother Ellen, deceased".

REF: Wills, Liber 27, folio 177.

MORGAN

Mathias Morgan of Bristol, Gloucestershire, Merchant, received 500 acres on the Choptank from the Lord Proprietary.

REF: Patents, Liber 7, folio 523.

William Morgan one time of Bristol, Gloucestershire, received land grants in 1680.

REF: Patents, Liber WC 2, folio 288.

MORRIS

Robert Morris, of London, Mariner, in January 1659, was granted by Lord Baltimore seigniory on Ratcliffe Manor then in Talbot Co.

REF: Patents Libers 15, folio 286, 19, folio 593.

Robert Morris, Talbot Co., Merchant, Apr. 17, 1749, declared himself to be the "Son of Andrew Morris, Mariner, and Maudlin his wife, both deceased, late of the town of Liverpool in the County of Lancaster and Kingdom of Great Britain". He furthermore bequeathed Legacies to his sister, Ellen Eccleston wife of Jonathan Eccleston, Butcher, Liverpool; sister Margaret Trout wife of George Trout at Mr. Timothy Hollis, Merchant. London; and cousins Ellen and Sarah, daughters of Easter Jackson, late of Liverpool; and also referred to Robert Morris Jr., employed by Robert Greenway, Merchant of Philadelphia.

"In Memory of Robert Morris Native of Liverpool, Great Britain, late Merchant of Oxford [Maryland]. . . . departed on the 12th day of July MDCCL".

REF: Wills, Liber 27, folio 347; Stone at Old White Marsh Church near Oxford, Talbot Co.; The Maryland Original Research Society, Bulletin 3, pub. 1913, p. 123.

William Morris of Baltimore Town by his will of January 19, 1851, bequeathed legacies to the children of his deceased brother, Alexander Morris, late of Glasgow, in the Kingdom of Scotland.

REF: Balto. Wills, Liber 24, folio 217.

MORRISITTE
Peter Morrisitte of Baltimore Town on November 25, 1797, declared himself a native of France.

REF: Balto. Co. Wills, Liber 6, folio 144.

MUDD
Thomas Mudd sailed from Bristol for Virginia between 1663-1679.

REF: Bristol & America, p. 111 (47).

NOTE: The progentior of the well knwn Mudd family of Maryland was Thomas; it is probable that he tarried in Virginia before his settlement in Maryland.

MUGENBROUGH
Martin Mugenbrough in 1674 at time of his naturalization declared that he was a native of Germany.

REF: Md. Archives, vol. 2, p. 400.

MUIR
Died 30 August 1810, aged 60 years, John Muir, came to Maryland at a young age from Scotland.

REF: Riley's The Ancient City, p. 227.

MULLETT
Madame Winifrede Mullet, widow of the Rev. William Mullett, was the daughter of Sir Thomas Wolseley, Knt, and Helen Broughton his wife, and granddaughter of Erasmus Wolseley, of Wolseley, Staffordshire, Esq. Her will, dated Charles Co., April 20, 1685, named her nieces Helen Spratt, Ann Knipe and Anne Brooke. The said niece, Anne Brooke, was the daughter of Roger Brook of Charles Co., who married a daughter of the brother of the testatrix.

REF: Wills, Liber 2, folio 244; Pyne 59, Public Record Office, London.

MUNDAY
Patrick Munday, born c1793, a native of County Fernanagh, Ireland, Parish of Dremrigan, died May 22, 1839, Washington Co., Md.

REF: Graveyard, Hancock, Md.

MUMFORD

James Munford who declared himself a subject of Great Britain and a Christian on July 1, 1785, took the Oath of Naturalization.

REF: Proceedings of Council, Md. Archives, vol. 71, p. 36.

MUNDELL

Thomas Mundell, a subject of Great Britain, declared himself a Christian on Oct. 22, 1792, and subscribed to the Oath of Naturalization. County domicile not stated.

REF: Council Proceedings, Md. Archives, vol. 72, p. 294.

MURDOCK

William Murdock, City of London, Merchant, who dwelt at Upper Bedford Place, Russell Square, Co. Middlesex, by his will dated July 25, 1822, requested to be buried in the protestant burying grounds, named his brother, Benjamin Murdock of Frederick Co., Md., and a number of Maryland kinsmen including the Potts, Tylers and Bruce and the children of his godson, Thomas Clagett of London, Merchant.

REF: Fred. Co. Wills, Liber HS no. 3, folio 398.

MURRY

The Rev. Leigh Murry, "educated at Oxford, Rector of Poplar Hill Parish, dyed January 10, 1752/3, aged 29 years".

REF: Poplar Hill Churchyard, St. Mary's Co.

MUSHET

John Mushet and his brother Dr. Mushet [Charles Co. 1747] were sister's sons of "Old Lendricks" of Stirlingshire, Scotland.

REF: Statement of Alexander Stewart, Jacobite of 1747, who was purchased by Benedict Calvert. see, Md. Hist. Mag, vol. 1, pp 349-352.

MUTTERSPAW

Philip Mutterspaw born 1744 in Germany and came to America with parents when he was 1 or 2 years of age, served in the Maryland Militia from Washington Co., during the war.

REF: Revolutionary Pension Claim S9435, National Archives.

MYERS

Jacob Myers, a native of Ireland, substituted for William Warden in accordance with "Act to procure Troops for the American Army", passed March Session 1778.

REF: Militia List, Md. Hist. Soc., Balto.

John Myers, Dorchester Co., Feb. 15, 1760, ". . . and for as much as there is the revision of a Real Estate that will be due to me after the decease of my Father and Mother John and Katherine Myers in the County of York and Town of Langston upon the Swale in the Kingdom of Great Britain my Father John Myers being Rector of the said Langston upon Swale"; he also mentioned brothers Anthony and William Myers.

REF: Wills, Liber 31, folio 157.

Philip Myers, a native of Mainz, Germany, born Nov. 3, 1759, came to the Colonies with parents in 1766, settled in Frederick Co., where he served in the Maryland Militia during the war; removed later to Luzerne Co., Penn.

REF: Revolutionary Pension Claim, W4554, National Archives.

MYNSKIE

John Samuel Mynskie of Annapolis, Blacksmith, Catherine his wife and Susannah his daughter "born in the Province of Brandenburgh in the Kingdom of Prussia" were naturalized in 1727, by an Act of the Assembly.

REF: Md. Archives, vol. 38, p. 407.

NANS

In 1682 a bill for the naturalization of Rowland Nans of Baltimore Co. was introduced and passed.

REF: Md. Archives, vol. 7, pp. 362, 444.

NAYLOR

Abraham Naylor, Anne Arundel Co., by will of May 5, 1683, devised his estate to his wife, Jane, but in the event of her marriage only her thirds, and the residue to the poor of Dranfiel Parish, Derbyshire.

REF: Wills, Liber 4, folio 18.

NEALE

In 1666 Captain James Neale, an English-born subject, then of Charles Co., petitioned the Assembly for the naturalization of his children, stating that he "hath lived divers yeares in Spain and Portugal following the trade of Marchandize and his Royal highness the Duke of Yorke in Several Emergent Affaires as by the commission herewith presented may appeare dureing which tyme of his abode in those he had four children borne by his lawfull wife Anna Neale, vizt, Henieretta Maria James Dorothy and Anthony Neale which four he hath now liveing in this Province of Maryland". His ancestry is listed in the Visitation of Bedfordshire.

REF: Md. Archives, vol. 2, p. 89-90; Harleian Pub. Soc., vol. 19, pp 33. 34, 185; Md. Hist. Magazine, vol. 7, p. 201.

NEEDHAM

William Needham, Montgomery Co., July 30, 1826, stated that he was entitled to a share of his brother's estate, Richard Needham, of Staffordshire, in England, deceased.

REF: Montgomery Co. Wills, Liber F, folio 195.

NELSON

Petition for the naturalization of Ambrose Nelson was read 1712 in the Lower House.

REF: Md. Archives, vol. 27, p. 150.

NENGFINGER

William Nengfinger of St. Mary's Co., in 1671 declared at time of naturalization that he was "borne in Holland and Under the Dominion of the States General of the united Provinces".

REF: Md. Archives, vol. 2, p. 270.

NICHOLSON

William Nicholson, Anne Arundel Co., Merchant, Sept. 25, 1719, appointed his sisters Mrs. Elinor Foster, Anne Nicholson, and Elizabeth Nicholson and Mr. William Hunt the executors of his estate in England".

REF: Wills, Liber 15, folio 325.

William Nicholson, Anne Arundel Co., Merchant, Dec. 28, 1731, provided for his sons at the age of 10 years to be sent to Edinburgh, then to College for three years, then to London for the study of law; sons to be brought up in the Established Church of Scotland; referred to his sister, Elizabeth Nicholson living at Berwick-on-Tweed, Northumberland.

REF: Wills, Liber 20, folio 306.

Joseph Nicholson of Chestertown, Kent Co., Md., Merchant, son of William Nicholson, late of Nicholson Manor, Baltimore Co., was brother to Benjamin Nicholson of Berwick-upon-Tweed, Great Britain and to Samuel Nicholson of Stockton-upon-Tease, Co. Durham, Great Britain, according to 1754 deed.

REF: Prov. Crt Deeds, Liber EI no. 9. folio 509.

NICODEMUS

Frederick Nicodemus, a member of the Reformed Congregation in Conogochick, in Frederick Co., received the church's sacrament on Aug. 18, 1765, and by taking the Oath of Abjuration became a subject of Great Britain.

REF: Prov. Crt Judgements, Liber DD no. 9, folio 13.

NINCONDUCE

Magnan Ninconduce, formerly of the French portion of St. Domingo but then of Frederick Co., declared that he imported negroes for his own use on 5 Nov. 1792.

REF: Fred. Co. Deeds, Liber WR no. 11, folio 755.

NISBET

"Alexander Nisbet born at Montrose, Scotland, June 26, 1777, Came to the United States in 1784; Died Nov. 22, 1857. Judge of the Baltimore City Court, President of St. Andrew's Society for 26 years".

REF: Burying Grounds at Montrose, Baltimore Co.

NIXON

July 29, 1738, "on this Day were married Jonathan Nixon and Mary Searitt Late of Leek in the County of Staford Shire in England by the Revd John Dantry".

REF: Register of St. John's Piscataway Parish, transcript of, folio 357, Md. Hist. Soc., Balto.

NOMERS

John Nomers in 1674 at the time of his naturalization stated that he was a native of Sweadland [Swedish Colony on the Delaware].

REF: Md. Archives, vol. 2 p. 400.

NORRIS

Daniel Norris Kent Co., 13 January 1706/7, "Whereas I expect some of my Sister's Children or their Children to Come from England within this twelve months", if they had not paid their passage then the testator's son and daughter were to pay such.

REF: Wills, Liber 12, folio 242.

NORTH

Robert North who settled in Maryland and died 1749 in Baltimore Co., according to Bible record, was the son of Thomas and Ellen North of Whittington, Lancashire.

REF: Va. Hist. Mag., vol. 25, pp. 438-9.

NORTON

Andrew Norton, Charles Co., Planter, Aug. 10, 1712, "formerly of ffairfield in the Parish of Stope in the County of Derby in the Kingdom of South Britain Eldest Son and Heir of Andrew Norton Sr., of ffairfield afsd Yeoman, it being now at the Sealing here of above twelve and near thirteen years Since my coming here....give and devise all those houses and Tenements and premises lyeing and being in ffairfield afsd which were purchased of one Bʊrk by my said ffather and by him conveyed to me in leiu of other lands....which I left in the hands of my kinsman William Morwood of burbige Green near Buxton in Derbyshire". Mentioned his son, Cornelius Norton, whom he placed under the guardian of "my ffather-in-law Cornelius White of Charles Co., Gent., but in the event of his death then "to my brother-in-law Luke Barber".

REF: Wills, Liber 14, folio 500.

NORWOOD

John Norwood who emigrated to Anne Arundel Co. 1650 from Virginia was born 1605 at Wykeham Abbey, Lincolnshire, and was the son of Tyringham Norwood (1576-1625) at Wykeham, Spalding, Line.

REF: Professionial English research commissioned in 1961 by Norwood descendant.

NOTLEY

Thomas Notley, St. Mary's Co., Apr. 3, 1679, "I give and bequeath unto my Loving sister Katharine Grugefield of London my owne natural sister £500 Ster."

REF: Wills, Liber 10, folio 7.

Walter Notley of "ffermanagh in the Realme of Ireland, Gent.," received 20,000 acres of land from the Lord Proprietary for transporting or promised to transport 100 men into Maryland and to enjoy the privileges of Court Leet and Court Baron to him and his heirs forever. Dated 5 November "14th yeare of the Reigne of Oʳ Soverign Lord, Charles by the grace of God of England, Scotland & ffrance and Ireland."

REF: Original parchment, Calvert Papers, Md. Hist. Soc., Balto; photoprint in possession of this compiler.

NOURSE

James Nourse by his will, 25 Mar. 1784, declared himself to be domiciled in "Piedmont in the County of Berkeley, Virginia, and of Annapolis, Maryland, formerly of Bedford Street, Covent Garden, London, and the Son of John Nourse of Weston in the County of Hereford, England.

REF: A.A. Co. Wills, Liber TG no. 1, folio 237.

NUTT

Job Nutt of London, Merchant, agreed to emigrate to Maryland, in 1657.

REF: Patents, Liber Q, folio 473.

NUTTER

John Nutter, Oxford, Talbot Co., Merchant, 11 Dec. 1725. "I give and bequeath to my father Mr. Ellis Nutter, Rector of Broughton in Yorkshire in the Kingdom of Great Britain, and to my mother Anne his wife £100 . . . . . to my brother Elias Nutter the sum of £100 Sterling and to my brother-in-law Mr. Richard Hartley of Greenhead in Lancashire £100 and to my siter Mary Hartley wife of the said Richard £40".

REF: Wills, Liber 18, folio 441.

O'BRIEN

Matthew O'Brian by his will, Baltimore 26 Sept. 1815, declared ". . . born in the County of Dublin in the Kingdom of Ireland now a resident of the City of Baltimore".

REF: Balto. Wills, Liber 10, folio 73.

OETH

John Oeth "born under the Dominion of the Emperour of Germany" was naturalized in 1721/2 by an Act of the Assembly.

REF: Md. Archives, vol. 38, p. 288.

OFFLEY

Catherine Offley, daughter of Thomas Offley, London Merchant, was the grandmother of Richard Edelen, by her marriage to the Rev. Philip Edelin (*sic*). The marriage is proved by the 1633-35 Visitation of London.

REF: Harleian Soc. Pub., vol. 17, p. 130.

OFFLEY-THOROWGOOD—YARDLEY

Madame Sarah wife of Francis Yardley and widow of Adam Thorowgood of Virginia, was born Sarah Offley and resided in Maryland when her last husband held office during the Puritan take-over, was descended from a Lord Mayor of London. Catherine Offley, mother of Richard Edelen, the Emigrant to Maryland, was of the same London family.

REF: Visitation of London 1633, Harleian Soc. Pub. vol. 41; Newman's Heraldic Marylandiana.

OGLE

Luke Ogle, of New Castle, Northumberland, Great Britain, Gent., by his will, dated June 13, 1719, probated in Maryland May 27, 1734, made his brother, Samuel Ogle, heir to his entire estate.

Samuel Ogle (1702-1752) Governor of Maryland, was son of Samuel Ogle, of Bousden, who represented Berwick-on-Tweed in the House of Commons and of his 2d wife, Ursula, daughter of Sir Robert Markham and the widow of Lord Althan.

REF: Wills, Liber 21, folio 87; Ogle and Bothal Families by Sir Henry A. Ogle, Bart., pub. 1902.

OGLEBY

John Ogleby Cecil Co., 19 Jan. 1744/5, "I give and bequeath to my Brother George's children Jane Ogleby and Dorcus Ogleby in Ireland".

REF: Wills, Liber 24, folio 31.

OLDSONE

In 1681 an Act was introduced in the Assembly to naturalize Peter Oldsone [Ouldson] and subsequently passed.

REF: Md. Archives, vol. 7, pp. 187, 216.

OLEY

In March 1701/2, the act and fee for the naturalization of Sebastian Oley, born in Germany, of Anne Arundel Co., came before the Lower House.

REF: Md. Archives, vol. 24, pp. 253, 280.

ONION

"Stephen Onion, Iron Master, born February 10, 1694, at Brewood in Staffordshire in England; departed this life Aug. 26th 1754, his Body here Interr'd".

Will dated Balto. Co. Aug. 24, 1754. "...to my Brother Thomas Onion of Braywood in Staffordshire £20 a year during his life"; nephew Zatheus Barret to inherit and take the name of Onion.

REF: Churchyard, St. John's, Kingsville, Baltimore Co.; Wills, Liber 29, folio 190.

ORME

James Orme was born "Jan. 21st 1691 as appears by the Register of England", said to have been in Wiltshire; was preacher of the first Presbyterian Church at Upper Marlborough.

REF: Original family records written by the Rev. Jaes Orme; see also "Zimmerman, Waters and Allied Families, by Dorothy E. Allen, pub. c1910.

O'ROURKE

Nicholas O'Rourke, son of Patrick and Marie Angele Renee (de Veteaux) O'Rourke, French refugee from Santo Domingo, settled in Baltimore, and buried in St. Peter's churchyard.

REF: Hartridge.

O'ROURKES

Patrick O'Rourkes by his will of January 29, 1806, Baltimore Co. stated that he was "a Native of Ireland and refugee from the French Island of Saint Domingo", and mentioned his wife Marie Angelique Renee Devezeana de Rancaugne. Buried in St. Peter's churchyard.

REF: Balto. Co. Wills, Liber 8, folio 116.

OTTEY

William Ottey, Baltimore Co., Jan. 16, 1773, "I give and bequeath unto my sister Ann Ottey* the whole residue of my estate during her natural life and at her demise to be divided into three equaled parts, one-third thereof I give and bequeath unto my cousin Jane Henderson of Ackington Park in Northumberland, if living at my or my sister's demise other wise to the children of her body....one-third to cousin Ann Hudson of Newcastle-upon-Tyne.

REF: Wills, Liber 39, folio 100.

*She married as his second wife Zachariah Maccubin of Baltimore.

OULDSON

In 1692 an act was passed the Assembly to naturalize John Ouldson of Kent Co.

REF: Md. Archives, vol. 13, p. 536.

OVERARD

Peter Overard, of Annapolis, Sadler, was naturalized in 1712 by an Act of the Assembly.

REF: Md. Archives, vol. 38, p. 165.

OWEN

Richard Owen of Balto. Co., on Aug. 17, 1703, transacted business with "John Owen of Tower Street, London, England, Merchant", when he signed "Your Dutiful Sonne". On Dec. 29, 1703, he requested his father to pay £15 to Mistress Catherie Stutt.

REF: Balto. Co. Deeds, Liber HW no. 2, folio 322; TR no. A, folio 72.

OWINGS

Richard Owings [Owen], born c1662 in Wales, died intestate 1716 in Baltimore Co., is placed as the 4th son of Owen ap Humphrey of Llwyn-du, Co. Merioneth, Wales. He married 1682 Rachel ap Robert, daughter of Robert ap Pugh of Llwyn-dedwydd. They settled first in the Welsh Tract in Pennsylvania and before 1688 in Anne Arundel Co. His widow Rachel Owings died testate 1729 in Baltimore Co.

REF: Welsh research commissioned by the late Donnell Owings, Ph. D., one-time of Oklahoma.

PACQUETT

Daniel Pacquett, a Labourer of Ann Arundell Co. was naturalized by act of 1709.

REF: Md. Archives, vol. 27, p. 481.

PAGE

Bartholomew Page "a native of the Parish of Portet in the Diocese of Tholouse an Inhabitant of the Parish of Lady Mary and Merchant residing in Jeremie, part of the Department of the South of the Island and Coast of Saint Domingo in America. Considering the dangerous circumstances in which I find myself without a hope of escaping from the Poniards of the Assassins who have already massacred all the unfortunate French Whites in every part of this Colony......Done in Jeremie in my Ordinary dwelling in the house of Colimant" Dated Apr. 22, 1804, probated in Baltimore Co., Md. June 15, 1805.

REF: Balto. Co. Wills, Liber 7, folio 418.

PAGETT

Petition for the naturalization of David Pagett, a Frenchman, of Queen Anne's County, his wife and daughter was introduced in 1711.

REF: Md. Archives, vol. 27, pp. 63, 66; vol. 38, p. 133.

PALMER

William Palmer who died in Maryland before Mar. 20, 1715/6, was brother to John Palmer of Towchester, Northamptonshire, Glazier. Other heirs or kinsmen were Daniel Collins of St. Martin's in the Fields, Middlesex, Ironmonger, and Samuel Palmer, of Black Frayars, London.

REF: Prov. Crt Deeds, Liber TP no. 4, folio 243.

PARANDIER

James Parandier and John Parandier "born under the Dominion of the French King" were naturalized in 1720 by an Act of the Assembly.

REF: Md. Archives, vol. 38, p. 261.

PARDEE

The English ancestry of Eli Stephen Pardee (1787-1862), one-time president of Washington College, Chestertown, is registered in the Parish of Pitminster, near Taunton, Somersetshire. He was the great-great grandson of George Pardee, baptized Feb. 19, 1623/4, in Pitminster Parish, the son of Anthony Pardee by his wife Anstice Cox, who the said George emigrated to the New Haven Colony, Conn., and died in 1700.

REF: Register of Pitminster Parish Church, near Taunton, Somersetshire, *see* also "The Pardee Genealogy", by Donald Lines Jacobus, pub. 1927, New Haven, Conn.

PARKS

John Parks was born at Dijon, Dukedom of Burgundy, Kingdom of France, according to petition to the session of the Council April-May 1666.

REF: Md. Archives, vol. 2, p. 144.

PARRAN

"Near this place lieth the body of Mr. Alexander Parran Son & Heir of John Parran of Boynton in the County of Oxon in England Esqr who departed this life ye 30th day of May 1720 aged 52 years Also near thereto lieth the body of Mary Parran daughter of Young Parran & Eliz his Wife who Departed this life the 25th of August 1744 aged 1½ year. Also under neath lyeth the body of Moses Parran son of the Above Alexander ob: the 28th Decemr 1740 aetas 32 years & 3 months".

REF: Tablet in Middleham Chapel, Calvert Co.

PARSON

William Parson, Town Point, Cecil Co., Gent., 7 Aug. 1716, "I give and bequeath unto my said five children William Parson, Jon Parson, Mary Parson, Margaret Parson and Catharine Parson my house with out houses and the pretenances thereunto belonging which was left me by my Grandfather being in the Kingdom of Old England in Branford in Dorchester".

REF: Wills, Liber 14, folio 299.

PARY

Samuel Sandford "sometime of Accomac Co., Va., and now of City of London" by will of March 27, 1716, "To John son of Thomas Pary my kinsman now in Maryland the two corn mills bought of my account of Ralph Foster of St. Mary's Co.

REF: P.C.C. Smith 98.

PASCAULT

Lewis Pascault, a subject of the King of France, on Apr. 14, 1792, declared himself a Christian and subscribed to the Oath of Naturalization. County domicile not cited.

Jean Charles Marie Louis Pascault, born on his father's plantation in Santo Domingo, emigrated from Le Cap circa 1794. He settled in Baltimore and died there in 1824. He became the ultimate heir to the title "Marquis de Poleon", but according to records he was last heard from in Santo Domingo in the 18th century. Inasmuch as trace of him had been lost his brother in France assumed the title. The brother left no male issue, therefore, the son of a daughter, the Marquise de Saint Georges, added Poleon to his own resulting in "de Poleon Saint Georges".

REF: John O'Donnel of Baltimore; His Forbears and Descendants, by E. Thornton-Cook, pub. London, 1934; Council Proceedings, Md. Archives, vol. 72, p. 264.

PATTERSON

William Patterson of Baltimore and the father of Madame Jerome Bonaparte in his will stated "My family were of the Episcopal Church, the established Religion of Ireland in which I was born and brought up with great care and attention. . . . my Father was a farmer in Country with a large family, his name was William, my Mother's name was Elizabeth, her maiden name was Peoples. They were both descended from a mixture of England and Scottish families who had settled in Ireland after the Conquest of that country. I was born on the first of November old style in the year 1752, at a place called Fanat in the County of Donegal, Ireland".

REF: Balto. Co. Wills, Liber 15, folios 254-77.

PAYNE

George Payne late of Anne Arundel Co., in 1768, had a brother, Robert Payne of Borough Helstone, Co. Cornwall, England, hatter.

REF: Prov. Crt Deeds, Liber DD no. 4, folio 591.

John Payne, styled Mr., Collector of the Patuxent, was murdered about 1694. He was brother to Dr. Payne of London who requested that the two criminals be brought to trial.

REF: Md. Archives, vol. 19, pp. 44, 49, 99, 470.

PEALE

Charles Peale, father of Charles Wilson Peale, the famous Maryland limner, was the son of the Rev. Charles Peale, of Edith Weston, Co. Rutland, of the Established Church. The birth of the painter was recorded in St. Paul's Parish, Queen Anne's County, (register now destroyed) as "Charles Wilson, eldest son of Charle Peale, and heir intail to the Manor of Wotton in Oxfordshire, estate of Charles Peale, Doctor of Medicine.

REF: Boyle's Biographical Sketches of Distinguished Marylanders, pub. 1877, pp. 123-4.

Charles Wilson Peale son of Charles Peale by Margaret, born Apr. 15, 1741, which say Charles as he says is the Eldest son of the Rev. Charles Peale, Rector of Edith Weston in the Co. of Rutland and heir-in-tail to the Manor of

Wotton in Oxford Shire the Estate of Charles Wilson Doctor of Physic who died at Hampford Town, Lincolnshire, March 1724.

Elizabeth Bennett aged 60 and plus certified that she knew Charles Peale who taught school and was married to Margaret by the Rev. Vaughan of Westminster.

REF: Prov. Crt Deeds, Sept. 1762, folio 237.

PEANE

In 1678 James Peane, Magdelen his wife and Anne Peane their daughter, natives of France, were naturalized by Act of the Assembly.

REF: Md. Archives, vol. 7, p. 79.

PEARCE

Joseph Pearce of Dartmouth in the County of Devonshire, Merchant, Sept. 24, 1674, died at the plantation of Thomas Hussey of Charles Co. left an estate in England to his wife Anne.

REF: Wills, Liber 2, folio 13.

PEARSON

Thomas Pearson, "formerly of Kingdom of England, now of Anne Arundel Co., Mariner", married Nov. 10, 1775, Mary Gassaway.

REF: West River Quaker Meeting, notes by Christopher Johnston, p. 22.

PEELE

Samuel Peele, late of Salem in New England, but now resident of Anne Arundel Co. Shipjoiner, appointed his brother, Roger Peele late of Salem, but now of Anne Arundel Co., Shipright, his lawful attorney to demand and receive of William Peele, administrator of my two uncles, Samuel and Robert Peele, late of London Town, Gent., all inheritance due him.

REF: Prov. Crt Deeds, Liber EI no. 3, (1737-1744) folio 173.

William Peele of London Town, South River, Jan. 26, 1748/9, by his will named his brother John Peele "Citizen and Founder of London in Great Britain" to whom he bequeathed £500; kinsmen Richard Peele "Citizen and Cowpers of London; and nephews Roger, Robert and Samuel sons of "my dear brother Roger Peele of Salem in New England, Mariner.

REF: Will, Liber 27, folio 574.

PEERCE

John Peerce, Chyrugen, Calvert Co., 1679 by his will bequeathed a legacy to his daughter, Martha Peerce, now "residing in England my watch and rings".

REF: Wills, Liber 10, folio 15.

PENCE

Michael Pence under the Act of George II (13th year) received the sacrament according to the Church of England, as certified by the Rev. Alexander Williamson, rector of St. Anne's Parish, and subscribed to the Oath of Abjuration Sept. 8, 1761, and became a naturalized subject, country of birth not noted.

REF: Prov. Crt Judgements, Liber DD no. 1, folio 492.

PENNINGTON

Joseph Pennington, a Quaker, who died in Maryland prior to 26th day 8th mo. 1711, leaving issue was brother to Isaac Pennington of Swarthmore, Lancashire, England.

REF: West River Quaker Records.

PENRUDDOCK

Anthony Penruddock by his will of December 29, 1641, devised his Maryland land to his daughters, Jane and Lucy, and referred to his legacy from Lord Windsor and also one from Lord Herbert, son and heir of the Earl of Worster, and 40 shillings to his only sister, Madame Elizabeth Seaborne, to purchase a ring. He declared that he lived and died a Roman Catholic.

REF: Cambell 60, Public Record Office, London.

PENTZ

Adam Pentz, a German Protestament, received the sacrament of the Reformed Congregation at York Co., Penn., on Apr. 1, 1763, and as prescribed by the Act of George II (13th year) took the Oath of Abjuration and became a naturalized subject.

REF: Prv. Crt Judgements, Liber DD no. 3, folio 125.

PERCEY

James Percey, a native of Muirkirk, Ayreshire, Scotland, died Cumberland, February 22, 1855, aged 64 years, 8 months and 5 days.

A. T. Percey, born Muirkirk, Ayreshire, Scotland, died May 9, 1858, aged 25 years.

REF: Gravestone, Rose Hill Cemetary, Cumberland, Md.

PERRIN

Edward Perrin of Bristol, Quaker Merchant, by will of June 8, 1702, devised his son, Thomas, all his land in Maryland, Virginia and Pennsylvania, as well as elsewhere in America.

REF: Lane 295, Public Record Office, London.

PERRY

Richard Perry of London, but late of Maryland on May 10, 1684, conveyed to Thomas Plowden and George Plowden of South Hampton, England, for £400 improved realty of 4000 acres and 500 acres of "The Farme" in Calvert Co. as granted to John Bateman of London, Haberdasher, also known as John Bateman of the Patuxent and also 200 acres on the west side of the Patuxent as granted to the said Richard Perry.

REF: Liber WRC no. 1, folio 341, Hall of Records, Annapolis.

PETER

Robert Peter, born 1726, at Crossbasket, Lanarkshire, Scotland, was a younger son to Thomas Peter of Crossbasket by Jane, daughter of James Dunlop of Garnkirke whose wife was Lillian Campbell of Blythewood, Lanarkshire. The said Thomas Peter was a younger son of Walter Peter of Chapel Hall, Parish of Mearn, Renfrewshire, all of the Lowlands.

Robert Peter emigrated to Georgetown when it was a part of Frederick County, became a wealthy merchant, large land and slave owner and first

Mayor of Georgetown. On December 27, 1767, he married Elizabeth, daughter of George Scott, a native of Malenie, Midlothianshire who died in Prince George's Co. 1771, naming his son-in-law Robert Pater.

REF: Family papers of Peter family, see also Scharf's History of Western Maryland, vol. 1, p. 732, pub. 1882.

PETERS

Christian Peters of Cecil Co. in August 1729 petitioned the Assembly for naturalization, being "born in Germany". Styled "Gent", his will May 1746, Cecil Co., declared "Born in Harborugh in the Dukedom of Luneburg, Germany" and devised his estate in Germany to "my half sister the Widow Matfields in Lavenbury or her children".

REF: Md. Archives, vol. 36, pp. 314, 316; Wills, Liber 25, folio 411.

PETERSON

Cornelius Peterson in 1674 upon naturalization stated that he was a native of Sweadland [Swedish settlements on the Delaware].

REF: Md. Archives, vol. 2, p. 400.

Hance Peterson of Baltimore made oath on Aug. 11, 1673, that he entered Maryland from Holland as a freeman in 1665 and that his wife, Ingaberus, entered Maryland from New York as a freewoman in 1661.

REF: Patents, Liber 17, folio 489.

James Peterson in 1674 when he petitioned for naturalization declared that he was a native of the Kingdome of Denmarke".

REF: Md. Archives, vol. 2, p. 400.

Mathias Peterson and his son Peter of Talbot Co. upon naturalization in 1671 stated that they were natives of Holland.

REF: Md. Archives, vol. 2, p. 282.

An act for the naturalization of Mathias Peterson and his children past the Lower House in 1683.

REF: Md. Archives, vol. 7, p. 487, 488.

PHEYPE

Marke Pheype imigrated in 1641 from Ireland.

REF: Patents, Liber ABH, folios 9, 102.

PHILLIPS

Nicholas Phillips became a naturalized subject of Britain after taking the Oath of Abjuration and having submitted certification that he was a member of the Lutheran Church of Frederick and had taken communiun on July 13, 1760, in accordance to the Act of George II.

REF: Prv Crt Judgements, Liber DD no. 1, folio 191.

PHILPOTT

Bryan Philpott of London, Merchant, mentioned his son Thomas Philpott in Maryland and also referred to a son Philip Philpott, Oct. 20, 1758.

REF: Wills, Liber 31, folio 338.

PICK

John Lodwick Pick, Minister, Frederick Co., Jan. 10, 1765, bequeathed the residue of his estate to his executor to be conveyed to Minister Gerock in Lancaster and then to "my youngest sister Eve Barbara Picken (sic) to be divided among all her children."

REF: Wills, Liber 33, folio 134.

PIERPONT

Henry Pierpont (Parpoynt, Perepointe) who emigrated to Maryland with his wife and family in 1665 was baptized May 27, 1629, in Bennington Parish, Hertfordshire, the son of Amos Parpoynt, Taylor.

REF: Parish Record, Bennington Parish, Co. Record, Herts.

PILE

John Pile, Privy Councilor, came out of Wiltshire before 1648, accompanied by the Tattershalls who are proved as natives of Wilts. John Pile named his plantation "Salisbury", and furthermore in 1680 when Lord Baltimore conferred seigniory upon his widow, Madame Sarah Pile, and the son and heir, Joseph, with court leet and court baron, they named their manor "Sarum", the ancient Roman name for Wiltshire.

REF: Visitation of Wiltshire, edited by G. W. Marshall.

PINAULT

Rene Pinault of Baltimore Co. by will of Aug. 30, 1805, bequeathed property to her sister Radegonde Pinault daughter of Oliver Pinault and Perpetue Dupont her mother "now residing in France".

REF: Balto Co. Wills, Liber 7, folio 444.

PINDER

John Pinder, Talbot Co., Husbandman, Apr. 2, 1711, "I will and Bequeath all my Lands and Livings in Old England in the County of Westmoreland and in Ravenstondale Called Bontherdalworth it being in six Closes there known by the name of Parrachmore & one known by the name of Adams' intake Bottom and another known by the name of Middle End and another known by the name of head end with all dwelling houses . . ." to be sold.

REF: Wills, Liber 13, folio 353.

PINEAU

Anne Catherine Pineau, refugee from Santo Domingo about 1794, married Edne Germain DuCatels, a compatriot.

REF: Hartridge:

PLESTO

The will of Edward Plesto of Kent Co., Md., Carpenter, was proved at the Prerogative Court of Canterbury on Aug. 2, 1727, by which he bequeathed Dorothy, daughter of his brother John £10 and his sister, Catherine Eales, both of Great Britain, "Tilghman's Farm" bought of Col. Richard Tilghman.

REF: Farrant 191, Public Record Office, London; Md. Wills, Liber 14, folio 638.

PLOWDEN

George Plowden who died 1713 in St. Mary's Co., was the grandson of Sir Edmond Plowden, Knt, dubbed 1630, a family which held estates in Salop and Oxon.

REF: 1634 Visitation of Oxon, British Museum, London.

Thomas Plowden and George Plowden of Southampton, England, on May 10, 1684, purchased several plantations in Calvert County from Richard Perry late of Maryland.

REF: Liber WRC no. 1, folio 341.

PLUNKET

David Plunket of Baltimore Co., Captain of the 4th Regt. Continental Dragoons, Revolutionary War, was a native of Enniskillen, Co. Ulster, Ireland.

REF: Family mss.

POLEMAN

Elias Poleman of Annapolis, Gent., by his will probated Dec. 19, 1712, bequeathed £100 Sterling to his sisters Elizabeth and Anne Poleman of London.

REF: Wills, Liber 13, folio 470.

POLKE

Magdalen Polke, [Lower Eastern Shore] 7 Apr. 1726, "I give and bequeath a Tract of Land Called Moaning in the Kingdom of Ireland in the barony of Rosse and County of Donegall in the Parish of Leford unto my Son Joseph Pollock (sic)."

REF: Wills, Liber 19, folio 125.

POPE

John Grisman Pope of Frederick Co. on Apr. 20, 1762, received the sacrament of the Church of England prior to his subscribing to the Oath of Abjuration in order to become a naturalized subject under the Act of George II (13th year).

REF: Prov. Crt Judgements, Liber DD no. 2, folio 94.

POPELY

Captain Richard Popely, Gent., who was granted Popley Island by Lord Baltimore deposed in May 1640 that he was aged 39 and a native of Wooly Parish, Yorks.

REF: Md. Archives, vol. 5, p. 225.

POTTINGER

John Pottinger of Sittingbourne, Co. Kent, sailed from Bristol, Sept. 24, 1684 in the "Maryland Merchant" for Maryland.

REF: Bristol & America, p. 174.

POTTS

In 1771 Sarah Potts widow, William Potts merchant, Sarah Eleanor Potts spinster, Benjamin Mackall and Rebecca his wife and Richard Potts an infant under the age of 21 were heirs to the undivided estate of Rebecca Potts, late of the Parish of St. Michael, Island of Barbadoes, widow.

On December 10, 1771, the aforesaid heirs sold for £380 the realty of the late Rebecca Potts which consisted of 3004 improved square feet in Bridgetown and 1947 square feet on Palmetta and Marl Hill Streets to Michael Arthur. The land bordered the estate of the Hon. John Truro, Esq. and Mary Coats, both deceased.

REF: Prov. Crt Deeds, Liber DD no. 5, folio 297; Prov. Crt Deeds, Liber 12, folio 297.

POULSON
In 1683 a bill was introduced in the Lower House and passed for the naturalization of Andrew Poulson alias Mullock and his children who had been in Maryland as early as 1662.

REF: Md. Archives, vol. 5, p. 175; vol. 7, p. 487; Patents, Liber 5, folio 175.

POUSTON
March 4, 1633/4. "Then was Granted to John Pouston Pattent of Dennizacon subject of the Kingdom of Scotland". Pattent estem eadem uerbatin mutatis mutandis Vt esb folio supra 160, pro Isaack Bedlo.

REF: Md. Archives, vol. 3, p. 490.

POWELL
Bernard Powell accepted the sacrament of the Church of England in St. Anne's Church and on Sept. 11, 1765, became a British subject.

REF: Prov. Crt Judgements, Liber DD no. 9, folio 5.

POWER
Henry Power of Frederick on Apr. 19, 1762, received the sacrament of the Church of England at St. Anne's, Annapolis, prior to his subscribing to the Act of Abjuration in order to become a naturalized subject under the Act of George II (13th year).

REF: Prov. Crt Judgements, Liber DD no. 2, folio 94.

POWICK
John Powick of London, Gent., emigrated in 1662 and received 300 acres from the Lord Proprietary.

REF: Patents, Liber 5, folio 124.

PRATHER
Jonathan Prather [Prater] was a native of Latton on the Eton River in Wiltshire; emigrated first to Virginia and later settled in Calvert Co., Md.

REF: Statement 1932 by professional genealogist, no documentation cited.

PRESTON
Anthony Preston, born Apr. 12, 1792, Kirby Stephen, Co. Westmoreland, Eng., died May 3, 1843.

REF: Congressional Cemetery, Washington, D.C.

PRICE
Mary Price, the mother of the Rev. James Jones Wilmer (1749-1814) was the daughter of John Price, late of Presteign, Co. Radnor, Wales, and the step-daughter of the Rev. Hugh Jones, one time rector of St. Stephen's Parish, Cecil Co. The said Mary (Price) Wilmer was sister to Edward Price of Aylesbury, Buckinghamshire, Gent., in whose care James Jones Wilmer was sent to

England for his education. Edward Price died testate 1774, Aylesbury, Buck, and bequeathed legacies to his nephews—James Jones Wilmer, John Lambert Wilmer, and Edward Pryor Wilmer of Maryland.

REF: Memories of the Rev. James John Wilmer.

PRITCHARD
John Pritchard, Prince George's Co., Gent., Oct. 10, 1741, "Appoint my Kinsman Anthony Donne in London my Executor for the distribution of my Effects in the hands of Arthur Vaughan, Esq."

REF: Wills, Liber 22, folio 397.

PRITCHELL
"John Pritchell the Son of Michael Pritchell born in herburn (sic) parrish in Stafford Shire was Joynd in holy mattrimony unto Eliza: Bener borne in Stepney parrish in Middlesex the 2d March annoq 1701".

REF: Register of St. John's Piscataway Parish, Pr. Geo. Co., transcript of, Md. Hist. Soc., Balto., folio 259.

PROTZMAN
John Protzman, born February 26, 1749, in one of the German States, died at Hancock, Washington County, Md. July 4, 1804, aged 55 years.

REF: Headstone in Hancock Cemetary.

PRYCE
Mary Pryce, daughter of Mr. John Pryce of Comb, Preston Parish, Co., of Hereford & Radnor, married Sept. 16, 1735, Simon Wilmer Jr. of Kent Co., Md.

REF: St. Stephen's Parish Register, Cecil Co.

PUMPHREY
Walter Pumphrey, a carpenter (architect and house constructor) was of Gloucestershire, England, and settled first in Burlington Co., West Jersey in 1678. Later he settled on Curtis Creek which eventually became under the jurisdiction of Broad Neck Hundred.

REF: Pumphrey Family Assn., no documentation cited.

PUTMAN
Andrew Putman, a German Protestant of Frederick Co., after certification that he was a member of the church in Frederick, took the Oath of Abjuration under the Act of George II (13th year) and on Sept. 4, 1762, was declared a naturalized subject.

REF: Prov. Crt Judgements, Liber DD no. 2, folio 352.

PYE
Walter Pye sailed from Bristol for Maryland between 1654-1663.

REF: Bristol & America. p. 96 (510).

The Pye family of Charles Co., was of The Mynde, Hereforshire, and well-connected in England. On July 18, 1769, Edward, 14th Duke of Norfolk, gave to "John Pye son and heir of Charles Pye and Mary Booth his wife of the Province of Maryland a part of His Majesty's Dominion in North America... of his free Bounty and goodness to the said John Pye and his family is mined to

142

make some provisions for his Daughters and younger sons to the extent of £500".

REF: Chas. Co. Deeds, Liber O no. 3, folio 584; Newman's Heraldic Marylandiana.

QUINN

Anne, wife of Michael Quinn and daughter of John and Mary O'Reilly, a native of Longford, Co. Craven, Ireland, died Oct. 20, 1851, aged 34 years.

Michael Quinn, a native of Longford, Co. Craven, Ireland, died Nov. 6, 1876, aged 80 years, 1 month.

REF: Holy Rood Cemetery, Georgetown, D.C.

RAAL

Adam Gottleib Raal of Baltimore was attorney for the heirs of Michael Kuensler, late of York Co., Penn., the said heirs residing in Mittelsin, Dutchy of Hanau, Germany, November 1813.

REF: Balto Co. Wills, Liber 9, folio 375.

RADDISH

Thomas Raddish of London, Mariner, now of Baltimore Co., Sept. 26, 1766, "I leave and bequeath unto my Sister Sarah Hill wife of John Hill the sum of £10 Sterling she living in Buckle Street nedir red Lyon Street White Chappel".

REF: Wills, Liber 35, folio 40.

RALPH

Rev. George Ralph, born in England, rector of North Sassafras Parish, Cecil Co. 1793; Washington Parish, D.C. 1795; Queen Anne's Parish, Pr. Geo. Co., 1797; President of Charlotte Hall Academy and rector of Trinity Parish, died 1813.

REF: Allen.

RAMSEY

John Ramsey "late of Bellabofey in the County of Donegal and Kingdom of Ireland now of the City of Baltimore" by will of Sept. 23, 1803, devised property in Co. Donegal.

REF: Balto Co. Wills, Liber 7, folio 241.

John Ramsey, a Jacobite, captured at Preston, Lancashire, in 1715, and sold in Maryland for seven years of servitude, petitioned for his freedom on August 3, 1721, which was denied.

REF: Md. Archives, vol. 34, p. 164.

RANKIN

"Was born Mary Walker Rankin, the daughter of George Rankin and Mary Bull on Friday [23 June 1775], her mother being the Daughter of Constantine Bull of the City of Norwich in the County of Norfolk and Catherine Walker his wife of Rothrop Hall near Dalton in Yorkshire".

REF: Original parish register, St. Anne's, Anne Arundel Co., p. 269.

RASHOON

Stephen Rashoon of Talbot Co., Planter, and his children were naturalized by an act of the Assembly 1711.

REF: Md. Archives, vol. 38, p. 143.

RASOLINI

Onorio Rasolini of Annapolis, born 1737 "in the Venetian Territories" was naturalized in 1732, by an Act of the Assembly; was guardian to the Hon. Elizabeth Calvert, died 1763.

REF: Md. Archives, vol. 37, pp. 389, 567; Bacon Laws Chap. 7, (1732); Chap. 20, (1747).

RAWLINS

John, Anthony and Richard Rawlins [Rawlings] sailed from Bristol, England between 1663-1679.

REF: Bristol & America.

RAYMAN

William Rayman of Annapolis "borne in Germany under the Dominion of the Prince Palatinate of Rhyne" was naturalized in 1728 by an Act of the Assembly.

REF: Md. Archives, vol. 38, p. 422.

READ

Richard Read whose will was written in 1711, but not probated in Prince George's Co. until 1732 declared himself of "Deptford Parish, Co. Kent, England".

REF: Wills, Box 4, folder 27; Newman's Heraldic Marylandiana.

READING

The Rev. Philip Reading, son of the Rev. Philip Reading Sr., librarian of Sion College, London, was one-time rector of St. Augustine's Parish, Cecil Co.; died 1778.

REF: Rightmeyer's Maryland's Established Church.

REEDE

William Reede, Dorchester Co., 21, Feb. 1728/9, "I William Reede of Dorchester County the son of William Reede of Chip in Candin, Glostershire" devised realty in Candin.

REF: Wills, Liber 19, folio 763.

REGNIER

Jacob Regnier, late of Lincoln's Inn, London, Esq., was a resident of Annapolis in 1701.

REF: A.A. Co. Deeds, Liber WT no. 1, folio 259.

REID

Oct. 14, 1718, Alexander Reid of Parish of Alfordshire, Aberdeen, stated that he was collateral cousin of the whole blood and heir-at-law to George Reid, late of Calvert Co., Gent., who was seized of Readbourne on the East side of the Chester River, who died intestate.

William Reid, Merchant, who possessed in 1722 "Reid Burne" [Readburne] and "New Seat" in Chester River and also "Reid's Point" in St. Mary's Co., was of "Aberdeem that part of Great Britain called Scotland".

REF: Prov. Crt Deeds, Liber EI no. 8, folio 6; Prov. Crt, Liber PL no. 5, folio 39.

RENELL

"A Memorial of John N. Renell a native of Great Britain. He was born at Topsham in Devonshire in April 1776 and died at Baltimore on the 5th of December 1818".

REF: Churchyard of St. Thomas' Garrison Forest, Baltimore Co.

RENTON

James Renton, a Jacobite, was captured at Preston, Lancashire, in 1715, and transported to Maryland to be sold into servitude of seven years.

REF: Md. Archives, vol. 25, pp. 347-349.

RETISFORD

William Retisford, Talbot Co., Oct. 6, 1674, declared himself formerly an "Inhabiter of Plymouth in the County of Devon...All that I have to my Dear Beloved Wife Mary Retisford now Living in Plymouth".

REF: Wills, Liber 2, folio 22.

REYNOLDS

Thomas son of Robert Reynolds late of the County of Fermanagh, Kingdom of Ireland, was buried 24 July 1719.

REF: Original register of St. Anne's Parish, Anne Arundel Co., p. 45.

RICAND

Benjamin Ricand, no county cited, 24 Jan. 1684/5, If his named children died without issue then "unto the heirs of my brother Thomas Ricand of ye City of London".

REF: Wills, Liber 4, folio 80.

RICH

Stephen Rich of Queen Anne's Co., Carpenter, "borne under the Dominion of the States Generall of the united Province" was naturalized in 1713 by an Act of the Assembly.

REF: Md. Archives, vol. 38, p. 181.

RICHAND

Benjamin Richand, placed as a planter of Kent Co., by his will dated Jan. 24, 1684/5, made his brother, Thomas Richand of London, Eng., heir to his Maryland estate in the event of his sons dying without issue.

REF: Wills, Liber 4, folio 80.

RICHARDS

On Sept. 24, 1762, James Richards of Baltimore Co., Gent., received the sacrament at St. Thomas' Church, same county, as certified by the Rev. Thomas Craddock, and at court subscribed to the Oath of Abjuration under the Act of George II (13th year) and was therefore declared a naturalized subject, country of birth no stated.

REF: Prov. Crt Judgements, Liber DD no. 2, folio 353-4.

RICHARDSON

Anthony Richardson, Talbot Co., Gent., Nov. 19, 1740, "I give devise and bequeath unto my well beloved niece Ann Richardson Daughter of my well beloved Brother Thomas Richardson, deceased, all right title Interest and Claim which I now have or ought to have of in and to any Land or Lands which did heretofore belong to my Brother Thomas, lying in the Kingdom of Great Britain"; executors" to place £400 Sterling in the hands of my Dear Sister Ann Spaulding of Whitehaven in the Kingdom of Great Britain for the use and benefit of my said niece Ann Richardson".

REF: Wills, Liber 22, folio 361.

Anthony Richardson of London, Merchant, Aug. 10, 1771, was the eldest son and heir of Anthony Richardson, of Talbot Co., Md., deceased, and Hannah his wife.

REF: Prov. Crt Deeds, Liber DD no. 5, folio 252.

Thomas Richardson, of Baltimore Co., but then at Kingston, Jamaica, Mar. 12, 1768, bequeathed legacies to "my mother in Scotland", but in the event of her decease then to his sisters, Ann, Jennet and Isabelle Richardson.

REF: Wills, Liber 35, folio 478.

Thomas Richardson, Talbot Co., Merchant, Oct. 1, 1734, "I give and devise to my dear Mother Abigail all the Field commonly called and known by the name New Close all that Close or field called the Severlands and the Meadow called the Ings lying adjacent thereto and all that close or field commonly called and known by the name of the Kemp-Garth and the Messuage thereon which are parts of a parcel of Land in Cumberland in the Kingdom of Great Britain called and known by the name of Byerstead. . . unto my well beloved Sister Lidia Salked £6 Sterling yearly during life. . . to my nephew Anthony Bacon £50. . . to Brother Anthony Richardson to be guardianship of sister Jane wife of Francis Dickinson of Cumberland, shoemaker".

REF: Wills, Liber 21, folio 306.

RICKEY

Joseph Rickey, native of Co. Tyrone, Ireland, born June 7, 1748, emigrated to Pennsylvania, 1771, and served in the Militia of Frederick Co. during the Revolution; later removed to Richland Co., Ohio.

REF: Revolutionary Pension Claim S4100, National Archives.

RICKS

John Ricks, Anne Arundel Co., Nov. 22, 1677, "I give £10 Sterling money of England to my loving Mother Elizabeth Ricks of Suffolk in Old England".

REF: Wills, Liber 9, folio 14.

RIDDELL

Alexander Riddell, born c1752, in Glasgow, one time associated with Robert & Alexander Riddell of Baltimore, returned to Glasgow and died testate in his 74th year. His will probated 1825, left legacies to his brother, Robert Riddell, and the nieces and nephews of his said brother. The latter died testate in Baltimore, "departed this life on the 5th instant [May 1809] in 49th years of his age for many years a respectable merchant of this city".

REF: Balto Co. Wills, Liber 8, folio 406.

RIDGELY
See, Skinner-Ridgely.

RIDOUT
John Ridout, Esq., a native of Dorset, England, died 7 Oct. 1797, and was buried at Whitehall, Anne Arundel Co.

REF: St. Margaret's Westminster Parish Register, transcript Md. Hist. Soc., Balto.

RIGGS
John Riggs, the progenitor of the Anne Arundel Co., branch, died "August 17 in the year of our Lord 1762. He was then in the 75th year of his age". Therefore, he was born in or about the year 1687. It may be more than a coincidence that the records of St. Duncan, Stepney, London, contain the marriage of John Riggs and Jane Warden on April 24, 1687, and that a son John Riggs was born December 13, 1687.

REF: Entries in a book by Richard Baxter, printed 1672, which belonged to the Riggs family; Register of St. Dunstan, Stepney; Riggs Family of Maryland, by John Beverley Riggs, pub. 1939.

RIND
Alexander Rind, a Jacobite, captured at Preston, Lancashire, in 1715, and sold in Maryland for seven years of servitude, petitioned for his freedom on August 3, 1721, which was denied.

REF: Md. Archives, vol. 34, p. 164.

RISTON
Edward Riston of Rangers' Forest, Baltimore Co., married Rachel, the daughter of Rinaldo Monk, late of London, England, before 1772.

REF: St. Paul's Parish Register, Balto Co.

RITCHIE
Benjamin Ritchie, a native Scotsman, substituted for John Wayman Sellman, in accordance with the "Act to procure Troops for the American Army", passed March Session 1778.

REF: Militia List, Md. Hist. Soc., Balto.

ROADES
Abraham Roades, St. Mary's Co., Apr. 29, 1705, devised to wife Frances during life, but "after my wife's decease my plantation I now live upon to Containe 100 acres to my Cozen Bloomer Goodacre living in the Kingdom of England".

REF: Wills, Liber 3, folio 661.

ROBERT
James Robert of Calvert Co., Planter and a French Protestant, was naturalized in 1708 by an act of the Assembly.

REF: Md. Archives, vol. 27, p. 369, 370.

ROBERTS
Edward Roberts, Charles Co., 15 Jan. 1676/7, "Any money that is fallen to mee in England by the death of my Uncle John Reade Son to my

Grandfather George Reade, deceased, as by the said Grandfather's Will will appear".

REF: Wills, Liber 5, folio 321.

William Roberts, domiciled in All Hallows Parish, Anne Arundel Co., was formerly a contract servant and the son of John and Letitia Roberts of England. In 1756 he was living in London and was a nephew of John Broughton, a wealthy Londoner, living in Warwick Street, Charing Cross. In 1756 Roberts sailed from England to Maryland aboard the "Betsy" and arrived in Annapolis in June of that year after a three-month crossing.

REF: See his letters to his uncle, Md. Hist. Magazine, vol. 74, pp., 117-131.

ROBINS

George Robins, Talbot Co., May 20, 1694, "Whereas I have one Sonn named John Robins and one Daughter Named Jane the wife of Edmond Chibsey in England and my will is that they have no part of my Estate real and personal in Maryland nor that my wife's Sonnes or Daughters in Maryland Claim any part of my Estate in England, But I have one house in Wellstreet in Buckingham in the Kingdom of England mortgaged to my sister Elizabeth ffreeze for £100 Sterling. . .to daughter Jane I give my house in Castle Street in Buckingham"; what other estate which would descend to said George Robins at the death of his mother to son John Robins and Daughter Jane Chibsey.

REF: Wills, Liber 7, folio 90.

ROBINSON

On July 26, 1699, Charles Robinson, formerly of Yarmouth in the Kingdom of England, "now of Talbot Co.", Woolen Draper, was domiciled in Maryland.

REF: Wills, Liber 6, folio 300.

Leonard Robinson, a Jacobite, captured at Preston, Lancashire, in 1715, and sold in Maryland for seven years of servitude, petitioned for his freedom on August 3, 1721, which was denied.

REF: Md. Archives, vol. 34, p. 164.

William Robinson, Nov. 29, 1696, "The remaining part to my Deare Loveing ffather William Robinson of the Kingdom of England in the County of York".

REF: Wills, Liber 7, folio 226.

ROBOTHAM

George Robotham, Talbot Co., Feb. 28, 1697/8, "I give and bequeath unto my Nieces Mary Erp and Anne Cooke Daughters to my Sister Anne Wilson of Findren in the County of Derby in Old England And to my niece Ann Cotton daughter of my Sister Mary Keeling in the County of Stafford in England all Estate in Old England real and personal Saveing to my two Sisters Anne Wilson and Mary Keeling Each of them £100 Sterling".

REF: Wills, Liber 7, folio 358.

ROCHE

John Roche, Fells Point, by will bequeathed "gold watch and said appendages to my nephew John Murphy of the Kingdom of Ireland...to the lawful children of my brother Adam Roche of the Kingdom of Ireland and to my nephew my sister's son John Murphy of the Kingdom of Ireland" $800.00. 12 July 1817.

REF: Balto Co. Wills, Liber 10, folio 346.

ROCHFORD

Michael Rochford, St. Mary's Co., Aug. 13, 1678, legacy "to my honored Mother Mrs. Helena Rochford in case she be living if not to my Brothers and sisters, viz Patrick, Christian and Kathereine Rochford all living in the Citty of Limerick in Ireland".

REF: Wills, Liber 9, folio 46.

RODAWAY

John Rodaway, Talbot Co., Oct. 20, 1675, "I give an bequeath unto my dear and Loving Mother Margaret Rodaway of the Citty of Bristoll Widdow all that shall be found my just due in the Province of Maryland" both personall and reall during life then to my sister Mary Rodaway and if his sister died without issue then to his sister Elizabeth Beaks of Bristol wife of Richard Beaks of Bristol, corwinder.

REF: REF: Wills, Liber 2, folio 375.

ROELANDS

Robert Roelands in 1669 upon naturalization stated that he was born in Brabant [now Belgium] within the Dominion of the said States Generall" of the United Provinces.

REF: Md. Archives, vol. 2, p. 205.

ROGERS

William Rogers of Annapolis who became the third husband of Mary, widow of Colonel John Contee of Prince George's Co., and Philemon Hemsley of Queen Anne's Co. was connected in some manner with Sir John Rogers, Bart, late of Burrough of Plymouth in Devonshire, whose father was of Purleigh, Co. Essex. At the death of Sir John, Madame Mary Contee, then widow of Colonel Contee, had in 1709 property of Sir John to the value of 6000 lbs. tob.

Mary, the widow of Sir John Rogers, Bart., married secondly Sir Edmond Pridaux, Bart, as his third wife, and as the executors of Sir John Rogers, sued Madame Contee.

Madame Mary (Townley) Contee-Hemsley-Rogers was sister to Frances Townley who as the wife of James Wotton of Ogburn St. George in the County of Wilts, Great Britain, Clerke, declared herself in 1731 as one of the coheiresses of the said Mary, the Widow Rogers. Judith (Townley) Bruce of Charles Co. was another sister and coheiresses to Mary, the Widow Rogers.

REF: Chas. Co. Deeds, Liber M no. 2, folio 294; Bond's, Maryland Court of Appeals, vol. 1, pp. 190-195; The Complete Bartonetage.

ROLLE

Francis Rolle of Maryland by his will dated November 1724, probated December 7, 1724, bequeathed his wife, Dorothy Rolle, her dowry and the residue to his four sons, Robert, Francis, Fhidemon and Henry. Arndolt Hawkins of William was named executor. Will not recorded in Maryland.

REF: Public Record Office, London, Boston 282.

ROSS

David Ross, M.D., Scottish native, one-time Merchant of Bladensburg, by his will dated February 23, 1778, bequeathed £250 to his son-in-law Cunningham Corbett, Merchant, as balance of his wife's portion to be paid at Glasgow.

REF: Chancery, Liber 48, folio 390; Pr. Geo. Co., Wills, Liber T no. 1, folio 107.

John Ross of Annapolis, Esq., was born August 13, 1696, the son of Henry Ross and Jane his wife, who were married August 11, 1695, at St. James' Westminster, London. At the latter church on October 18, 1720, the said John Ross married Alicia Arnold and sailed for Maryland shortly thereafter. Ancestors of Francis Scott Key.

REF: Parish Register; Md. Hist. Mag., vol. 9, pp. 109-110.

ROUND

James Round of Maryland and Mary his wife were devised land by the Rev. John Wood of Dorking, Surrey, the father of Madame Mary Round, by will of October 28, 1695. The said devise was to descend to the heirs of the body of Mary (Wood) Round and in default of heirs then to another son-in-law, William Round, and his wife Martha, another daughter of the said Rev. Mr. Wood.

REF: Archdeaconry of Surrey 1695-1699, no numbered folios.

James Round, Somerset Co., 5 Apr. 1780, "I give an bequeath unto my Nephew Edward Morris son of Zachariah Morris of London, Iron Monger" £50; "I give and bequeath to my nephews and nieces children of my brother Edward Round, Iron Monger of London" £20.

REF: Wills, Liber 11, folio 106.

ROUSBY

Christopher Rousby and John Rowsby emigrants to Maryland were brothers to William Rousby, Citizen and Grocer of London, circa 1680.

REF: Md. Hist. Mag., vol. 17, p. 29; Liber TP no. 4, folio 1, Hall of Records.

ROWAN

Hugh Rowan born c1800 at County Mayo, Ireland, settled in Washington Co., Md., died June 4, 1862.

REF: Gravestone, Roman Catholic Cemetery, Cumberland.

RUSSELL

James Russell, born Apr. 23, 1708, son of James and Anne (Wightman) Russell of Kingseat and Slipperfield, Fifeshire, Scotland, settled about 1730 in Nottingham Town, Prince George's Co., and intermarried into a branch of the Maryland Lees.

REF: Article by Prof. Jacob M. Price, University of Michigan, Md. Hist. Mag., vol. 72, p. 165.

Mrs. James Carstairs. Cupar [Co. Fife] 20 May 1818. "We acknowledge to have received from you Twenty pounds sterling to enable us to go out to America which sum we oblige us to repay to you, within Twelve Months with Interest, from this date till repaid". Your ob^t Servts. Michael Russell and Jenet Russell.

REF: Private papers of the Russell family of Md.

RYE

Charles Rye, Dorchester Co., 23 Dec. 1708, "...the other part of my Estate unto my Dear Mother Mrs. Caroline Rye of England and in case of her decease I give and bequeath the said half part of my Estate to my Sister Mary Take and her heirs forever and I desire and order my Dear Wife Immediately after my decease to send word to my mother".

REF: Wills, Liber 12 pt. 2, folio 146a.

SAGER

The Rev. George Sager became a naturalized subject on Sept. 10, 1762, after subscribing to the Oath of Abjuration in accordance to the Act of George II (13th year) and after receiving a certification from the Rev. Thomas Bacon, rector of All Saints' Parish, Frederick, then officiating at St. Anne's, Annapolis, that he had taken the sacrament under the rites of the Church of England.

REF: Prov. Crt Judgements, Liber DD no. 2, folios 89-90.

SALENAVE

Bernard Salenave aged 40 years about to make a voyage to Saint Domingo declared himself a "native of Bayonne in the Department of Lower Pynches, son of Peter Salenave and Miss Jane Maria Mazans his wife", 21 Nov. 1816.

REF: Balto Wills, Liber 10, folio 106.

SALTER

Cornelius Salter who died testate Oct. 6, 1801, in Baltimore Co., declared himself to be a native of the Kingdom of Prussia.

REF: Balto Co. Wills, Liber 6, folio 432.

John Salter, Queen Anne's Co., 13 Dec. 1715, Failing issue "then my will is that my Sister Son Jonathan Gunthrope who is a pewter and lives near Ractiff Cross in London shall have possession and enjoy ye above Lands Tenements and hereditments".

REF: Wills, Liber 14, folio 78.

SAMPSON

Jeremiah Sampson, Mariner, late of Annapolis and also Parish of St. Mary's London and Rotherbith, County Surrey, possessed lot 64 in Annapolis. By his will of September 18, 1717, he devised it to his wife, Saraah, who was daughter of Samuel Paul of Parish of Camberwell, County Surry.

REF: Wills, Liber 14, folio 493; A.A. Co. Deeds, Liber RB no. 1, folio 80.

SANCTON

Thomas Sancton, subject of Great Britain, on Aug. 10, 1790, declared himself a Christian and subscribed to the Oath of Naturalization. County domicile not cited.

REF: Council Proceedings, Md. Archives, vol. 72, p. 132.

SANDERS

John Sanders [Saunders] "of ye City of Bristol, England, Merchant, on Mar. 9, 1674/5, bought "Nonsuch" of 106 acres in Charles Co. from Thomas Brooke, of Calvert Co., Gent. On February 19, 1676/7, he bought water mill and dam in Charles Co. from John Allen of the same county, Gent. On Jan. 10, 1678/9, John Sanders of Bristol, England "now of Charles Co., Gent." deeded "Nonsuch" to William Wells of Charles Co.

REF: Chas. Co. Deeds, Liber F no. 1, folios 73, 243; Liber H no. 1, folio 6.

Peter Sanders of Talbot Co., Planter, and his children were naturalized by an Act of the Assembly in 1711.

REF: Md. Archives, vol. 38, p. 143.

SANFORD

Samuel Sanford by his will of March 27, 1716 who styled himself "sometime of Accomack Co., in Virginia now in London" devised to John, the son of his kinsman Thomas Parry, "now in Maryland" two corn mills bought of Ralph Foster of St. Mary's Co., in Maryland.

REF: Smith 98, Public Record Office, London.

SAUGHIER

"My Dear and loving Father George Saughier, born in Newport in ye Isle of Wight A^O Dom^n 1600 in March. And arrived in Virginia in Decemb^r 1620. And departed this life ye 24 December 1684 and was buried ye day following being ye Christmas Day. His daughter, Margaret Saughier, was born "in Virginia at the trimbell Spring"*** 11th 1646. She married March 5*** Thomas Beson Jr. of South River Maryland.

REF: Small leather-bound book among the papers of the late Edmund Law Roger; Md. Hist. Mag., vol. 14, p. 76 (1919).

SAUL

John Saul of Dublin, Ireland, presented his certificate on 2d day 9th mo. 1714, at a Quaker Meeting at West River.

REF: West River Quaker Records.

SAUNDER-SLYE

Mistress Jane Saunders of Worcestershire, England, emigrated to Maryland in company with Mr. Massey, a Roman Catholic priest, and Frances, presumably her maid-servant. She was first a house guest of Lord and Lady Baltimore at Mattapani and then resided with Colonel John Jourdain and his family in St. Clement's Manor. About 1676 at the home of Captain Jourdain she married Captain Gerard Slye of Bushwood. She, Captain Gerard Slye and their two sons returned to England, where Captain Slye died.

In 1732 Charles Slye son of Capt. Gerard and his wife, returned to Maryland to claim his birthrights. Several interesting depositions were made. The maid-servant later became "Goody Frances Roads wife of Abraham

Roads. Mistress Saunders brought with her a large box of goods from England given her by her Cousin Boukey". James French of St. Mary's Co., deposed that he knew Mistress Jane Saunders, a Gentlewoman, that came out of England and who was reputed to have had a great fortune. She was a little woman, fair and a little round-shoulder. The white wet-nurses of the two sons of Captain Slye testified.

Madame Elizabeth Cole, widow, aged 53, sister of Captain Gerard Slye, deposed that 3 years after the marriage her sister-in-law returned to England to adjust her affairs and returned afterwards with "goods and effects and servants".

Edward Field of St. Mary's Co., aged 74 swore to the marriage and that Mistress Saunders persuaded Captain Slye to name a portion of Bushwood "Siper's Hill" in remembrance of an estate in Worcestershire. Other interesting and human interests depositions were made, especially Major Nicholas Sewell's visit to his mother and step-father, Lord and Lady Baltimore, in London.

REF: Chancery, Liber PL no. 4, folio 754.

SCAMPER

By an Act of the 1701 Assembly Peter Scamper of Prince George's Co. was naturalized.

REF: Md. Archives, vol. 24, p. 204.

SCARBOROUGH

Anne West who married first Thomas Sparrow and secondly William Sellman both of Anne Arundel Co. and who died in that county 1749 was a daughter of Matilda Scarborough by her husband Colonel John West of Accomac Co., Va. Her Scarborough ancestors were from North Walsham, Co., Norfolk, prior to their emigration to Virginia.

REF: Visitation of Norfolk, Harleian Soc. Pub., vol. 86, pp. 193, 194.

SCHEE

A bill was presented to the Assembly March 1701/2 for the naturalization of Hermanus Schee, Gent.

REF: Md. Archives, vol. 24, pp. 245, 253, 279.

SCHELL

Eva Margareth Schell, widow, born Nov. 24, 1729, in Langen-Candel in Hochfueratl, Platz, Zweybruckischer Herrschaft [Kandel Germersheim], daughter of Johannes Weiss and his wife, Anna Elisabeth. Her father died Aug. 10, 1749. In 1752 she, her mother and two brothers, George Heinrich and Johann Dieter came to his country. In Jan. 1754 she married Carl Schell, a locksmith, who embarked to eternity before her on Jan. 19, 1783. She died of pains in her limbs and diarrhea the 12th Aug. 1795, at 5 P.M.

REF: Evangelical Luther Church, Frederick.

SCHLEY

George Schley after certification that he had received the sacrament of the Calvinistic Church of Geneve on Sept. 15, 1762, took the Oath of Abjuration under the Act of George II (13th year) and thus on Sept. 16th was declared a naturalized subject.

REF: Prv. Crt Judgements, Liber DD no. 2, folio 350.

SCHNEIDER
Gerard Joseph Schneider, M.D., a native of Dusseldorf, Germany, died December 26, 1821.

REF: History of Western Maryland, vol. 1, p. 472, by Scharf.

SCHRADER
Henry Schrader, born in Kingdom of Prussia, April 15, 1754, emigrated to America in 1776, and died August 19, 1824, Funkstown, Md.

REF: Methodist Cemetery, Funkstown.

SCHULTZE
Christopher Schultze "late of Magdeburg in Lower Saxony now of the City of Baltimore, Merchant", willed legacy to brother John Ernest Christian Schultze, by will of Jan. 18, 1802.

REF: Balto Co. Wills, Liber 7, folio 453.

SCOTT
Elizabeth Scott, Talbott Co., Quaker, Dec. 17, 1717, ". . .to Thomas Willson (nephew). . .due to me in Cumberland in Ould England".

REF: Wills, Liber 16, folio 40.

George Scott, born 1700 at Melenie, Midlothianshire, Scotland emigrated 1730 to Maryland and died Prince George's Co., 1771; father-in-law to Robert Peter of Georgetown.

REF: History of Western Maryland, by Scharf, vol. 1, p. 732.

Robert Scott, St. Mary's Co., Clerk, 7 Nov. 1733, "Any overplus if any to be Divided equally between my sister Ann Scott of Dundee in North Britain, if she be living and my sister Margaret Gutherie if she be living and my niece Susanna Murray".

REF: Wills, Liber 20, folio 836.

Samuel Scott, Calvert Co., 19 Jan. 1698/9, requested that William Dakins take charge of all goods that "have come to my hands belonging to my Brother Robert Scott and Hugh Calverly of London, Merchant".

REF: Wills, Liber 6, folio 185.

Upton Scott of Anne Arundel Co., was a native of Co. Antrim, Ireland; died Feb. 23, 1814 in his 92d year; "for 60 years a distinguished and respected inhabitant of Annapolis".

REF: Headstone, St. Anne's Cemetery, Annapolis.

Walter Scott of "Province of Maryland but at present residing in London, Merchant", by will of February 26, 1752, devised to Walter Scott & Co., Glasgow, 2 lots at Portobacco, Charles Co.; to James Armour & John Steward of London, Merchant, land granted "to me by Henry Wynne and Sarah Wynne in Portobacco," that is "Simpson's Delight" of 300 acres, "Warroll" of 200 acres, "London" of 100 acres, "Blorksith" of 100 acres, also land at Nanjemoy "Lover Point" of 200 acres, land at the head of the Wicomico called

"Burtons" of 90 acres; "Sudmooe's Adventure" of 37 acres, and also the benefit of an assignment from Henry Wynne, and all money due from the Hon. Benjamin Young, Esq., of Maryland.

REF: Public Record Office, London, Bettesworth 78.

SCRIVENER

Benjamin Scrivener, St. Botolph without Aldgate, Co. Middlesex, Eng., Merchant, on Dec. 22, 1686, devised his wife, Grace, one-third of his estate Hartley Wintney in Co. Southampton and in Maryland.

REF: Pett 107, Public Record Office, London.

Thomas Scrivner of Anne Arundel Co., Gent., on April 6, 1689, deeded to Thomas Couch of Anne Arundel Co., Mercht improved land at Hartly Rowe, Hampshire, Engl., given the said Scrivner by Francis Coates late in the possession of Edward Subb.

REF: Prov. Crt, Liber TL no. 2, folio 33.

SEALE

John Seale, Queen Anne Co., Dec. 27, 1774, bequested estate to his children, but if they died without issue "it is my Will that all my Lands or all such part as may not be sold or Disposed of as aforesaid shall Descend to my Heir-at-law now in England provided only my Said Heir-at-law shall come over and dwell".

REF: Wills, Liber 41, folio 362.

SEDGWICK

John Sedgwick, Sept. 28, 1753, declared himself "now of Anne Arundel County in Maryland late of London, Mariner".

REF: Wills, Liber 30, folio 511.

SEMPLE

John Semple one time of Dublin, Ironmonger, settled first in Maryland but later in Prince William Co., Va., mortgaged extensive tracts of land during 1769 in Western Maryland. In 1811 a lenghty lawsuit developed over the property by his heirs some of whom were domiciled in Ireland and others in Maryland.

REF: Chancery, Liber 46, folios 161-268, Hall of Records.

SETH

An act was introduced at the 1684 Assembly for the naturalization of Jacob Seth.

REF: Md. Archives, vol. 13, p. 126.

SEWELL

Charles Sewell, Gent., aged 29 years, sailed to Maryland on the ship "Industry" for "employment".

REF: Emigrants from England 1773-1776, by Gerald Fothergill, p. 35.

Henry Sewell [Sewall], of Mattapany-Sewell Manor and one-time Secretary of Maryland, was born about 1630, son of Richard Sewell of Nuneaton, Warwickshire. In 1652 he claimed an estate of his elder brother,

Richard, at Corley, Warwickshire, which had been sequestered in 1644, as his brother had fought with the Rebels under Cromwell.

REF: 1619 Visitation of Warwickshire, Harleian Soc. Pub., vol. 12, p. 343; Waters' Gleanings in England, vol. 1, pp. 153, 811.

John Sewell of the Barbados by will of Aug. 20, 1715, named his brother Cuthbert Sewell of St. Mary's Co. all his land in Fenwick Manor and his sister Mary Green of Charles Co., and all other brothers and sisters residing in "this Island" and elsewhere. The will was probated in Maryland before Thomas Bordley on Sept. 13, 1721.

REF: Wills, Box S, folder 25, Hall of Records.

SEYMOUR

Governor John Seymour, Esq., 12 Dec. 1708, "And as for the rest of my personal Estate either in Maryland or Great Britain and not by my Said Will or this Codicil disposed. . . I give and bequeath the Same to my Dear and Living Son Berkeley Seymour".

REF: Wills, Liber 12 pt. 2, folio 155a.

John Seymour, Plymouth, Devonshire, M.D., by will of Aug. 27, 1741, devised his three daughters the plantation in Maryland willed him by his late aunt, Anne Lynnes, widow of Philip Lynnes of Charles Co., Md.

REF: Spurway 243, Public Record Office, London.

SHAFLOE

John Shafloe, a Jacobite, captured at Preston, Lancashire, in 1715, and shipped to Maryland to be sold into servitude, was deceased at his arrival in the Potomac River.

REF: Md. Archives, vol. 25, pp. 347-349.

SHALCROSS

Thomas Shalcross "late of the West Indies now of the City of Baltimore" according to his will of Aug. 7, 1805.

REF: Balto Co. Wills, Liber 7, folio 434.

SHANK

Christian Shank, born Jan. 1, 1751, in Germany and served in the Militia from Middletown, Frederick Co., later domiciled in Morgan Co., Va.

REF: Revolutionary Pension Claim W19344, National Archives.

SHEHAWNE

Thomas Shehawne was among a ship load of Irish servants who were transported in 1678 by Phillip Popleston, Master of Ship Encrease" of Youghall, Co. Cork, Ireland, and assigned to William Sharpe of Talbot Co.

REF: Patents, Liber 20, folio 184.

SHEPARD

Thomas Shepard, Nov. 14, 1756, "Know ye that I Thomas Shepard of the said County of Cecil. . .I give and bequeath to my Cousin Thomas Shepard son of John Shepard in Devonshire in the Kingdom of Old England £50".

REF: Wills, Liber 30, folio 168.

SHOTT

Christian Shott of Frederick Co. received the sacrament of the church as prescribed by the Act of George II (13th year) upon taking the Oath of Abjuration at court and becoming a British subject.

REF: Prv. Crt Judgements, Liber DD no. 1, folio 185.

SICKS

John Sicks "late of England Subject of the Royall Empire of Jermany" on January 30, 1663/4, was granted letters of denization.

REF: Md. Archives, vol. 3, p. 489.

SIMMS

James Simms, Annapolis, Taylor, 4 Apr. 1735, "I give and bequeath to my sister Elizabeth who married one John Young a Clothier in Monistrose in the Shire of Angus in North Britain all the rest and residue of my Estate".

REF: Wills, Liber 21, folio 457.

SIMPSON

William Simpson of Catocin Furnace, Frederick Co., on March 21, 1828, acknowledged a debt to Andrew Sharp of Dremahill, Co. Antrim, Ireland, and mentioned his brothers and sisters — Thomas, Hugh, Archibald, Sarah and Elizabeth — who were living in Ireland when he left it two years ago.

REF: Fred. Co. Liber GME no. 1, folio 1.

SIMSON

Thomas Simson, Cecil Co., Gent., eldest son of Thomas Simson, late of Jamacia, deceased and residuary legatee of the said Thomas Simson, Merchant, "On 15 July 1726 at Jamacia purchased of my own mother Ann and her present husband Peter Vallete their full Right of Dower . . . . . . left me by my said own deceased father's last will and testament . . . . . . I give unto my late divorced wife Ann (the Own Daughter of Mary), the widow of Jeremiah Pearce late of the City of Bristol in the Kingdom of Great Britain, Merchant, deceased" a legacy.

REF: Wills, Liber 19, folio 649.

SINGLETON

Jacob Singleton, Cecil Co., May 14, 1678, bequeathed the residue of his estate "unto my Dear ffather Mr. John Singleton of Goldsmith . . . neare ffleete Streete in London".

REF: Wills, Liber 10, folio 34.

John Singleton of Whitehaven, Co. Cumberland, England, married Feb. 14, 1774, married Bridget Goldsborough.

John Singleton married Dec. 30, 1790, Anna Goldsborough.

REF: St. Peter's Parish Register, Talbot Co.; Md. Archives, vol. 54.

SINKLOR

John Sinklor, a Jacobite, captured at Preston, Lancashire, in 1715, and sold in Maryland for 7 years of servitude petitioned for his freedom on August 3, 1721, which was denied.

REF: Md. Archives, vol. 34, p. 164.

SIPHERSON

On July 29, 1661, Marcus Sipherson "late of New Amstell and Subject of the Crowne of Sweden" was issued letters of denization. In 1674, upon naturalization he stated that he was a native of Sweadland [Swedish settlements on the Delaware].

REF: Md. Archives, vol. 2, p. 400; vol. 3, pp. 429-430.

SKINNER — RIDGELY

Ann Skinner, daughter and heiress of Aquilla Skinner of Collington, Devonshire, emigrated to Maryland and married Henry Ridgely as his second wife. They became the parents of Henry Ridgely II the son and heir. Her father Aquilla Skinner in 1666 gave his daughter Ann a house and lot in Newport Street, Tiverton, County Devon, which was later claimed by her grandson Henry Ridgely III.

Aquilla Skynner (sic) aforesaid was the son of Richard Skynner of Collington who died testate in 1630 naming Aquilla as his youngest son. The Parish Church at Collington contains tombs and memorials to the Skynner family.

REF: Litigation by Henry Ridgely III in chancery 1727 to claim his grandmother's property at Tiverton which was then used as the Meeting House of the Anbaptists; see also "History of the Baptist Church in Tiverton", publish London by the Baptist Union.

SKIRVIN

William Skirvin, Somerset Co., Jan. 13, 1720/1, referred to a debt due to his wife (Margaret) by her sister Mary Brown in Scotland".

REF: Wills, Liber 16, folio 297.

SLEYCOMB

George Sleycomb, a subject of a German State, was naturalized during the 1697 May-June Session of the General Assembly.

REF: Md. Archives, vol. 19, p. 596.

SLEYTER

Peter Sleyter was the subject of the Act of the 1684 Assembly for naturalization.

REF: Md. Archives, vol. 13, p. 126.

SLUYTER

Henry Sluyter and Jacob Sluyter Jr. of Cecil Co. were naturalized in 1694 by an Act of the General Assembly.

REF: Md. Archives, vol. 19, pp. 85, 104.

SLYCER

Thomas Slycer, son of Robert Slycer of Tewkesbury, Gloucestershire, England, married June 16, 1737, Mary Harris.

REF: Nottingham Quaker Records, Cecil Co.

SLYE

Clement Slye, baptized at Rowington, Warwickshire, May 7, 1648, was son of George Slye, baptized at Lapworth Parish, Nov. 16, 1617, and Hannah his wife. Clement Slye settled in Maryland but died leaving only female issue. He is reputed to be a nephew of Robert Slye of Bushwood Plantation, St. Mary's Co.

REF: Transcript of Parish Registers, Society of Genealogists, London.

Robert Slye, baptized July 8, 1627, at Lapworth Parish, Warwickshire, son of George Slye, emigrated to Maryland in 1654, bringing with him a number of retainers. He named his dwelling-plantation "Bushwood", a portion of St. Clement's Manor, after Bushwood Hall, an estate in Warwickshire and another plantation "Lapworth" after his native parish.

In his will dated St. Mary's Co., Jan. 18, 1670/1, "If they (daughters) dye without heirs lawfully begotten and my further will is that my said two daughters have 30,000 lbs. tob., a piece out of my estate and that and that the same be shipt for England the first next year after my death . . . . . and Consigned to Coll. Henry Meese and my kinsman Mr. Strangwayes Mudd of London for the use of my Said Children . . . . I give and bequeath my Tract of Land called Rich Neck upon St. Mary's Manor to the Eldest son of my dear sister Mrs. Elizabeth Russell of London".

REF: Entries of Lapworth Parish Register, Warwickshire; Patents, Liber Q, folio 208; Wills, Liber 1, folio 422.

SMALL

Andrew Small, born August 28, 1794, Lockee, Liff Parish, Scotland, died Washington, D.C., April 6, 1847, emigrated 1829. Founded the Andrew Small Academy of Darnestown; buried in Presbyterian Churchyard, Darnestown, Montgomery Co.

SMITH

Anthony Smith, Anne Arundel Co., 6 May 1711, in event of the death of son without issue "goe and redound by Equally and every parts to the children of my sister Mary Hunter in habitant of the City of London in the Kingdom of Great Britain".

REF: Wills, Liber 13, folio 331.

On February 16, 1662/3, Emperour Smith "Subject to the States of Holland" was issued letters of denization.

REF: Md. Archives, vol. 3, p. 470.

Robert Smith, Harford Co., Aug. 29, 1776, bequeathed the residue of his estate "to my uncle David Owens at con water near Belfast in the Kingdom of Ireland and his children".

REF: Wills, Liber 41, folio 146.

Samuel Smith, Mariner, was in Maryland by 1658, and deposed to be age 24 at court held in Charles Co. during that year. At his death 1661/2, an inquisition stated that Robert Slye of Bushwood Plantation was "cousin" which could be defined as nephew or cousin as it is used today.

REF: Archives of Md., vol. 53, p. 36.

Thomas Smith was among a ship load of Irish servants who were transported in 1678 by Phillip Popleston, "Master of Ship Encrease" of Younghall, Co. Cork, Ireland, and assigned to William Sharpe of Talbot Co.

REF: Patents, Liber 20, folio 184.

William Smith, a member of the British Army, born 1755 at Buckinghamshire, was captured by the Americans in 1777, and as a prisoner in New York he defected and enlisted in a Maryland regiment as a drill sergeant; later lived in Chatham Co., N.C.

REF: Revolutionary Pension Claim R9874, National Archives.

William Smith, Charles Co., Gent., Jan. 2, 1694/5, "It is my Will that after all my Debts are Paid That William Smith, the son of Adam Smith of Berkshire in the Kingdom of England, be the whole heire of all my remaining parte of my Estate . . . . if said William Smith be dead . . . then divided equally between Adam Smith the Elder Brother of the said William Smith and his sister whose Christian name I know not".

REF: Wills, Liber 7, folio 74.

The heir-at-law of William Smith, late of Charles Co., Md., was Adam Smith of Reading in the County of Berks, Great Britain, Gent., the elder brother and heir-at-law of William Smith, Gent., who was the nephew and devisee of the said William Smith, Gent., late of Charles Co. 6 Dec. 1719.

REF: Chas. Co. Deeds, Liber H no. 2, folio 338.

The Rev. William Smith, born Aberdeem, Scotland, circa 1727, was one-time rector of Chester Parish, Kent Co. and founder of Washington College. He married a Tilghman. He was elected June 1783, Bishop of Maryland, but declined the ofice. He later accepted a parish in South Carolina and became the first Anglican bishop of that State. He died 1803, aged 76 years.

REF: Rightmeyer's Maryland's Established Church; Diocesian Library, Balto.

SMITHERS

On May 1, 1704, a bill was endorsed for the naturalization of Christopher Smithers, of Annapolis, Taylor.

REF: Md. Archives, vol. 24, p. 402.

SMITHSON

John Smithson of London, Merchant, emigrated to Maryland 1677.

REF: Patents, Liber 15, folio 394.

Thomas Smithson, Talbot Co., Nov. 1, 1713, "I give to my sister Dorothy the wife of Michael ffetcher of Richmond in Yorkshire in Great Britain and to ye said Michael her husband and to any husband she may happen to have for their lives . . .".

REF: Wills, Liber 13, folio 649.

SMYTH

Joseph Smyth, Baltimore, 11 March 1818, referred to property in Jamaica, America and England belonging to John M. Smyth in the Parish of St. Anne's, deceased "left to me by the will of my late brother, deceased, Alexander McLeod of Dawkins Camanas Sugar Estate nine miles from Kingston, Spanish Town Road," and money belonging to him in England.

REF: Balto. Co. Wills, Liber 10, folio 438.

Martha Smyth, Kent Co., 22 Jan. 1723/4, "I give and bequeath unto my loving brother William Thomas one hundred pounds Sterling money now in England."

REF: Wills, Liber 18, folio 245.

SNELSON

John Snelson of London, Mariner, November 16, 1700, bequeathed his sister, Mary Ogle, £1 and to his wife Elizabeth Snelson all land in Maryland on the east side of Blackwater River.

REF: Dyer 9, Public Record Office, London.

SNOW

Justinian Snow died enroute to Maryland, consequently his rights to a manorial grant was given in 1640 to his brother and heir-at-law, Abel Snow, Gent., of the Cursitor's Office, London.

REF: Calvert Papers no. 119, Md. Hist. Soc., Balto; Patents Liber 1, folio 55, Liber 2, folio 116.

SOMERFIEL

Ralph Somerfiel and Hannah his wife presented their certificates from Kettesing of West Riding, Yorkshire, England, on the 6th day 5th mo. 1712 to the Quaker Meeting at West River.

REF: West River Quaker Records.

SOMERSET — LOWTHER — SMITH

Madame Maria Johana Smith, 3d wife of Captain Richard Smith of Calvert Co., and widow Colonel John Lowther of the English Army, was a daughter of Charles Somerset of Acton Park, Middlesex, who was grandson of Henry Somerset, 1st Earl of Worcester and on her maternal side a descendant of Thomas, Lord Arundel of Wardour. Her marriage to Richard Smith occurred about 1697 in Calvert Co.

REF: The Complete Peerage; Chancery, Liber PC, folio 849-50.

SOMERVILLE

John Somerville, younger son of James Somerville, Laird of Kennox, Ayrshire, Scotland, was involved in the Jacobean Uprising of 1715, captured and exiled to Maryland by the English. He was shipped in the "Good Speed" of Liverpool in 1716 to be sold into servitude for 7 years. He became a merchant of St. Mary's Co. and died in 1788 leaving issue.

REF: Md. Archives, vol. 25, pp. 347-349.

SORRELL

Richard Sorrell of Anne Arundel Co., died intestate in 1715 possessed of a large estate which resulted in litigation. Administration was granted to Thomas Robinson and Rachel his wife of Anne Arundel County. Edward Skydmore of Kent County claimed that the deceased had married his sister. The said John Sorrell was the son of John Sorrell and Dorothy his wife of Parish of Stebbing, Co. Essex, England. The English heirs of Great Baddow, Co. Essex, appointed John Bond of the Parish of St. Mary's Magdaline Permondsey, Co. Surrey, marine, their attorney.

REF: Testmentary Papers, Box 21, folder 20; Testamentary Proceedings, Liber 22, folio 338; Inventories & Accounts, Liber 33B, folio 144.

SOUTH

Alexander South, born in England, substituted for Capt. Nicholas Maccubin in accordance with the "Act to procure Troops for the American Army", passed March Session 1778.

REF: Militia List, Md. Hist. Soc., Balto.

SPAVOLD

James Spavold, Baltimore Co., M.D., July 26, 1772, "to the heirs of my brother Robert Spavold of Seaflwarth in Nottinghamshire in Great Britain; mentioned friend Mr. John Foss of Bawtry in Yorkshire.

REF: Wills, Liber 28, folio 896.

SPRIGG

Thomas Sprigg who settled in Maryland about 1650 after some years in Virginia was a native of Ketterling, Northamptonshire, where the Sprigg family had been seated for several generations. He gave the name of "Kettering" to one of his plantations and "Northampton" to another — both in Prince George's County.

STANLEY

Known as Charles Stanley of Chestertown, Md., on February 11, 1828, stated that he was born in Stockholm, Sweden, and wished his name changed to Carl Ludwig Standberg, likewise, those of his children.

REF: Laws of Maryland 1828, chapter 40.

STANSBURY

The emigrant ancestors of the Stansbury family of Baltimore County were Detmore Sternhergen and Rense his wife who emigrated in 1658 with their son Tobias. Social-economic factors would indicate that they were from Holland then under the States General of the Spanish Bourbon dynasty. The spelling underwent several changes such as Sternberge, Stanborrow, Stanber until it ultimately acquired the English orthography of Stansbury.

History records that a number of enterprizing Britishers settled in the Low Countries for commercial purposes and also history proves that the Dissenting English Pilgrims who disapproved of the formality and Ritualism of the Established Church settled in 1607-8 at Leyden, Holland.

After a few years dissatisfaction arose when their children acquired Dutch characteristics and were mating with Dutch youth. The leaders turned their thoughts to settlement under English sovereignty. When John and Sebastian Cabot explored the North American Continent in 1497 they claimed it for Queen Elizabeth I and named the undefined boundaries as "Virginia". Settlement had already been made at Roanoke Island in 1585 and on the James River in 1607. The Leyden dissenters obtained a Charter from the London Company and thus founded the Pilgrim Colony at Plymouth in 1620.

It is not unlikely that some of the English around Leyden or descendants of British tradesmen failed to sail on the initial voyage of the Mayflower to now Massachusetts. While no definite documentation has been found in the Dutch Archives, it is the belief of the Stansbury family historians that Detmar or Rense were scions of once English ancestry who had acquired Dutch cognomen after considerable Holland domicile.

The Stansbury name is Cornish of armorial heritage where the family had dwelt in Cornall around Taunerton for a number of years. The early Cornish orthography was Stanberge and Stanbery. The family was registrants at the Heraldric Visitations of Cornwall.

REF: Harliean Soc. Pub., vol. 9, p. 213; Vivian's Visitation of Cornwall, p. 443; British Museum mms 1164, folio 64, London.

STAPLES

John Staples, born May 18, 1754, at Islington, now part of London, England, landed in the Colonies in 1777 and enlisted at Annapolis in the Artillery; removed to Northampton Co., Penn.

REF: Revolutionary Pension Claim W4518, National Archives.

STEDMAN

Richard Stedman of Yearley Parish, Co. Southampton, England, married Aug. 29, 1744, Ann Kenison.

REF: Nottingham Quaker Meetings, Cecil Co.

STEELE

John Steele, Anne Arundel Co., Goldsmith, 20 Jan. 1721/2, "Whereas I have left me by my grandfather Fabean Steel of Great Britain, Gent., £230 Sterling....to my friend Cesare Ghiselin of City of Annapolis, Goldsmith....whereas my father left to me when he died one house and lot in Carlyle in Great Britain after the decease of my brother Bagean Steele Called and known by the name of Steele's Acre".

REF: Wills, Lilber 18, folio 122.

STEELMAN

John Hans Steelman and John his son of Cecil Co. were naturalized in 1695 by an Act of the General Assembly.

REF: Md. Archives, vol. 19, p. 281.

STEPHEN

Rev. John Stephen, Scotchman, settled in Maryland 1766 from the West Indies, and was rector of All Faith's Parish, St. Mary's Co.; died 1784, aged 43 years.

REF: Allen.

STEPHENSON

William Stephenson of St. George's Hundred, St. Mary's Co., emigrated from Tertudos with his wife (unnamed) and her children Christopher, Mary and Frances; he applied for landrights in 1654.

REF: Patents, Liber ABH, folio 396.

STERRITT

Stewart Sterritt, native of Londonderry, Ireland, born circa 1752, came to Frederick Co. with his father, James, and his brother, James, and served in the Militia of Frederick Co., during the Revolutionary War, later of Harrison Co., Ind.

REF: Revolutionary Pension Claim S31991, National Archives.

STEVENSON

Henry Stevenson (1721-1814), born in Ireland emigranted 1750 to Baltimore.

REF: Md. Hist. Mag., vol. 24, p. 14.

STEWART

Alexander Stewart, a Jacobite, was transported in 1747 to Maryland in irons. He was sold to Benedict Calvert for £9/6/- but "sympathetic friends purchased his freedom".

REF: The Jacobite Convicts, Md. Hist. Mag., vol. 1, pp. 346-352.

Anthony Stewart, Annapolis, Merchant, son of James Stewart of Edinburgh, Esq. Attorney to his Majesty's Courts of Exchequer, Scotland. In Maryland prior to the Revolution and owner of the famed Peggy Stewart of Tea-party fame.

REF: Register of All Hallow's Parish, Anne Arundel Co., p.146.

David Stewart of Glaslough, Co. Monaghan, Ireland, is stated to be the son of Sir John Stewart, Bart., and Isabella, daughter of Captain David Conyngham of Ballyhenny and Letterkenney. He was born Oct. 22, 1746, and emigrated to Maryland prior to 1774 with his kinsmen, David Plunket and David Hayfield.

REF: Bookplate of Redmon Conyngham Stewart, Md. Hist. Soc., Balto.

Edward Stewart of Millington, Kent Co., Md. emigrated from Scotland prior to the Revolution in which war he fought. He died about 1792. The family later changed the orthography to Stuart.

REF: Md. Hist. Mag., vol. 12, p. 390; Family Bible record.

George Stewart who figured as a defendant in the lawsuit instituted by Jonathan Rawlings was not a native of Maryland. Capt. John Ijams Sr., aged 66 of Anne Arundel Co., stated on July 3, 1778, that he had known the said George Stewart "since he came to America".

REF: Chancery Liber 14, folios 90, 105.

George Hume Steuart of Kilmadock, Perthshire, Scotland, settled about 1722 in Maryland and married Anne Digges of Warburton Manor, Prince George's Co.

REF: Memoirs of Dr. Richard Sprigg-Steuart (1797-1876); Clan Steuart-Stuart, by Gladys Melker, pub. 1970, p. 24.

William Stewart, native of Leeds, England, emigrated to Maryland and was a musican portrait painter; died in Western Maryland, April 17, 1824.

REF: Scharf's History of Western Maryland, p. 472.

William Stewart and his brother, Dr. Stewart of Annapolis in 1747 were brothers to David Stewart of Ballachalum, Nontieth, Scotland.

REF: Estate of Alexander Stewart, Jacobite of 1747, which was purchased by Benedict Calvert, see, Md. Hist. Mag., vol. 1, pp. 349-352.

STIER-CALVERT

Rosalie Eugenia Stier, daughter of Baron Henri Joseph Stier, Seigneur d'Artzelaer et Cleydael of Belgium, fled with her parents to Annapolis upon the approach of the Napoleonic Armies. In 1799 she married George Calvert, a direct descendant of five Barons of Baltimore and one of the *enfants d'armour* of Charles II of England.

REF: Newman's Heraldic Marylandiana; Calvert private papers.

STILLE

Axel Stille on July 22, 1661, was granted letters of denization. In 1674 when he was naturalized he declared that he was born "in the Kingdom of Sweadland" [Swedish settlements on the Delaware].

REF: Md. Archives, vol. 2, p. 400.

STIRLING

Thomas Stirling, Calvert Co., 24 January 1684/5, if my children died without issue then "my whole Estate of land and plantacons fall to the heirs of John Buchanan or James Bowlell in the Kingdom of Scotland".

REF: Wills, Liber 4, folio 150.

STOCK

Robert Stock and Tabitha his wife in 1712 brought their certificates from Horselewe Down, London, to the Quaker Meeting at West River.

REF: Quaker Notes, by Christopher Johnston, Md. Hist. Soc.

STOCKETT

The elder of the four Stockett brothers who settled in Maryland after their exile in France with Charles II is listed in the Visitation of Kent which carries the lineage to an ancestor to the time of Elizabeth who served at her court as Surveyor of the Works.

REF: Hasted's Kent, vol. 3, pp. 131-3; "Anne Arundel Gentry", vol. 2 and "Heraldic Marylandiana", published by Newman; All Hallow's Parish Register, Md. Hist. Soc.; Visitation of Kent, Harleian Soc. Pub., vol. 42, p. 184.

STONE

John Stone, a native of Germany and resident of Frederick Co., took the Oath of Abjuration on Sept. 1, 1765, and became a subject of Great Britain.

REF: Prv. Crt Judgements, Liber DD no. 9, folio 8.

Captain William Stone, 3d Governor Maryland and Lord of Poynton Manor, was granted power of attorney in 1647 by his nephew, Thomas Stone, of Cateaton Street, London.

REF: Visitation of London; Parish Register of Croston, Lancashire; The Stones of Poynton Manor, by Newman.

Hugh Heyes of Presbury, Cheshire, England, by his 1637 will bequeathed a cow to the son of "my cozen William Stone in Virginia". The said Stone was later Governor of Maryland. The testator also named his mother Alice Heyes.

REF: Va. Hist. Mag., vol. 15, p. 428.

William Stone of Baltimore Co., by his will dated Dec. 3, 1819, probated Oct. 27, 1821, stated that he was formerly of the Island of Bermuda. He married Hannah (Owings) Cockey, the widow of William Cockey who died 1775.

REF: Balto. Co. Wills, Liber 11, folio 318.

STONESTREET

Thomas Stonestreet, a redemptioner, who settled in Charles Co., with his wife Eleanor, about 1662, was of Bethersden, Co. Kent, England.

REF: Canterbury Marriages; Berry's Sussex Genealogies.

STORER

Arthur Storer, Calvert Co., Nov. 25, 1686, bequeathed property to his mother, Catherine Clarke (presumably of England), to "Joseph Clarke apotherary in Lough Bourrough in Lancashire 500 lbs. tob. to be sent him by my executor", also a legacy to Mr. Samuell Taylor, Druggist, at the Signe of the Greyhound within Newgate in London.

REF: Wills, Liber 6, folio 68.

STORK

Robert Stork and his wife Tabitha with certificate from the Horselews Down, London, were accepted into the community of Quakers of West River, on 2d day 11 mos. 1712.

REF: West River Quaker Records.

STORY

Walter Story, the progenitor of the family in Southern Maryland, was originally from London and was styled Merchant when he purchased a plantation in Charles County on Feb. 2, 1663/4 from Henry Pearre. Inference is rather strong that he was a younger son of James Story who in 1633 was a London haberdasher and who was an armorial registrar at the 1633 Herald's Visitation of London. The said James Story was the son of Walter Story of St. Ines, Co. Huntingdon.

REF: Charles Co. Deeds, Liber B no. 1, folio 259; 1633 Visitation of London, vol. 17, pub. by Harleian Soc., London.

STRACHAN

James Strachan, a Jacobite, was transported in 1747 to Maryland in irons.

REF: The Jacobite Convicts, Md. Hist. Mag., vol. 1, pp. 346-352.

STRIBY

The Rev. James Striby, born 1701, King's Co., Ireland, was rector of All Hallow's Parish, Anne Arundel Co., at the time of his death about 1743: both wives were Maryland maidens.

REF: All Hallow's Parish Register.

STRONG

"Here lyeth Interred the Body of Capt. James Strong of Stepney in the County of Midd: Marine, second son of Capt. Petter Strong. Departed this life ye 8 day of Jan. 1684, A . . . . . . yeare 2 months XI dayes".

REF: Lloyd Burying Grounds, Wye House, Talbot Co., Md.

STUART D'AUBIGNY

Alexander Stewart, Baron Stuart d'Aubigny, a Scottish exile in France supported the Young Pretender in his attempt to wrest the British Throne in

1743. He was captured and later transported to Maryland to be sold as a bonded servant. Ultimately he settled in Annapolis.

REF: Newman's Heraldic Marylandiana.

STURMAN

Richard Sturman one-time of Maryland, later of Westmoreland Co., Va., by will Mar. 5, 1668/9, devised land in Britain and named "brother Thomas Hall and his son Thomas Hall of London, Merchant, to be overseers of his estate.

REF: Westmoreland Co., Va. Wills, Liber 1668.

Thomas Sturman of Kent Isle, cooper, May 1640, deposed that he was aged 56, a native of Hadman Parish, Bucks, and had arrived in America on the "Sarah Elizabeth".

REF: Md. Archives, vol. 5, p. 181.

SUIRE

Edmund Suire, late of Leogne, Island of St. Domingo, but now of Baltimore Town, named his sister Louisa Laporte and mother in the Isle of St. Domingo. 11 Dec. 1798.

REF: Balto Co. Wills, Liber 6, folio 147.

SUMER

John Sumer on March 29, 1762, received the sacrament of the Reformed Congregation at Frederick Town and in accordance with the Act of George II (13th year), he took the Oath of Abjuration and became a naturalized subject.

REF: Prv. Crt Judgements, Liber DD no. 2, folio 187.

SUTHERLAND

John Sutherland, a native of Scotland, came to the Colonies in 1773 and settled in Prince George's Co., where he served in the Militia and also the 7th Maryland Regiment during the Revolution; removed to Washington Co., Penn.

REF: Revolutionary Pension Claim S 6173, National Archives.

SUTOR

"In Memory of our father J. Nicholas Sutor a native of Germany, born Dec. 4, 1756, died at Havre de Grace, Md. Mar. 23, 1831, in the 75 year of his age".

REF: Spesutia Church yard, Perryman, Baltimore Co.

SWALE

William Swale, St. Mary's Co., Gent., 12 Aug. 1728, "I give unto my loving Sister Elizabeth Honson (Howson) in Lambeth Parish in the County of Surry in the Kingdom of Great Britain the sum of £20".

REF: Wills, Liber 19, folio 490.

SWANN

Robert Swann of Annapolis, Oct. 7, 1763, "I give and bequeath unto my Nephews Christopher and Robert Johnston sons of my sister Jane Swann wife of John Johnston, deceased, in Moffat in that part of Great Britain called

Scotland the sum of two hundred pounds Sterling each; . . . unto my Cousin Robert Neilson Merchant in Paisley Street, Glasgow . . . unto the three eldest children of my sister Elissa Thompson, deceased, living nigh Dumfries in Scotland the sum of fifty pounds Sterling. . . I give and bequeath unto the Minister, Elders and Deacons of the Parish of Thothocall in that part of Great Britain called Scotland where I was born £100 Sterling for the maintenance of school in that parish".

REF: Wills, Liber 32, folio 152.

SWINEYARD

John Swineyard of Baltimore Co., Planter, "born under the Dominion of the King of France" was naturalized in 1724, by an Act of the Assembly.

REF: Md. Archives, vol. 38, p. 346.

SWORD

Humphry Sword, a Jacobite, captured in 1715 at Preston, Lancashire, and transported to Maryland for seven years of servitude, ran away.

REF: Md. Archives, vol. 25, pp. 347-349.

SWORMSTEDT

Christian Swormstedt of Calvert Co. "Chyrugeon a German by birth and borne out of her Majtys allegiance" was naturalized by act of the Assembly in 1710.

REF: Md. Archives, vol. 27, p. 578.

TABB

The Rev. Moses Tabb, a native of Ireland, was rector of Popular Hill Church, St. Mary's Co., died testate 1779.

REF: Rightmeyer's Maryland's Established Church.

TAILLOR

Sept. 9, 1709, "Thomas Taillor late of the Colony of Maryland in parts beyond the Seas but now of London in the Kingdom of Great Britain son of Thomas Taillor", for natural love and affections plus 5 shillings deeded to his son, John Taillor land on the Ridge in the Colony of Maryland of 600 improved acres, also 1800 acres and an additional 2000 acres including all negroes, stocks and household goods.

REF: Prov. Crt Deeds, Liber TY no. 4, folio 94.

TALBOT

Sir William Talbot, of St. Mary's Co. and Cartown, Co. Kildare, Ireland, Bart., Secretary of Maryland 1670-1673, was son of Garrett Talbot by Margaret, daughter of Henry Gaydon of Dublin, and nephew and heir of Sir Robert Talbot, Bart. who married Grace, daughter of George Calvert, 1st Baron of Baltimore.

REF: Complete Baronetage, vol. 1, p. 247.

William Talbott, Baltimore Co., Nov. 8, 1713, "I give and bequeath unto my Brother Thomas Talbott's children in Lancashire to them and their heirs forever. . . Melomdey" and the other called Middle Ridge both containing 600 acres.

REF: Wills, Liber 13, folio 642.

TALBOT—DARNALL

The Hon. Ann Talbot who married Henry Darnall of Prince George's Co., before Aug. 2, 1735, and became identified with "His Lordship's Kindness" was the daughter of John Talbot of Longford in the County of Salop, Esq. She was also the niece of the 13th *de juro* Earl of Shrewsbury and first cousin to the 14th Earl. The marriage settlement of Henry Darnall, the father of the groom, was £500, whereas the dowry of the bride was at least £90.

A deed which deserves clarification recorded in Prince George's Co., in 1735, however, would infer the bride to be the niece of the 14th Earl. "Henry Darnall, Gent., son and heir apparent of Henry Darnall of Prince George's Co., Ann Darnall wife of Henry Darnall and the Rt. Hon. George Earl of Strewsbury and John Talbot of Longford in the County of Shrewsbury, Esq." executed a tripartitie deed . . . "in consideration of a marriage sometime since had and solemnized between the said Henry Darnall and said Ann Darnall his present wife".

Gilbert Talbot, was first cousin and heir to Charles Talbot, 12th Earl of Shrewsbury; the said Charles died without issue in 1717. Gilbert, the heir-at-law, was a member of the Society of Jesus and ultimately became a priest of the Roman Catholic Church. He was never vested in the robes of the earldom nor assumed his noble prerogatives and was never recognized by the House of Lords. During his lifetime his brother and heir-at-law, George Talbot, was unofficially styled the Earl of Shrewsbury, but like his brother, Gilbert, was never seated by the House of Lords.

George Talbot, self-styled Earl of Shrewsbury, predeceased his brother Gilbert of Holy Orders and the *de jure* Earl. Edward Harley, Earl of Oxford, wrote that "George [Talbot] because his brother did not assume the title did pretend to it. His widow is so silly as to pretend to it, and suffered her three daughters to be called ladies, and put the Earl's coronet over the glasses and upon plate, but durst not put it upon the achievement (coat-of-arms) nor coach".

Gilbert, however, remained the *de jure* Earl until his death without issue in 1743. Thereupon his nephew, George, son of the aforesaid George Talbot, succeeded to the earldom on July 22, 1743. He was recognized by the House of Lords and vested in the robes as the 14th Earl of Shrewsbury. He likewise died without issue in 1787.

Ann Talbot, consort of Henry Darnall of "His Lordship Kindness" was therefore a niece of Gilbert the *de jure* 13th Earl of Shrewsbury and Earl of Waterford and first cousin to George, the 14th Earl. The citation in the 1735 deed of the Rt. Hon. George, being the 14th Earl of Shrewsbury was an assumed honor, although he was the heir-apparent, yet he never received the robes of investiture.

REF: Pr. Geo. Co. Deeds, Liber T, folio 305; The Complete Peerage (2d ed), vol. 11, pp. 725-751.

TALBURT

On Febr. 2, 1696, when John Talburt married Sarah Lockyer, he declared himself to be the son of Paul Talburt of Pockington, Yorks.

REF: Register of St. John's Piscataway, Transcript Md. Hist. Soc., Balto.

TAME

Edward Tame, a native Englishman, substituted for Dr. James Murray, in accordance with the "Act to procure Troops for the American Army", passed Marsh Session 1778.

REF: Militia List, Md. Hist. Soc., Balto.

TASKER

Thomas Tasker by his will of May 1679 and probated August 1700 in Calvert Co., stated: "I give my Mother Widdow Ann Tasker Ten pounds per annun during her natural life to be paid by Capt. Keye". No residence of his mother was cited, but probably London or environs, as he had accounts with Peggin, Hyde, Keye and Miller, Merchants of London.

Thomas Tasker at his death was one of the wealthy planters and merchants in Maryland and his children contracted marriages with the aristocratic families of that generation. He had arrived in Maryland during 1673 as a redemptioner under what circumstances research has not produced any definite reason.

The name Tasker does not appear in the 1633, 1634 or 1635 London Visitations nor is it listed among the armorial families in Burke. The arms on the tomb of Colonel Thomas Tasker (died 1768) in St. Anne's churchyard at Annapolis, according to Papworth's British Armorials, vol. 1, p. 155, is "Adams alias Tasker" and is impaled with that of Bladen.

REF: Wills, Liber 11, folio 137.

TAWERS

On May 1, 1704, a bill was endorsed for the naturalization of John Tawers [Jawert] of Cecil Co. Gent.

REF: Md. Archives, vol. 24, pp. 402, 410.

TAYLARD

William Taylard by his will, dated November 11, 1711, no county cited, devised his wife, Audry "all my reall Estate in the Kingdom of England and in the Province of Pensilv^a or Maryl^d and appointed his son-in-law, Richard Liuellan, to assist his widow in the administration of the estate.

REF: Wills, Liber 13, folio 338.

TAYLOR

Brian Taylor, Baltimore Co., 4 Dec. 1736, made a will in England before emigrating to Maryland and referred to "my Couzen Elizabeth Smith" who had his snuff box and "my Couzen Margaret Rogers may have a Gold Ring".

REF: Wills, Liber 21, folio 694.

Joseph Taylor of Prince George's Co., and patentee of "Taylor's Hall" in Baltimore Co., was deceased by 1725, when his brother, Benjamin Taylor of Warwick, England, and William Taylor of Theobalds of Hertfordshore, England, granted power of attorney to dispose of his estate.

REF: Balto Co. Deeds, Liber IS no. H, folio 189.

Philip Taylor of Accomac Co., Va., and later of Maryland, was son of Philip of Marden Parish, Herts. In May 1640 Philip Taylor Jr. deposed that he was aged 30 and gave his nativity as Marden Parish. He died before Sept. 29, 1649, leaving a widow who was born Jane Fenwick.

REF: Md. Archives, vol. 5, p. 220; Md. Hist. Mag., vol. 33, p. 280.

William Robeson Taylor, native of Gloucestershire, born 1746, but was raised near London, came to Baltimore at the age of 16, and served in the 7th Maryland Regiment, Revolutionary War; later of Ashe Co., N.C.

REF: Revolutionary Pension Claim S7687, National Archives.

TETTERSHALL
William Tettershall of Bretton Bay, St. Mary's Co., May 30, 1670, "And in Case my said Children shall chance to dye before they come of lawful age that then their Parts of the Said Estate to go & descend to my brother John Tettershall of Oddstocke in Wiltshire his oldest son for Ever".

REF: Wills, 1, folio 391.

THOMAS
Philip Thomas of Anne Arundel Co., by will of September 6, 1674, bequeathed the revenue of two houses in Bristol, England, to his wife during life and then to be sold and the proceeds divided equally among his children.

REF: Wills, Liber 2, folio 350.

William Thomas of St. Mary's Co., June 3, 1764, assigned three plantations including "Granall Walk" to Ann Callon of St. John Hacking Parish, Co. Middlesex, England. On Aug. 7, 1769, Ann Callon conveyed to Peter Wood of Charles Co.

REF: Chas. Co. Deeds, Liber O no. 3, folio 596.

THOMPSON
George Thompson, a Jacobite, captured at Preston, Lancashire, in 1715 and sold in Maryland for 7 years of servitude, petitioned for his freedom on August 3, 1721, which was denied.

REF: Md. Archives, vol. 34, p. 164.

Richard Thompson [Tomson], Isle of Kent, May 1640, deposed to be aged 27 years and a citizen of Norwich in Co. Norfolk.

REF: Md. Archives, vol. 5, p. 204.

"In memory of Richard W. Thompson a native of Dublin, Ireland, who departed this life Oct. 12th 1826, in the 51st year of his age".

REF: Tombstone Whitemarsh Churchyard, Talbot Co.

THOMSON
William Thomson, born May 22, 1735, the son of the Rev. Samuel Thomson, was ordained deacon and priest of the Church of England at the Bishop of London's Palace in Fullam in December 1759; he married at Lancaster, Penn., Susanna, the daughter of the Rev. George Ross, rector of St. Mary Anne's Parish, Cecil Co.

REF: St. Mary Anne's Parish Register, Cecil Co.

THORNBERRY
Jane Thornberry of the Clifts, Calvert Co., 16 Oct. 1702, "I give my loving sister in England Dorothy Thornberry all the rest of my estate".

REF: Wills, Liber 11, folio 246.

THORNBURGH

Rowland Thornburgh, Back River, Baltimore Co., July 25, 1695, "To descend unto the next a kin of the family of Thornburgh at Hampsfeild in Lancashire in England to them and theire heires lawfully begotten for Ever and failing this family aforesaid then the land to descend to the next a kin of the Thornburgh at Selsad in Kindale in Westmoreland in Old England".

REF: Wills, Liber 7, folio 200.

THOROLD

George Thorold, Anne Arundel Co., June 16, 1737, devised all estate in Prince George's and Anne Arundel Co., to friend Richard McColymeux of Charles Co., "except that part of my real estate in England formerly conveyed by deed duly executed to the Hon. Lord Cardigan".

REF: Wills, Liber 22, folio 527.

THOROWGOOD

Although the Thorowgood family is more closely identified with Virginia, several lived on the Eastern as well as the Western Shore and Cyprian Thorowgood was one of the Adventurers on the Ark and the Dove in 1634. Francis Thorowgood held office in Maryland and married a Maryland maiden. The family was settled in Co. Norfolk, but more remotely in Herts.

REF: Harleian Soc. Pub. vol. 14, p. 707; vol. 86, p. 220; Farrer's Monumental Brasses, pub. 1890; Branch of the Douglas Family with its Maryland & Virginia Connections, by Newman, pub. 1967; Harleian Soc. Pub. vol. 17, p. 286.

THRELKELD

John Threlkeld, clergyman, native of England, settled first in Virginia and later officiated at Prince George's Parish, Montgomery Co., Md., died in that county in 1783.

REF: Allen.

THURSTON

Thomas Thurston, Baltimore Co., 21 Dec. 1692, "If all my children died without issue...I give unto my brother Samuel his children to bee Equally divided amongst them living at the Towne called Thornberry in Gloucester".

REF: Wills, Liber 6, folio 22a.

THWAITES

George Thwaites of Baltimore Town, 15 Oct. 1816, "I give and bequeath to my Brother Thomas Thwaites now or lately of St. Giles Parish of West Minster in the Kingdom of Great Britain and to my Brother William Thwaites now or late of Leeds in Yorkshire and Kingdom of Great Britain and to my sisters Elizabeth Thwaites and Margaret Thwaites now or lately living in or near Kerby in York", residue of estate.

REF: Balto Co. Wills, Liber 10, folio 227.

THOM

Henrick Thom, a native of Germany and member of the Lutheran Church, subscribed to the Oath of Abjuration on Sept. 7, 1765, and became a British subject.

REF: Prov. Crt Judgement, Liber DD no. 9, folio 11.

TICK

William Tick in 1674 when he petitioned for naturalization stated that he was born "att Amsterdam in Holland under the Dominions of the states General of the united Provinces".

REF: Md. Archives, vol. 2, p. 400.

On April 19, 1669, William Ticke "late of Amsterdam Belonging to the states of Holland" was granted the rights of a free denizen.

REF: Md. Archives, vol. 5, p. 37.

TILGHMAN

Dr. Richard Tilghman, the Emigrant, whose plantation "The Hermitage" in Queen Anne's Co. is well known, was of Snodland, Co. Kent, though at the time of his emigration he was styled "Citizen and Chirurgeon of London". He was the son of Oswald Tilghman of Snodland. When he was granted seigniory by Lord Baltimore, he named his manor "Canterbury", the cradle of his Christian faith in his native county.

Samuel Tilghman, his kinsman, was appointed Admiral of Maryland by Lord Baltimore, and was granted in 1659 manorial rights on "Tilghman's Fortune". About 1660 he was styled of Ratcliffe [Lancaster], Eng., ship captain", when he filed suits in Maryland and named an attorney.

REF: Letters between the English and American branches of the Tilghman family 1697-1764, Md. Hist. Magazine, vol. 33; Register of All Saint's Parish, Snodland; 1574 Visitation of Kent; Harleian Soc. Pub. vol. 42, p. 37; Md. Hist. Magazine, vol. 23, p. 36.

TILLINGEN

George Tillingen of Frederick Co. was naturalized a British subject in April 1763, under the Act of George II (13th year) after subscribing to the Oath of Abjuration and filing certification that he had received the sacrament of the Church of England at St. Anne's, Annapolis, on Apr. 13th.

REF: Prov. Crt Judgements, Liber DD no. 3, folio 128-9.

TOADVIN

Nicola Toadvin [Todvine] who settled in Somerset Co. prior to 1675 from all circumstances was a native of the Channel Islands. His racial background was therefore French, though the Islands had been English possessions since the Norman Conquest. In 1682 he gave the name of "Gernsey" (sic) to his plantation and in 1694 by another grant from the Lord Proprietary he gave the name of "Jersey".

REF: Patents Liber CB no. 2, folio 540; Liber B no. 23, folio 50.

TODD

Thomas Todd of Baltimore Co., by his will dated Feb. 26, 1675/6, devised his wife, Anne, "one parcel of land lying in old England which the said Robert Gorsedy is now possessed of". His wife also was bequeathed £176 Sterling in the possession of Robert Gorsedy.

REF: Wills, Liber 5, folio 227.

TOLSON

"Francis Tolson borne at Wood Hall in Cumberland in Bright Church parrish the son of Henry Tolson, Esq., Was Joynd in holy Mattrimony to Mary Clark Daughter to Robert Clark this pish Sept. 22d 1707".

REF: Register of St. John's Piscataway Parish, Pr. Geo. Co., transcript of, Md. Hist. Soc., Balto, folio 265; Visitation of Cumberland, by Foster, p. 154.

Thomas Tolson, of London, Merchant, received 100 acres from the Lord Proprietary 1664.

REF: Patents, Liber 7, folio 526.

TORESON

On July 29, 1661, Andrew Toreson "late of New Amstell and Subject to the Crowne of Sweden" was issued letters of denization.

REF: Md. Archives, vol. 3, pp. 429-430.

TOULSON

Andrew Toulson of Baltimore Co. in 1671 declared himself a native of Swedeland [Swedish settlements on the Delaware and Schuyekill Rivers].

REF: Md. Archives, vol. 2, p. 282.

TOWNLEY

Edmund Townley who emigrated to Maryland prior to 1772 appears as the fourth son of Francis Townley of Littleton, Co. Middlesex, and Catharine, daughter of Thomas Forster of Hunsdon, Co. Hertford, one of the Justices of the King's Bench, in the 1634 Visitation of Middlesex, England. Entitled to Townley and Ruxton Arms.

REF: Harleian Soc. Pub. vol. 64. p. 170.

Francis Townley, wife of the Rev. James Wootton of Ogburn St. George in Wiltshire, England, in 1731 became one of the coheiresses of her sister, Mary Rogers, wife of William Rogers of Annapolis, formerly Mary Contee of Charles County, widow.

REF: Chas. Co. Deeds.

TOWNSEND

Henry Townsend, a subject of Great Britain, on May 17, 1791, declared himself a Christian and subscribed to the Oath of Naturalization. County domicile not cited.

REF: Council Proceedings, Md. Archives, vol. 72, p. 194.

TRIMBLE

Matthew Trimble, native of Co. Tyrone, Ireland, resided in United States for 42 years, died Dec. 26, 1858, aged 56 years.

REF: Congressional Cemetery, Washington, D.C.

TRUMAN

Entries of the births of the Truman brothers' ancestry who settled in Maryland are found in the register of Godling Parish, Nottinghamshire, England.

REF: Original Parish Register, England.

TRUMAN-GREENE

Charles Greene of King's Lynn, Co. Norfolk, Esq., Apothecary and Elizabeth his wife, one of the daughters of James Truman, late of the Province of Maryland, Gent., and one of the legatees of Thomas Truman and Nathaniel Truman, both late of Calvert Co., Md., on Sept. 17, 1697, conveyed their inheritance to Thomas Greenfield of Prince George's Co. Robert Sparrow, Mayor of King's Lynn, witnessed and certified to the identity of the grantors.

REF: Pr. Geo. Co. Deeds, Liber A, folio 97.

TURNER

Thomas Turner, St. Winifred, St. Mary's Co., Oct. 2, 1662, "Whereas there is an Estate Due to me in the Kingdom of England & lying in several parishes about and in Essex (as may appear by my father's will). . . I give to my Sonne Thomas Turner".

REF: Wills, Liber 1, folio 167.

Thomas Turner of Anne Arundel Co. in 1671 upon naturalization declared that he was born in Holland under the Dominion of the States General.

REF: Md. Archives, vol. 2, p. 282.

Thomas Turner presented his certificate from England in 1703 to the Quaker Meeting at West River.

REF: Transcripts by Christopher Johnston, Md. Hist. Soc., p. 164.

UBBEN

Barnard Ubben "Subject to the States of Holland having transported himselfe wife and children" was issued on February 17, 1662/3, patent of Denization.

REF: Md. Archives, vol. 3, p. 470.

UNDERWOOD

Anthony Underwood clerk to Barrister Robert Rideley on March 1, 1687, declared at court that he served councilors-at-law at Gray's Inn prior to his Maryland settlement. The family was registrants at the 1633-35 Visitation of London.

REF: Harleian Soc. Pub., vol. 17, p. 303.

URINSON

On July 29, 1661, John Urinson "late of New Amstell and Subject of the Crowne of Sweden" was issued letters of denization.

REF: Md. Archives, vol. 3, pp. 429-430.

URY

Michael Ury "a Greek" of Prince George's Co., was naturalized in 1725, by an Act of the Assembly.

REF: Md. Archives, vol. 38, p. 377.

VALLETTE

Elie Vallette, a German Protestant, on 22 April 1764, received the sacrament of the Church of England at Annapolis, and subscribed to the Oath of Abjuration and thus became a British subject.

REF: Prov. Crt Judgements, Liber DD no. 5, folio 282, 284.

VAN BEBBER

Henry van Bebber, Cecil Co., 28 Apr. 1720, declared that he made a will in Holland before emigrating to Maryland.

REF: Wills, Liber 21, folio 645.

In March 1701/2, the act and fee for naturalization of Isaack Van Bebber, Gent., of Cecil Co., born of Dutch parents, came before the Lower House.

REF: Md. Archives, vol. 24, pp. 253, 280.

In March 1701/2, the act and fee for the naturalization of Mathias Van Bebber, Mercht, born of Dutch parents, came before the Lower House.

REF: Md. Archives, vol. 24, pp. 253, 280.

VAN BURKELO
Herman Van Burkelo of Cecil Co. was naturalized in 1694, by an Act of the General Assembly.

REF: Md. Archives, vol. 19, pp. 85, 103.

VANDENBUSSCHE
Peter Vandenbussche, formerly of Cape Francois, Domonican refugee to Baltimore about 1793.

REF: Hartridge.

VANDERHEYDEN
In 1692 an act was passed by the Assembly to naturalize Mathias Vanderheyden of Cecil Co.

REF: Md. Archives, vol. 13, p. 536.

VAN SWERINGEN
Garret van Sweringen in 1669 upon petition for naturalization stated that he "was born in Reensterswan in Holland under the Dominion of the states Generall of the united Provinces and that his daughter, Elizabeth, and son, Zachariah, were "born at Newanstell in Delaware Bay then under the Government of the States Generall".

REF: Md. Archives, vol. 2, p. 205.

VARLOW
James Varlow, Calvert Co., 14 Nov. 1676, "I give and bequeath unto James Varlow the son of Philip Varlow of the Citty of Norwidge one tract of land called Sewell's Point lyeing in the County of Kent within this Province".

REF: Wills, Liber 5, folio 117.

VAYRAUD
M. R. Vayraud, a subject of the King of France, on Nov. 7, 1791, declared himself a Christian and subscribed to the Oath of Naturalization. County domicile not stated.

REF: Council Proceedings, Md. Archives, vol. 72, p. 233.

VERBRACK
At 1684 Assembly an act was introduced for the Naturalization of Nicholas Verbrack.

REF: Md. Archives, vol. 13, p. 126.

VICTOR
Frederick Victor of Annapolis, Gent., "a foreigner of the Protestant or Reformed Religion" was naturalized in 1762.

REF: Md. Archives, vol. 48, p. 206.

VON SCHMIDT

Marianna, born 1775, died Apr. 19, 1847, wife of Peter von Schmidt, both natives of Courtland, Russia.

REF: Congressional Cemetery, Washington, D.C.

WADE

John Wade, Chirurgeon, Sept. 4, 1658, "I give unto my Son Edward Wade and his heirs all and whatsoever did belong to me or Mary my wife given unto us and to our heirs by Edward Attkins of Chilvercoton, Warwickshire as will appear by a Will and deed of Guift Intrusted in the hands of Mr. George Warde lieving in Chilverscoton Street at the Sign of the Sunn"; mentioned brother William Wade "who Liveth in Cecill in Warwickshire". The testator died at sea.

REF: Wills, Liber 1, folio 101.

Zachary Wade of Charles Co., named his 1200-acre plantation "Market Overton" after his native parish in Rutlandshire, Eng.

REF: Patents, Liber 5, folios 170, 262.

WALKER

Rev. Francis Walker, born in Scotland, came to Maryland from Ireland, rector of South Sassafras Parish, Kent, 1784; William and Mary in Charles Co. 1786; St. Andrews Parish, St. Mary's Co. 1790, and Christ Church Parish, Calvert Co., 1797; and St. Andrew's Parish, St. Mary's Co. 1803.

REF: Allen.

John Walker, born Bermuda, May 1782, died Washington, Jan. 1845.

REF: Congressional Cemetery, Washington, D.C.

William Walker, native of Co. Donegal, Ireland, died Dec. 2, 1816, aged circa 47 years.

REF: Congressional Cemetery, Washington, D.C.

William Walker from Raby, Co. Durham, England, in 1711 presented his certificate to the Quaker Meeting at West River.

REF: Quakers Transcripts, by Christopher Johnston, p. 168, Md. Hist. Soc., p. 168.

WALLIS

John Wallis, Somerset Co., 3 July 1685, declared himself "late of the Kingdom of Ireland and now Monokin River in the Province of Maryland".

REF: Wills, Liber 4, folio 169.

WARD

Matthew Ward of Cecil Co., was the son of Francis Ward, of South Walsham, Co. Norfolk, Gent., who was admitted to Gray's Inn Apr. 20, 1657.

REF: Register of Gray's Inn, folio 282; Md. Archives, vol. 51, p. xiv.

WARDROP

John Wardop of All Hallow's Staining, England, and Calvert Co., named his nephew Andrew Whyte in his will of Sept. 2, 1754, the house in Lower Marlborough, Calvert Co., his sister, Jean Kelly, and her three youngest children; John and Jean Holden near Dundee; niece Jean Symmes and nephews Alexander and Andrew Symmes, children of the testator's sister, Jean Symmes.

REF: Public Record Office, London, Legard 288.

WARING

Sampson Waring of Calvert Co., was a registrant of the 1623 Visitation of Salop, the ancestral seat being Woodcote near Shrewsbury.

REF: Harleian Soc. Pub., vol. 28, p. 486; Newman's Heraldic Marylandiana.

WARREN

Humphrey Warren of Charles Co., the Colonist, was a merchant of London prior to his settlement in Maryland where he likewise traded as a merchant. On Jan. 14, 1660/1, "Humphrey Warren of London, Merchant" gave power of attorney to Captain Nicholas Guyther to collect debts due him in Maryland. He died in 1671, and was of the ancient family of Wood Plumpton Parish, Lancashire, and also Stockport, Cheshire.

REF: Visitations of Cheshire 1580, 1612, 1663; Watson's Ancient Earls of Warren and Surrey, pub. 1782; Md. Archives, vol. 41, p. 437; Newman's Charles County Gentry, pub. 1940.

WASSE

James Wasse, Citizen and Chururgeon of London, purchased Ratcliffe Manor, from Robert Morris and Martha his wife, in August 1674.

REF: Patents, Libers 15, folio 286, 19, folio 593.

WATERS

James Waters, Charles Co., Oct. 3, 1740, if his children married a Protestant their devises were to become null and void, "...for Want of Such Heirs to the Name of Waters that any Relation of that to them and their heirs for Ever living [in] County Sloughah in the West of Ireland".

REF: Wills, Liber 22, folio 295.

Richard Waters of Somerset Co. by his 1720 will devised his sons, Richard and Littleton, £250 out of the estate in England left the said Richard Waters by his uncle, William Marriott, late of Towcester [Morthamptonshire] then in the hands of William Cooper.

REF: Wills, Liber 16, folio 201, Hall of Records; Pub. Rec. Office Marlborough 227, London.

WATERTON

John Waterton, Baltimore Co., Gent., June 1, 1682, "to my two Nephews in ye Isle Weight in ye Kingdom of England all my Lands and housing equally estate being in Hampshire".

REF: Wills, Liber 4, folio 85.

WATTS

Richard Watts, St. Mary's Co., Dec. 2, 1771, "...unto my son Richard Watts a tract of land and house in or near Brigham in the County of Cumberland in Old England the deed of which Land and Houses in and near Brigham, Brother William Watts has in his possession".

REF: Wills, Liber 38, folio 702.

Thomas Watts of "Perth in Perthshire in Scotland in the Kingdom of Great Britain" devised his estate "unto Elizabeth Inch daughter of John Inch of the City of Annapolis", Silversmith. Jan. 4, 1760.

REF: Wills, Liber 31, folio 85.

WAYNE

On Dec. 23, 1776, John Wayne, native of Great Britain, then of Balto Co., near Joppa, "attached to the cause of Liberty" was recommended for lieutenant of the Maryland forces.

REF: Md. Archives, vol. 12, p. 549.

WEBB

John Webb, Talbot Co., Sept. 20, 1678, "...Doe hereby give and Bequeath unto my Deare Mother Anne Webb in Banbury in Oxford Shire in Old England".

REF: Wills, Liber 9, folio 113.

Peter Webb, late Merchant of London, son of Paddington Webb of Little Baddow, Co. Essex, England, married July 6, 1704, at Choptank Quaker Meeting House, Sarah Stevens, daughter of William and Sarah Stevens.

REF: St. Peter's Parish Register, Cecil Co.

WEEDON

James Weedon of Pocomoke by his will proved Somerset Co., 1670, bequeathed property to his brother, William Weedon, of England, Gent., and appointed said brother one of the executors of his estate; the testator possessed "Nonsuch House" on London Bridge.

REF: Wills, Liber 1, folio 478.

WEEKLER

Frederick Weekler, born March 6, 1818, at Wurtenborg, Germany, November 6, 1818, died June 29, 1871, Boonsboro.

REF: Gravestone, Boonesboror, Md.

WEISENTHAL

Charles Frederick Weisenthal, Physician, of Baltimore Town, "born in Germany" was naturalized in 1771. Surgeon to Gen. Smallwood's Regt. Feb. to Dec. 1776.

REF: Md. Archives, vol. 63, p. 281; Heitman.

WELLER

Jacob Weller on Apr. 15, 1761, subscribed to the Oath of Fidelity and declared that he was a German Protestant, a "Minonist" [Minorite] and professed the Christian faith, as prescribed by the Act of George II (13th year), thus he was declared a British subject.

REF: Prov. Crt Judgements, Liber DD no. 1, folio 188.

WELSH

Martin Welsh by his will of Balto Co. dated Sept. 12, 1797, declared himself a native or Ireland.

REF: Balto Co. Wills, Liber 6, folio 25.

WELTY

John Welty, "native of Eppingen, Germany", died Jan. 16, 1817, aged 94 years.

REF: St. Joseph Catholic Churchyard, Emmitsburg, Md.

WEST

"These are to certifie whom (it may) concern That the Bearer hereof Stephen West son of John West of the parish of Horton in the County of Bucks, Gent. (who hath an estate here of one hundred pounds p annum or upwards) was born and educated in our said Parish of Horton and that during the time he was amongst us he was always modest in behaviour sober and civill in his life and conversation, a frequenter of the Church of England, as now be . . .law established, and generally. . .our Neighbourhood and that he never was married or contracted to any. . .to our knowledge and that we do give this testimonial to no other than to do him Justice. Witness our hand this first day of August Dom 1711". Signed by the Vestry of Horton Parish.

REF: Parchment in possession of descendants.

WHEELER

On July 29, 1661, John Wheeler "late of New Amstell and Subject of the Crowne of Sweden" was issued letters of denization.

REF: Md. Archives, vol. 3, pp. 429-430.

WHETCROFT

James Whetcroft, a subject of Great Britain, on Sept. 3, 1793, declared himself a Christian and subscribed to the Oath of Naturalization. County domicile not cited.

REF: Council Proceedings, Md. Archives, vol. 72, p. 347.

WHETENHALL

John Whetenhall of St. Mary's Co., Gent., was of East Peckham, Co., Kent, and a descendant of Sir Henry Whetenhall, knighted 1609 by James I. By his will of 1750 he bequeathed personalty to his kinsman, Henry Jerningham. The latter is placed as the nephew of Sir George Jerningham, of Co. Norfolk, Bart.

John Whetenhall had interest in the project of Charles Carroll 2d to receive a large grant from the King of France in Louisiana embracing what is now the State of Arkansas and over-lapping territory. They were to establish a sovereign State restricted solely to members of the Roman Catholic faith subject to the King of France. Carroll expected to receive a French title of nobility and be made absolute ruler of the State.

REF: Wills, Liber 28, folio 20; Harleian Soc. Pub., vol. 54, pp. 114, 178.

WHIPS

Elizabeth Whips, Calvert Co., widow, November 11, 1729, "I give unto my younger Brother and Sister William and Jane Madcaff Living in Yorkshear in Winsht all in the Upper part of Yorkshear near Askring all my Estate" except certain legacies expressed.

REF: Wills, Liber 19, folio 855.

WHITE

Andrew White, subject of Great Britain, on Aug. 10, 1790, declared himself a Christian, and subscribed to the Oath of Naturalization. County domicile not noted.

REF: Council Proceedings, Md. Archives, vol. 72, p. 132.

Jerome Whyte, Surveyor General of Maryland and member of His Lordship's Council, named his manor, granted in 1662, "Portland" commemorating the dignity and honour of his maternal grandfather, Richard Weston, Earl of Portland, KG, Lord High Treasurer under Charles I. He was son of Sir Richard White, of Hutton, Knt, who with his consort is buried in the Church of Santa Maria Maggiore, Rome, being exiles from Puritan tyranny.

REF: 1634 Visitation of Essex, Harleian Soc. Publ., vol. 13, p. 521; Complete Peerage; Berry's Essex Pedigrees.

WHITMORE

Michael Whitmore became a naturalized subject Sept. 10, 1762, after subscribing to the Oath of Abjuration under the Act of George II (13th).

REF: Prov. Crt Judgements, Liber DD no. 2, folio 89.

WHITTINGHAM

Heber Whittingham of Somerset Co., Md. by his will 1749 styled himself a Merchant, late of Moorsborough, Parish of Middlewick [Cheshire] England, and also referred to property left him by Gilbert Symkin in Co. Cornwall.

REF: Wills, Liber 27, folio 150.

WIDMEYER

Dr. Michael Widmeyer, born Nov. 1711 in the City of Marchgroeningen in Wurttemberg, Markfroningen Ludwigsburg), married May 3, 1740, his surviving widow; died Mar. 18, 1778, of dropsy.

REF: Evangelical Lutheran Church, Fred.

WILDMAN

John Wildman, Worcester Co., Md., declared himself of "Parrish of Stephney and County of Middlesex, Weaver", 3 Feb. 1732/3.

REF: Wills, Liber 24, folio 43.

WILKINSON

Thomas Wilkinson, a native of Newcastle-on-Tyne, County Northumberland, England, died Washington County, December 31, 1877.

REF: Gravestone, Rose Hill Cemetery, Cumberland.

The Rev. William Wilkinson, the first Anglican clergyman to officiate in Maryland, was the son of the Rev. Gabriel Wilkinson of Yorkshire and onetime vicar of Woodburne, Bucks.

REF: The Maryland Dents, by Newman, pub. 1963, p. 7.

WILLIAMS

Joseph Williams sailed from Bristol for Maryland between 1663-79.

REF: Bristol & America p. 105 (11).

Ralph Williams, 13 Aug. 1672, "Ralph Williams of Bristoll Merchant now Resident in the County of Anne Arundell. . . unto my youngest Daughter Rebecca Williams now resident in Bristoll £400. . . money shall be comitted unto the Custody of my Loving Cousen Thomas Day of Bristoll Merchant. . . unto my married daughter Elizabeth Millen Living in London residue of estate. . . if daughter Rebecca dies before coming of age or marriage then my Cousen John Willcoks of Bristoll his children. . . poor of Chepstow Parish £10".

REF: Wills, Liber 1, folio 599.

WILLOUGHBY

John Willoughby, Anne Arundel Co., 2 Jan. 1702/3, "I give and bequeath £80 Sterling to my sister and brother in England and their representatives".

REF: Wills, Liber 11, folio 224.

WILSON

Rev. Thomas Wilson, 1st minister of Manokin Presbyterian Church, was a member of the Presbytery of Laggon, North Ireland, and minister of the Congregation at Killybegs, Donegal, Ireland.

REF: Torrence's, Old Somerset, p. 227.

WINCHESTER

William Winchester is reputed to have been born in London, Eng., Dec. 22, 1710, emigrated to Baltimore Co., and in 1747 married Lydia, daughter of Edward Richards of Baltimore Co. He died Sept. 2, 1790, at White Level, Westminster, Md.

REF: Family records.

WINTER

Martin Winter, Balto Co., on Sept. 14, 1761, subscribed to the Oath of Abjuration after having proved that he had taken the sacrament of the Church of England at St. Anne's, Annapolis, and thus became a naturalized subject in accordance with the Act of George II (13th year).

REF: Prov. Crt Judgement, Liber DD no. 1, folio 497.

James Winters of Baltimore Town, Aug. 10, 1765, ". . . unto my loving wife Anne Winters all my estate both real and personal to her heirs and assigns forever she paying unto my loving mother, Mary Winters, Widow of London, the sum of £20 Sterling if she be living at time of my death".

REF: Wills, Liber 34, folio 217.

WINTOUR

Frederick and Edward Wintour, brothers, were youthful Adventurers on the Ark and the Dove and were sons of Lady Ann Wintour, according to Lord Baltimore. By being sons of Lady Ann, it would indicate that she was widowed at the time of the youths' sailing.

REF: The Flowering of the Maryland Palatinate, by Newman, p. 271; Relation to Maryland, reprinted in "Narratives of Early Maryland, by Hll, p. 101.

Captain Robert Wintour, Esq. who died testate 1638 in St. Mary's Co. is placed as the son of Sir Edward Wintour of Lydney, Gloucestershire, Knt. and Lady Ann Wintour, daughter of Edward Somerset, Earl of Worcester.

His title of "Captain" may imply an officer of the Provincial forces or from a maritime career.*

According to Sir John Coke, Captain Robert Wintour was in "charge of the Companie" [Adventurers] of the Ark and the Dove. In my "Flowering of the Maryland Palatinate" I interpreted the statement as he was Captain of the Ark, particularly when he was addressed as Captain. John D. Kreugler in his "To Live Like Princes", pub. by the Enoch Pratt Free Library, 1976, throws a different light on the statement, asserting that Robert Wintour was merely in charge of certain formalities of the Adventurers prior to sailing. His interpretation reflects certain truths.

Captain Wintour was the author of "A Short Treatise sett downe in a letter written by R. W. to his worthy friend C. J. R. Concerning the new plantation now ercting under the Right Hoble the Lord Baltemore in Maryland". The original Treatise of 16 pages is deposited in the Enoch Pratt Library, Balto.

REF: "The Flowering of the Maryland Palatinate, by Newman; "To Live Like Princes" by Kreuger.

WISEMAN

Robert Wiseman, one of the Gentlemen of Fashion on the Ark, was a son to Sir Thomas Wiseman, of Canfield, Essex, Knt., dubbed by James I at Whitehall 1604.

REF: Relation of Maryland, pub. 1635 in London; Narrative of Early Maryland (1633-1684), pub. by Chas. Scribner, 1910; Visitation of Essex, Harleian Soc. Pub., vol. 13, p. 326.

NOTE: The aforesaid references inadvertently states Henry Wiseman instead of Robert Wiseman.

WOLF

In October 1727 a bill was introduced in the Assembly for the naturalization of John Wolf of Annapolis, Shoemaker, Hannah Wolf his wife, and their children — Peter, Annelesa and Hannah — also for Maudlin Wolf spinster and Garrett Wolf of Annapolis, Shoemaker, "being borne in Germany under the Domion of the Emperour".

REF: Md. Archives, vol. 36, pp. 24, 25, 38; vol. 38, p. 406.

WOLSELEY

Mary Wolseley, the wife of Philip Calvert, youngest son of George, 1st Baron of Baltimore, was daughter to Sir Thomas Wolseley, Knt., (dubbed 1617), of Wolseley, Staffordshire, and Helen Broughton, daughter of Humphrey Broughton of Longdown, Staffordshire.

Mary Wolseley, wife to Roger Brooke (1637-1700), was a niece of the aforesaid Madame Calvert and daughter of Walter Wolseley, Esq., of Staffordshire and Ravenston, Leicestershire, son to Sir Thomas, aforesaid.

REF: Visitation of Staffordshire, Harleian Soc. Pub., vol. 63, p. 252; Md. Hist. Mag., vol. 9, p. 113.

WOOD

Joseph Wood who married Francina, daughter of Augustine Herman of Bohemia Manor, Cecil Co., and who died in New Castle, Del. 1721, was the son and heir of William Wood of Darby, County Chester, Penn. The said William Wood while in England purchased 500 acres from William Penn. His descendants settled in Cecil Co., Md.

REF: Deeds, Liber A, folio 108, Chester Co., Penn.

WOODSTOCK

19 January 1792. On Friday 6th inst. died in this city (Annapolis) Mr. Henry Woodstock in his 56th year. He was a native of England, but had resided in America from early manhood.

REF: Md. Gazette, Annapolis.

WOODWARD

Abraham Woodward, Anne Arundel Co., Jan. 26, 1744, devised his son, William, all interest he maintained in Great Britain which came from the estate of his deceased father, William Woodward, of Britain.

REF: Wills, Liber 24, folio 7.

William Woodward of Annapolis, Gent., whose wife was Jane – – – –, and Mary Holmes of Newington Butts, Co. Surrey, England, were children and heirs to their mother, Mary Woodward, late of London, and sister to Amos Garrett, late of Annapolis, Merchant. On February 10, 1764, William Woodward of Annapolis as attorney for his sister, Mary Holmes, and his aunts conveyed their interest in "Land of Goshen" and "Common Delight" plantations in Anne Arundel Co.

REF: Prov. Crt Deeds, Liber DD no. 3, folio 378.

WOOTON, WOTTON

The Rev. James Wotton of Ogburn St. George, Wiltshire, Eng., whose wife was Frances Townley, was brother-in-law to Mary (Townley) Contee-Rogers and Judith (Townley) Brice of Charles Co., per deed of Dec. 13, 1731.

REF: Charles Co. Deeds.

WRIGHT

Arthur Wright, Kent Isle, 23 Aug. 1676, "I give and bequeath unto my three Sisters I have in England Alice, Anne and Barbary the Summe of fifteen pounds".

REF: Wills, Liber 5, folio 292.

Barbara Wright, Baltimore Co., widow, Feb. 14, 1670/1, "...unto my well beloved Niece Margaret Penry of the Parish of St. Andrews in Glamorganshire".

REF: Wills, Liber 1, folio 445.

Francis Wright, Baltimore Co., July 25, 1666, "I will and bequeath unto my Younger Brother Raphael Wright of Bovill in the Parish of St. Andrews Glamorganshire in Wales my house and lands known by the name of Clayfall in the County of Baltimore".

REF: Wills, Liber 1, folio 298.

John Wright, executor of the estate of Jonas Pennington, stated in 1817, that he, John Wright, was a native of Ireland, aged 63, naturalized in Baltimore Co., and came to America as early as 1789.

REF: Chancery papers no. 3951.

Nathaniel Wright with his brother, Solomon, later of Talbot and Queen Anne's Counties, was transported to Maryland prior to 1673. A Nathaniel Wright, baptized Jan. 25, 1623/4, was listed as the third son of Nathaniel Wright Sr., London Merchant, the latter being a registrant at the 1635 Visitation of London.

Fairclough appeared as a Christian name in the Wright family and it may be more than coincidence that Affabell Fairclough was likewise a registrant at the 1635 London Visitation.

The origin of the Wright family was Co. Essex, while the origin of the Fairclough family was Hertfordshire.

REF: Harleian Soc. Pub., vol. 17, p. 371; vol. 92, p. 156.

WYNE

Francis Wyne of Charles Co., by will November 14, 1681, devised his son, Henry Wynne, of London, estates at Prithley, Northamptonshire, England. His widow married Henry Hawkins and at her death bequeathed legacies to her Wynne grandchildren in England.

REF: Wills, Liber 2, folio 173.

WYVILL

Marmaduke Wyvill who settled in St. James' Parish, Anne Arundel Co., in 1774 became the rightful heir to Sir Marmaduke Wyvill, Bart., who died unmarried on February 23, 1774. The baronetcy remains dormant, inasmuch as the American claimants have not proved their rights and honours to the English courts.

The 1965 edition of Debrett states that the rightful owner of one of Britain's oldest titles is probably an American, Newton d'Arcy Wyvill, of Winchester, Va. "If he takes steps to prove his right to the title, he will rank as our 10th most senior baronet". His descent can be traced to Sir Richard Wyvill who was slain in 1461 during the War of the Roses.

REF: The Complete Baronetabe.

YATE

George Yate, Deputy Surveyor of Anne Arundel Co., who died testate 1691, was of the Yate of Buckland, Berks, the lineage of which was listed in the 1665 Visitation of Berks. A branch of the Yate of Buckland through Samuel Yate, the registrant, was also listed at the 1633 Visitation of London, with the Yate arms and quartering.

REF: REF: Harleian Soc. Pub. (Berks Visitation); vol. 52.

YEEDON

George Yeedon, St. Mary's Co., 1 September 1685 named his brother Thomas Yeedon "living att Gallway in Ireland".

REF: Wills, Liber 4, folio 159.

YOUALL

Thomas Youall of Kent Isle, May 20, 1640, deposed aged 22 and that he was a native of Willbarsonne [Wilbarston] Parish, Northamptonshire.

REF: Md. Archives, vol. 5, p. 189.

YOUNG

Rebecca Young on Mar. 20, 1793, produced her certificate to the Baltimore Meeting of Quakers from Coalbrookedate, Shropshire, England.

REF: Md. Hist. Magazine, vol. 4, p. 21.

ZENGER

John Peter Zenger of Kent Co., "an alien Borne in the upper palatinate on the Rhine" was naturalized in 1720 by an Act of the Assembly.

REF: Md. Archives, vol. 38, p. 277.

ZIMMERMANN

Jacob Zimmermann, born Feb. 25, 1722, in Eckershausen on the Neckar in the Palatinate, son of Valentin Zimmermann and his wife, married Lea, daughter of Thomas Thee and his wife, Margarett; died Nov. 6, 1795.

REF: Evangelical Lutheran Church, Frederick.

APPENDIX

ROLLE

At the death of the last Baron of Rolle of Stevenson in Britain without male issue notices were placed in the news media for the American heir who was believed to have gone to Maryland to claim the baronage.

REF: The Complete Peerage; Burke's Dormant and Extinct Baronage; Newman's Heraldic Marylandiana.

WEEMS

Elizabeth, the Widow Weems, with her three children David, James and Williamina about 1720 emigrated to Calvert County, Md., to join her brother, Dr. William Loch, and to escape the unsettled social and economic as well as warlike conditions which embroiled Scotland and England. William, her husband, had been killed in 1715 in combat to place James, the Old Pretender, on the British Throne, and was descended on the distaff side from John, 1st Earl of Wemyss and also from James Wemyss, the 1st Lord Burntisland.

REF: The Scottish Peerage, by Douglas; The Complete Peerage (2d ed), vol. 12, pt. 2, p. 405; History of the Weems Family, by Douglas A. Weems, pub. 1945; Wills, Liber 20, folio 480.

INDEX

Jacobites and Felons

Allen, James 3, 8; John 9
Aloule, Edward 7
Ammonon, Alexander 7
Angus, Ann 10
Arbuthnot, John 8
Atkin, William 9
Bagwell, Mary 9
Bailey, George 9
Baker, Mary 10
Ball, Elizabeth 10
Barber, Mary 10
Beard, William 7
Bennett, Elizabeth 10; John 9;
  William 10
Berry, Thomas 5
Beverly, William 8
Bilby, William 9
Birch, Richard 5
Black, James 9
Blandell, John 3
Boggs, Miles 5
Boswell, Ann 10
Bottle, Sarah 10
Bow, Bowe James 5; John 8, 9
Boy, Robert 8
Brace, John 10
Brand, James 9
Brandy, John 8
Brody, John 9
Brown, Andrew 9; Ninian 5
Buccanon, John 9
Buchanan, Alexander 8
Burnet, John 8
Butler, Thomas 4

Cameron, Donald 8; Dougle 9;
  Duncan 8; Finley 4; John 5, 8,10;
  Malcolm 9
Campbell, Alexander 8; John 9;
  Saunders 8
Carnages, Alexander 8
Carnes, Mary 10
Carry, John 9
Chambers, John 5; William 8
Chaperton, James 8
Chop, James 9
Clark, James 10; Mary 10; William
  10
Clover, Robert 10
Cocke, Nathaniel 10
Collins, John 10
Connack, Ann 10
Connell, William 8
Cook, Thomas 10
Cooper, Patrick 3
Couchan, John 4
Courtley, Samuel 10
Cowan, William 8
Craigin, Robert 8
Craith, Bridget 10
Crampson, James 5
Crawford, Susannah 10
Crisp, Sarah 10
Cristy, James 9
Critton, James 9
Cudday, Sophia 10
Cumming, Jane 8; William 3
Davidge, Charles 8
Davidson, Andrew 4; William 3

187

Davis, John 10; Robert 8
Daw, Andrew 4
Degeey, John 3
Deleny, Davis 10
Denholm, James 3
Dick, David 9
Dixon, James 5
Donalson, Charles 4
Donaldson, James 9; Thomas 4
Dow, John 9
Duff, John 8; Robert 9
Dunbar, Jeremiah 3
Duncan, John 9; Peter 9
Dunkin, John 8
Ellis, Jane 10
Erwin, James 8
Fairall, John 10
Ferguson, Dunkin 8; Duncan 5;
  Henry 4; Patrick 8; William 5
Fitzsimmonds, James 9
Fleming, Alexander 9
Fling, John 9
Flower, Annie 10
Forbes, Thomas 3; Foster, John 8
Franklin, Charles 9
Gaddick, Alexander 9
Gardiner, Nicholas 9; Pter 8
Gazey, Samuel 10
Gibson, John 9
Gloiney, John 3
Godley, Jasper 10
Golder, John 9
Gordon, Alexander 3
Gover, Ann 16
Graham, David 5
Grant, Allen 8; Angus 8; Daniel 6;
  John 8; William 3, 9
Gray, John 8, 9
Gregory, Ann 10
Halton, John 9
Hame, Thomas 6
Hamilton, Robert 8
Hargrove, Thomas 10
Harrison, William 10
Harvie, John 10
Haughton, William 10
Hay, John
Heath, Charles 10

Hector, John 8
Henderson, Rot 3
Hendry, James 3
Henry, John 10
Herring, James 8
Hiags, Mary 10
Hill, James 4
Hodges, James 10
Hodgson, George 5
Holden, Thomas 10
Hunter, Patrick 4
Irwin, George 8
Jacob, Cirnelius 10
Johnson, Richard 9; William 5
Jones, John 10; Samuel 10; Thomas
  10; William 10
Judge, Judith 10
Kukes, Benjamin 10
Keath, James 9
Kelligrew, Hannah 10
Kemno, Joseph 9
Kennedy, Daniel 5
Kenny, John 5
Kendall, Mary 10
Kent, William 10
King, James 8
Knoles, William 9
Lamb, John 10
Lammon, John 9
Land, Thomas 9
Lander, David 5
Lansdale, Henry 4
Lawrence, Nathaniel 10; Richard 10
Lawson, William 9
Learn, James 5
Lemon, Thomas 10
Longdon, Joseph 9
Low, Edmond 10
Lowe, Abraham 3; James 3
Lowry, Thomas 3
Lowther, Sarah 9
Luckey, John 9
McAnnis, Arch 8
Macbayn, John 3
McBain, Fran 5
McBean, William 3
McCloud, Angus 8
McCloud, Ann 8

McCloughaton, Peter 8
McCollin, John 5
McColon, Malcolm 5
McCowan, William 8
McCoy, Peter 8
McCullum, Gilbert 8
McDaniel, Angus 8; Daniel 8; John 8; Mary 8
Mac Donald, Alexander 9; Augish 9; Donald 9; John 4, 9; Ronald 9
Macdonall, Archibald
MacDormott, Angus 5
McDuff, James 8
McDugall, Hugh 5
McFerrist, Roderick 8
McGarrist, Roderick 8
McGeles, Daniel 8
Mc Giffin, Alexander 6
Macgilvary, Frag 3; William 3, 4
McGregor, Duncan 8
McGregor, John 5, 8
McGuerrish, John 8
McGuire, Lackland 10
Machen, Alice 3
MacInney, Alexander 9
McIntergath, Patrick 8
McIntire, Archie 8; Donold 8; Finley 5; Hugh 5; John 4
MacIntosh, Alexander 5, 9; Dunkan 8; James 5; Lauglin 5
McKewan, John 5
MacKiney, Donald 9
McKinsey, Ann 8
McKown, Kate 8
McKoy, Patt 5
MacLain, John 9; Malcolm 9
Maclean, Hugh 8; John 4
Macluff, Kenard 9
McNabb, John 8; Thomas 4
MacPherson, John 9; Will 5
MacQueen, Hector 4
McQuin, Flora 8
Magham, James 10
Magrige, Duncan 9; Mark 9
Maltone, James 5
Mare, William 4
Marr, Alexander 8
Mason, John 10

Massey, George 10
Matthew, Margaret 10
Mean, John 8
Melvil, William 8
Mertison, John 4
Mill, James 8
Miller, Farquar 9
Mills, David 3
Mitchell, Elizabeth 10; George 9; James 3, 10
Mobbery, William 3
Montgomery, Francis 10
Morgan, Patrick 8
Mortimer, Alexander 4
Mullings, William 10
Murdoch, William 8
Murray, Elizabeth 9; Henry 2, 4; Patrick 8
Nave, Alexander 3
Nesmith, John 8
Newman, John 8; William 10
Nicolson, George 5
Nithery, James 3
Norvil, Adam 8
Ogilvie, John 9
Orack, Alexander 5
Paddison, William 10
Paddy, John 9
Page, Ann 10
Patent, John 9
Pebworthy, Mary 10
Poss, John 4
Potts, Thomas 3
Price, Ralph 9
Prior, Samuel 10
Ramsey, John 2, 3
Randwell, Robert 10
Read, John 10
Reind, Alexander 3
Remon, James 6
Robert, Roberts, Charles 10; Hugh 10
Robertson, Donald 4; James 4; John 3; Nall 8; Rowland 5
Robins, Nathaniel 10
Robinson, Leonard 3
Ronubson, Daniel 9
Ross, Edward 10; Thomas 8

Ruddock, Pater 8
Russell, John 9
Rutherford, James 6
Sawyer, James 10; William 10
Seale, William 10
Scott, David 9
Scudder, William 10
Shade, William 9
Shaw, James 4, 5; Margaret 8; Mary
  8, 10; Thomas 5; William 5
Sheppard, John 9
Simpson, William 5
Sinclair, James 5; John 3
Small, James 3
Smith, Alexander 3, 8; Andrew 9;
  James 9; Patt 5; Thomas 4;
  William 3, 9
Somervill, James 5, 6
Spalding, Alexander 3
Spank, Thomas 3
Stal, Michael 8
Steward, Stewart, Alexander 7, 9;
  Daniel 5; David 4; John 5
Stobbs, Robert 4
Strachan, James 7
Stretton, James 8
Strong, Ann 10
Stroon, James 9
Stuart, William 8
Studder, John 10
Suter, John 8
Sutherland, Aaron 8

Swinger, Alexander 4
Sword, Humphrey 5, 6
Taylor, John 8, 10; Saunders 8
Thaler, Jane 10
Thompson, George 3; Susan 10;
  William 9
Tillery, Andrew 8
Tuker, Peter 10
Vaughan, Edward 10
Walker, Saunders 8
Wall, Mary 10
Waller, George 9
Warner, John 8
Waters, Richard 10
Watson, George 8
Watt, John 8
Webb, William 10
Webster, James 3
Welch, John 10
Wethersher, Joseph 10
Wheeler, Ann 10
White, Ann 10; Elizabeth 10; Hugh
  6: James 3, 4; Robert 9
Whitely, William 10
Whittingham, Richard 5
Williams, John 10; William 10
Wilson, Henry 3
Wise, Ninian 8
Wood, David 9
Wright, Ann 10; John 10
Yates, Francis 9
Yeats, William 8